METHODS FOR MATTHEW

Today's biblical scholars study the Gospel of Matthew with a wide variety of methods that yield diverse and exciting insights. *Methods for Matthew* offers a primer on six exegetical approaches that have proved to be especially useful and popular. In each case, a prominent scholar describes the principles and procedures of a particular approach and then demonstrates how that approach works in practice, applying it to a well-known text from Matthew's Gospel. As an added bonus, each of the chosen texts is treated to three different interpretations so that the reader can easily compare the results obtained through one approach to those obtained through other approaches. The reader will learn a great deal about two stories from Matthew ("the healing of a centurion's servant" and "the resurrection of Jesus") and will also learn enough about each of these six approaches to understand their function in biblical studies today.

Dr. Mark Allan Powell, Professor of New Testament at Trinity Lutheran Seminary, is an internationally recognized theologian and Bible scholar. The author of more than twenty-five books and a hundred articles, Dr. Powell has served as a visiting professor at numerous American universities, as well as at schools in Estonia, Tanzania, and Russia. He is best known for his work in literary criticism, Matthean studies, and historical Jesus studies.

METHODS IN BIBLICAL INTERPRETATION

The *Methods in Biblical Interpretation* (MBI) series introduces students and general readers to both older and emerging methodologies for understanding the Hebrew Scriptures and the New Testament. Newer methods brought about by the globalization of biblical studies and by concerns with the "world in front of the text" – like new historicism, feminist criticism, postcolonial/liberationist criticism, and rhetorical criticism – are well represented in the series. "Classical" methods that fall under the more traditional historical-critical banner – such as source criticism, form criticism, and redaction criticism – are also covered, though always with an understanding of how their interactions with emerging methodologies and new archaeological discoveries have affected their interpretive uses.

An MBI volume contains separate chapters from six different well-known scholars. Each scholar first elucidates the history and purposes of an interpretive method, outlines the promise of the method in the context of a single biblical book, and finally shows the method "in action," by applying it to a specific biblical passage. The results serve as a primer for understanding different methods within the shared space of common texts, enabling real, comparative analysis for students, clergy, and anyone interested in a deeper and broader understanding of the Bible. A glossary of key terms, the translation of all ancient languages, and an annotated bibliography – arranged by method – help new, serious readers navigate the difficult but rewarding field of biblical interpretation.

Volumes in the series

Methods for Exodus, edited by Thomas B. Dozeman
Methods for the Psalms, edited by Esther Marie Menn
Methods for Matthew, edited by Mark Allan Powell
Methods for Luke, edited by Joel B. Green

Methods for Matthew

Edited by

MARK ALLAN POWELL
Trinity Lutheran Seminary, Columbus, Ohio

CAMBRIDGE
UNIVERSITY PRESS

CAMBRIDGE UNIVERSITY PRESS
Cambridge, New York, Melbourne, Madrid, Cape Town, Singapore, São Paulo, Delhi

Cambridge University Press
32 Avenue of the Americas, New York, NY 10013-2473, USA

www.cambridge.org
Information on this title: www.cambridge.org/9780521716147

First published 2009

Printed in the United States of America

A catalog record for this publication is available from the British Library.

Library of Congress Cataloging in Publication data

Methods for Matthew / edited by Mark Allan Powell.
p.   cm. – (Methods in Biblical Interpretation)
Includes bibliographical references and index.
ISBN 978-0-521-88808-0 (hardback : alk. paper)
1. Bible. N.T. Matthew – Hermeneutics.   2. Bible. N.T. Matthew – Criticism, interpretation, etc.
I. Powell, Mark Allan, 1953–
II. Title.   III. Series. BS2575.52.M48   2009
226.2'0601 – dc22   2009009365

ISBN 978-0-521-88808-0 hardback
ISBN 978-0-521-71614-7 paperback

Contents

Methods in Biblical Interpretation

A New Series from Cambridge University Press

BACKGROUND

From the mid-nineteenth century until the 1980s, the historical-critical method dominated the study of the Hebrew Bible and New Testament. A legacy of J. P. Gabler, F. Schleirmacher, J. Wellhausen, and their immediate intellectual heirs as well as of philologists studying nonbiblical ancient texts, the historical-critical method can best be understood as an unproblematic quest for the provenance of scripture. A product of Enlightenment thinking, it attempts to find the "true," original political and social contexts in which the Bible was created, redacted, and first heard and read.

The "linguistic turn" – or, the use and abuse of different critical theoretical approaches to texts – was relatively late coming in the scholarly interpretation of the Bible. When, in the 1970s, biblical scholars began experimenting with methodologies borrowed from philosophy, anthropology, and literary studies, the results were at times creative and invigorating, as theoreticians demonstrated how biblical texts could yield new ethical, political, aesthetic, and theological meanings. Sometimes, valuable older interpretations that had been effaced for many years by historical-critical concerns were recovered. Frequently, however, the results could also be painfully derivative and the authors' motivations transparent. Students' and scholars' strange vocabulary and obfuscations could not hide unexamined political and theological (or antitheological) commitments.

Thanks to the globalization of biblical studies and the emergence of concerns rooted in issues related to ethnicity, gender, economics,

and cultural history, the quest for the Bible's meaning has intensified and proliferated. Both within the academy and within a larger,
more interconnected, religiously inquisitive world, the methodologies
used to study biblical texts have multiplied and become more rigorous
and sophisticated. Their borders may be porous, as a single scholar
may work with two or more methodologies, but several schools of
criticism in biblical studies are now established and growing. Interest
in new historicism, feminist criticism, rhetorical criticism, postcolo-
nial/liberationist criticism, and several other methodologies that focus
on the "world in front of the text" has consistently provided paradigm-
shifting questions as well as contingent, but compelling, answers. This is
not to say that older historical-critical scholarship has simply evaporated.
Most scholarship in the United States, and an even larger majority of
work done in Europe, still falls comfortably under the historical-critical
banner. So, the practice of "classic" historical approaches, like source
criticism, form criticism, and redaction criticism, is still widespread,
though much of their findings have been altered by coming into contact with the emerging methodologies as well as by new archaeological
discoveries.

RATIONALE

What, then, is needed at this time is a group of short books that would
introduce the best work from within these various schools of criticism to
seminarians, graduate students, scholars, and interested clergy. *Methods
in Biblical Interpretation* aims to fill that need.

The key to reaching the full, wider spectrum of this readership is to
build these books around the most widely studied books of the Bible,
using the best possible writers and scholars to explain and even advocate
for a given perspective. That is, rather than long, separate introductions to methodological "schools," like postcolonial criticism, rhetorical
criticism, and source criticism, *Methods in Biblical Interpretation* publishes separate, shorter texts on the most popular biblical books of the
canon, with chapters from six leading proponents of different schools of
interpretation.

DESCRIPTION

In order to make the volumes truly introductory, comparative, *and* original, each of the chapters is divided into two parts. The first part of the
chapter introduces to students the given method, a bit of its history, and
its suitability and promise for the entire book under discussion. This
part gestures toward various ideas and possibilities of how this particular methodological approach might interact at various points with the
biblical book.

The second part of the chapter, building on the background material
presented in the first, then shows the method "in action," so to speak.
It achieves that by asking each contributor to focus this second part of
the chapter on one of two passages from within the biblical book. The
comparative and pedagogical value of this second section of each chapter
allows students to view different methods' interactions with the same
biblical verses.

The two-part chapters offer opportunities for scholars both to explain
a methodology to students and to demonstrate its effectiveness and
cogency; that is, the chapters do not merely offer bland, shallow overviews
of how a theory might work. Subjective, opinionated scholarship, especially in the second half of each chapter, is in full display. Authors,
however, have also written their contributions for a student and general
audience, and thus have explained and distilled theoretical insights for
the uninitiated. So, lucidity and accessibility are equally manifest.

Each of the *Methods of Biblical Interpretation* volumes also contains
an annotated bibliography, arranged by methodology, and placed at the
end of the book. Such material, as well as a short glossary, provides
students with tools to understand the application of any given theory or
methodology and to further investigate the history of its development.

It is not desired, nor probably even possible, to have the same methodologies included in every volume of the series. Certain biblical books lend
themselves much more easily to certain forms of criticism (e.g., rhetorical
criticism and Paul's letters, narrative criticism and the synoptic Gospels).
Therefore, there is some flexibility on which methods will be included
in a volume. The selected methods depend, of course, on the choice of
contributors and are determined by the volume editor in consultation
with Cambridge University Press. Such flexibility helps ensure that the

best people, writing the most exciting and compelling scholarship, are contributing to germane volumes. Following these considerations, the series aims to have half of the essays closely related to historical-critical work and half devoted to more recently emerging methodologies.

It is hoped that these carefully structured volumes will provide students and others with both a sense of the excitement involved in such a wide spectrum of approaches to the Bible and a guide for fully making use of them.

Abbreviations

ABD	*Anchor Bible Dictionary*
AcBib	Academia Biblica
AJT	*American Journal of Theology*
ANRW	*Aufstieg und Niedergang der römischen Welt*
ATFS	Australian Theological Forum Series
BA	*Biblical Archaeologist*
BALS	Bible and Liberation Series
BDAG	Bauer, Danker, Arndt, and Gingrich, eds, *Greek-English Lexicon*
BETL	Bibliotheca ephemeridum theologicarum lovaniensium
Bib	*Biblica*
BibInt	*Biblical Interpretation*
BIS	Biblical Interpretation Series
BJS	Brown Judaic Studies
BRS	Biblical Resource Series
BTB	*Biblical Theology Bulletin*
BZ	*Biblische Zeitschrift*
BZNW	Beihefte zur Zeitschrift für Religions- und Geistesgeschichte
CBQ	*Catholic Biblical Quarterly*
CRINT	Compendia rerum iudicarum ad Novum Testamentum
DBI	*Dictionary of Biblical Interpretation*
ETL	*Epehemerides theologicae lovanienses*
EvT	*Evangelische Theologie*
ExpTim	*Expository Times*
FBBS	Facet Books, Biblical Series
GBS	Guides to Biblical Scholarship

GC	Gender and Culture
IBS	*Irish Biblical Studies*
JBL	*Journal of Biblical Literature*
JETS	*Journal of the Evangelical Theological Society*
JFSR	*Journal of Feminist Studies of Religion*
JR	*Journal of Religion*
JSNT	*Journal for the Study of the New Testament*
JSNTSS	*Journal for the Study of the New Testament Supplement Series*
JTS	*Journal of Theological Studies*
LCL	Loeb Classical Library
LEC	Library of Early Christianity
LTT	Library of Theological Translations
NovT	*Novum Testamentum*
NTL	New Testament Library
NTOA	Novum Testamentum et Orbis Antiquus
NTS	New Testament Studies
PTMS	Pittsburgh Theological Monograph Series
RB	*Revue biblique*
SBEC	Studies in the Bible and Early Christianity
SNTSMS	Society for New Testament Studies Monograph Series
TTod	*Theology Today*
TLZ	*Theologische Literaturzeitung*
TU	Texte und Untersuchungen
TynB	*Tyndale Bulletin*
VC	*Vigiliae christianae*

About the Contributors

Craig A. Evans is Payzant Distinguished Professor of New Testament at Acadia Divinity College, Acadia University, Wolfville, Nova Scotia. He is the author or editor of more than fifty books, including *Jesus and His Contemporaries: Comparative Studies* (Brill, 1995), *Ancient Texts for New Testament Study: A Guide to the Background Literature* (Hendrickson, 2005), and *The Encyclopedia of the Historical Jesus* (Acadia Divinity College, 2008).

Donald A. Hagner is George Eldon Ladd Professor Emeritus of New Testament at Fuller Theological Seminary in Pasadena, California. His areas of expertise include exegetical method, Christian-Jewish relations, and New Testament use of Old Testament writings. He is the author and editor of numerous books, including the two-volume commentary on Matthew's Gospel published in the Word Biblical Commentary series: *Matthew 1–13* (Word, 1993) and *Matthew 14–28* (Word, 1995).

Bruce J. Malina is Professor of Biblical Studies at Creighton University in Omaha, Nebraska. He is a past president of the Catholic Biblical Association and chairs a seminar on the Social Sciences and New Testament Interpretation for that organization. He is also the founder of the Context Group: Project on the Bible in Its Cultural Environment. His numerous publications include *The New Testament World: Insights from Cultural Anthropology* (3rd ed., Westminster John Knox, 2001) and *The Social World of Jesus and the Gospels* (Routledge, 1996).

Mark Allan Powell is Robert and Phyllis Leatherman Professor of New Testament at Trinity Lutheran Seminary in Columbus, Ohio. He has chaired both the Historical Jesus Section and the Matthew Group for the Society of Biblical Literature. His publications include *What Is Narrative Criticism?* (Fortress, 1990) and *Chasing the Eastern Star: Adventures in Biblical Reader Response Criticism* (Westminster John Knox, 2001).

Fernando F. Segovia is Oberlin Graduate Professor of New Testament and Early Christianity in the Divinity School and the Graduate Department of Religion at Vanderbilt University. His areas of expertise include method and theory, with a strong focus on ideological criticism. He is the author of numerous books and articles and serves as coeditor of *Postcolonial Biblical Criticism: Interdisciplinary Intersections* (T & T Clark, 2007) and *A Postcolonial Commentary on the New Testament* (T & T Clark, 2007).

Elaine M. Wainwright is Richard Maclaurin Goodfellow Professor in Theology and Head of the School of Theology at the University of Auckland in Auckland, Australia. She is the author of *Towards a Feminist Critical Reading of the Gospel of Matthew* (DeGruyter, 1991), *Shall We Look for Another: A Feminist Re-reading of the Matthean Jesus* (Orbis, 1998), and *Women Healing/Healing Women: The Genderisation of Healing in Early Christianity* (Equinox, 2006).

Stephen E. Young is Adjunct Instructor in New Testament at Fuller Theological Seminary, Pasadena, California, where he teaches at the Center for the Study of Hispanic Church and Community. Born and raised in Latin America (Ecuador and Argentina), he has a particular interest in the interpretation of the New Testament from a Latino/a perspective.

Introduction

MARK ALLAN POWELL

*T*HE GOSPEL OF MATTHEW REMAINS ONE OF THE MOST STUDIED and most influential books of the New Testament. Although a few matters remain controversial, there is generally more agreement among scholars regarding fundamental critical questions concerning Matthew than would be the case with Mark, Luke, or John, and this allows for a breadth of discussion that does not get stalled before it has a chance to begin. Furthermore, Matthew's Gospel probably had more influence on the development of Christian theology than the other Synoptic Gospels, and for this reason it continues to be a primary text for ecumenical and doctrinal discussions.

ACADEMIC STUDY OF MATTHEW'S GOSPEL

The academic field of New Testament study has developed into a discipline that encompasses different approaches and employs a variety of methods. Thus, students of Matthew's Gospel will discover that interpretive claims regarding the book have been arrived at by different avenues. Sometimes, at least, what appear to be conflicting interpretations of the book are simply responses to different questions.

To illustrate this, let us imagine that a student asks, "What is the meaning of Matthew 5:5 ('Blessed are the meek, for they will inherit the earth')?" Three scholars might answer this question differently. One might try to explain what Jesus meant when he said this to a group of Galilean peasants sometime around c.e. 30. Another might seek to explain why the author of Matthew's Gospel included this "Jesus quote" in the book that he composed for Christians living in the city of Antioch around C.E. 85. And a third scholar might offer some ideas about what this verse of scripture means for modern Christians living in the world today. All three scholars would think that they were answering the student's question but they would have different insights to offer regarding the meaning of Matthew 5:5, and they may have arrived at those insights through the use of different exegetical methods.

This book offers students a primer on six approaches that are often used in Matthean studies today. In each case, the approach itself is first discussed in some detail: the theoretical basis for the approach is presented and basic principles and procedures are outlined. In fairly short compass, the reader will learn both *why* scholars use the approach and *how* they do so. Then, each chapter turns its attention to the Gospel of Matthew, explicating how an approach that is used in New Testament studies generally is employed in study of this one particular book. Application of the approach is illustrated with reference to a specific Matthean text: three approaches are applied to the story of the resurrection of Jesus in Matthew 27:57–28:15, and another three are applied to the account of Jesus healing the servant (or son) of a centurion in Matthew 8:5–13.

By way of introduction, we will say something about all six of these approaches now so that the reader can get "the big picture" of methodological diversity before focusing on each approach individually. Initially however, we should consider what all the approaches have in common. There are certain fundamental aspects to Gospel study employed by scholars who use any or all these approaches.

First, all Matthew scholars study the Gospel in Greek, not in English (or any other translation). This means that, whatever approach they are using, Matthew scholars often must rely on the insights of people with expertise in such fields as linguistics, philology, and semantics. They need to determine the meaning (or, often, the possible "range of meanings") for each individual word, and they need to determine the effect of grammatical and syntactical constructions that bring the words into relationship with each other to form phrases, sentences, and larger linguistic units. When the author of Matthew's Gospel uses the genitive case, scholars will ask what type of genitive construction is intended (e.g., does the expression *theou tou zōntos* in Matt. 16:16 mean "God of the living" or "the living God"?). Likewise, they will enquire as to what kind of action is implied by the use of various verb tenses (especially

since, in Greek, verb tenses do not always correlate with *time* as closely
as they might in English). Further, scholars often want to compare the
way words are used in Matthew's Gospel with the way they are used
in other ancient writings: does Matthew's Gospel use the word *ekklēsia*
("church") the way Roman authors used it to refer to a general assembly
of people, or does he use it the way Paul used it to refer to a specific
Christian congregation, or the way later Christian writers used it to refer
to "all believers in Christ"?

Second, virtually all Matthew scholars would agree that the version
of Matthew's Gospel they are interested in studying is that which comes
closest to the original manuscript produced by the evangelist. Of course,
we do not have that original manuscript; we have only copies of copies
that were made over the years. In fact, we have thousands of copies, dating from the fourth century through the fourteenth century; and no two
are exactly alike. Scholars do not just pick one of those copies and comment on it; instead, they work with a composite manuscript that has been
painstakingly reconstructed by *text critics*, scholars who have examined all
the various copies of Matthew's Gospel and determined which words are
most likely to represent the original reading of the text. The current version of this composite manuscript is published as both the twenty-seventh
revised edition of the *Nestle-Aland Novum Testamentum Graece* and the
fourth revised edition of the United Bible Societies' *Greek New Testament.*
Almost all Matthew scholars today would view their task as being to interpret this reconstructed text of Matthew's Gospel – a version believed
to be very close to what was contained in the original manuscript –
but we should also note that at numerous junctures this reconstructed
Greek text of Matthew lists "variant readings" derived from possibly reliable manuscripts. For example, many of our most reliable manuscripts
of Matthew's Gospel list a man named Thaddaeus as being among Jesus's
twelve disciples in Matthew 10:3, but some usually reliable manuscripts
give that man's name as Lebbaeus (or, sometimes, as "Lebbaeus called
Thaddaeus"). Text critics may conclude that the disciple's name was
probably Thaddaeus, but that this is not a sure thing; the "variant reading"
(Lebbaeus) *could* be correct. Thus, Matthew scholars are attentive not
only to the main text of Matthew that has been reconstructed by text
critics but also to the numerous variants that represent possibly correct
readings.

Finally, all Matthew scholars are interested in knowing as much as possible about the world in which this book was written and the world about which it reports. Many Matthew scholars would not know how to excavate a city or date a piece of pottery, but they regularly rely on the insights of archaeologists and other ancient historians who do know how to do these things and who are able to provide them with reliable data concerning the first-century world. Matthew scholars also study the libraries of ancient literature (e.g., the Dead Sea Scrolls and the writings of first-century authors like Josephus, Philo, Seutonius, and Tacitus). Basically, Matthew scholars need to be well informed with regard to at least two historical contexts: first, and most obviously, they need to know as much as possible about the culture of Palestine during the time of Jesus: what did Pharisees and Sadducees believe? Who were the Samaritans? What did centurions do? How was a synagogue constructed and what sort of activities were held there? But Matthew scholars also need to know about the Greco-Roman environment in which this book was written some fifty years *after* the time of Jesus: how did Jewish and Gentile Christians relate to each other and how did they relate to Jewish neighbors who did *not* believe in Jesus? How had they been affected by the persecution of believers in Rome in the mid-1960s? What did they think of the Jewish war with Rome and the destruction of the Jerusalem temple?

In a nutshell, all Matthew scholars are attentive to basic questions of *text* and *context.* They are committed to studying the most reliable text of Matthew's Gospel that can be produced, to understanding it in its original language, and to interpreting it in light of accurate data regarding the story it presents and the circumstances of those for whom the book was originally written. Scholars who respect these fundamental concerns, however, may differ greatly with regard to which approach and interpretive method they adopt for their study.

THE FIRST THREE APPROACHES

Our first three approaches may be understood in terms of a somewhat simplistic paradigm. It is often said that interpretation of the Bible (or of any literary work for that matter) involves the analysis of a "communication event." An *author* (in this case, the person we call

"Matthew" – though we do not actually know who he was or what his name might have been) composes a *text* (in this case, the book we call "the Gospel of Matthew") to be received by *readers* (initially, Christians who lived in the Roman Empire during the latter part of the first century c.e., but, eventually, all sorts of people who would live in many different places and times). Students trying to make sense of different approaches to Gospel study might find it helpful to start out by thinking that the historical-critical method emphasizes the *author* part of this triad, while literary approaches emphasize the *text* aspect, and feminist approaches focus on the *reader*. Ultimately, this scheme breaks down, and if taken in an absolute sense, it can be misleading. Still, it does provide an initial perspective that can be fine-tuned with appropriate caveats later on.

The Historical-Critical Method

From the mid-nineteenth century until the 1980s, the historical-critical method was the dominant approach to academic study of Matthew's Gospel. The method (or more properly, group of methods) developed as a product of Enlightenment thinking and as a reaction against dogmatic interpretation of scripture according to which the Bible was simply mined as a resource for supporting the doctrinal views of various Christian sects. When applied to the Gospel of Matthew, the goal of historical-critical studies was either to determine what actually happened (a topic treated later under "Historical Jesus Studies") or to discern what the author of this book intended to communicate by writing such a work. One of the great benefits of this methodology was that it allowed scholars with divergent confessional views to work together in pursuit of common goals. While Roman Catholic scholars might continue to believe that Matthew 16:17–19 provides a sound biblical *basis* for the doctrine of the papacy, they could at least agree with Protestant interpreters that the primary intention of the historical author of Matthew's Gospel was not to establish such an institution (which he could hardly have envisioned, since he thought the world was coming to an end). Likewise, John the Baptist's brief reference to one who would "baptize with the Holy Spirit" (3:11) was not intended as an endorsement of Pentecostal revivalism, nor was Jesus's call to "be perfect" (5:48) intended as an expression of Wesleyan views on sanctification, nor was this Gospel's single reference to a primitive baptismal formula (28:19) intended as a summation of post–Nicene Trinitarian theology. Without necessarily challenging the legitimacy of the Bible being used in dogmatic and devotional ways, the development of the historical-critical method established parameters for the Bible to be used in nondogmatic, nondevotional ways. Although the historical-critical method entailed many aspects (including source, form, and genre criticism), the discipline known as redaction criticism would ultimately prove to be most significant for Matthean studies. By the mid-twentieth century, most Gospel scholars had become convinced that the author of Matthew's Gospel had actually used a copy of Mark's Gospel as one of his sources and had edited that volume in obvious, discernible ways. By tracing that editorial activity, redaction critics discovered that they had a fairly objective and intelligible means for discovering clues to Matthew's priorities and preferences. In fact, Matthew's redactional tendencies proved so accessible that his Gospel would become the preferred text for pedagogical instruction in the historical-critical method.

Literary Approaches

Around 1980, the interests of many scholars who had been trained in the historical-critical method shifted away from what they regarded as an "obsession with authorial intent" toward a more intense focus on literary dynamics of "the text itself." Most of these scholars borrowed heavily from movements in the secular field of modern literary criticism, including structuralism, narratology, and a discipline called New Criticism. All these approaches maintained that authors create texts that ultimately transcend their explicit intentions; texts come to mean things the author did not envision, and so *meaning* should not be constrained by authorial intent but should be determined by analysis of a work's literary features. A play is judged to be a tragedy because it has the literary characteristics of a tragedy (not because its author is known to have intended the work to be tragic). The meaning of a poem needs to be determined through engagement of the poem itself, apart from any biographical information regarding the poet or extraneous knowledge concerning circumstances of the poem's composition: the poet's life and circumstances might be interesting for other reasons, but the meaning of the *poem* is arrived at by analyzing it as a freestanding work of art.

One reason that this approach to literature caught on in Matthean studies was that, in the case of Matthew's Gospel, very little can be known with certainty about the author's intentions; the Gospel of Matthew is anonymous and its author gave no interviews. A focus on "literary features" rather than authorial intent seemed to many scholars to involve less guesswork. This penchant for objectivity did not last long, however, because by the end of the twentieth century secular literary criticism had shifted decisively away from a focus on "texts" toward a new orientation on readers. The main interest of literary theorists was now in *reception*, and it was often said that *readers* ultimately determine what any text means (regardless of what an author might have intended or what textual dynamics might imply). Biblical studies sometimes followed suit and various reader-oriented literary approaches were employed for interpretation of the Gospels. Still, in Matthean studies, the most popular literary approach would remain "narrative criticism," a basically text-oriented method that seeks to understand the Gospel from the perspective of an "implied reader" reconstructed from the text itself.

Feminist Approaches

In many ways feminist approaches to biblical studies developed ahead of the curve with regard to the just-mentioned growing interest in reception. This might not be immediately obvious because, in a certain sense, "feminist approaches" remains a transcendent category that overlaps all the other approaches discussed in this book: there are feminist scholars who use the historical-critical method; there are feminist scholars who use literary and/or social-scientific approaches; and there are feminist scholars who pursue historical Jesus studies and postcolonial criticism. Still, most varieties of feminist criticism are attentive to one significant aspect of *reception*: virtually all feminist critics attempt to discern how texts are received by one particular subset of readers, namely readers whose understanding of the text is informed by feminism. Thus, feminist historical critics may not be content simply to identify the authorial intention of a Matthean text; they may want to dialogue with that intention, challenge it, resist it, or simply identify circumstances that allow the author's intention to be viewed in broader scope. Feminist literary critics may be especially attuned to noticing textual dynamics related to gender or, indeed, to dynamics that are informed by particular understandings of gender.

THREE MORE APPROACHES

The next three approaches to be considered in this book might be envisioned as focusing on contexts for the communication event described previously. Historical Jesus studies is usually said to focus on "the world behind the text," that is, on what happened in the world before the Gospel of Matthew was written (on the words and deeds of Jesus to which the Gospel claims to bear witness). Postcolonial criticism is often said to focus on "the world in front of the text," that is, on what has happened in the world *since* the Gospel of Matthew was written (on decisive changes in perspective and ideology that affect how that book is now understood). In between these two, we will consider social-scientific approaches, which often focus on other analogous worlds that help to shed light on all contexts associated with Matthew's Gospel.

Historical Jesus Studies

The main character of Matthew's Gospel, Jesus, is regarded as a significant historical figure in ways that transcend the interests of theology or religious faith. Historians who want to study Jesus use documents like the Gospel of Matthew in the same manner they would use other primary sources from ancient history: they analyze the book in order to extract information pertinent to a credible reconstruction of who Jesus was and what happened in the world because of him. The goal of historical Jesus studies, then, is not to understand the Gospel of Matthew itself, but to use the Gospel of Matthew to understand the historical phenomena to which it testifies. Historical science is skeptical by nature, and historians are generally cautious about accepting unsubstantiated reports from authors who are reporting things that would have helped to promote their particular cause. Thus, from a historian's perspective, Matthew's Gospel must be classed as "religious propaganda," and what it reports must be tested in accord with various criteria to see if it can be deemed historically credible apart from biases of religious faith. In doing this, most historians recognize that Jesus might have said and done things reported in the New Testament that cannot be regarded as historical, simply because there is insufficient evidence to verify or confirm what is reported there. The search for "the historical Jesus" is basically a quest for the "historically verifiable Jesus." Still, as a result of such studies, a considerable amount of material in Matthew's Gospel – especially that which is associated with the "Q source" – has been deemed to be of extraordinary value for reconstructing a credible and verifiable portrait of the historical Jesus.

Social-Scientific Approaches

Scholars who use social-scientific approaches to study Matthew's Gospel draw on a number of theories and models derived from the fields of sociology and anthropology. As with the "historical-critical method" and "historical Jesus studies" the goals of social-scientific study are generally historical in nature: scholars who use these approaches want to understand the world that produced the Gospel of Matthew and the world that is described in that book, but the understanding they seek goes deeper than a simple discovery of "what happened" or "the message the author (writer) intended to convey." They seek to understand the values, institutions, social systems, and interconnected relationships that are intrinsic to the New Testament world and to read the Gospel of Matthew in light of that understanding. At one level, such scholars are attentive to matters that characterized the social world of the Roman Empire during the New Testament era: the phenomenon of the *Pax Romana*, the diaspora migrations of Jewish people, the military occupation of Palestine, and an economic system that virtually eliminated the middle class. They also study such cultural phenomena as kinship relations, power structures, gender roles, economic systems, and strategies for education. With regard to Matthew's Gospel, they have analyzed the purity codes that defined what most people considered to be "clean" and "unclean" and the social value system that led people to prize acquisition of honor above all else. It is sometimes said that those who employ social-scientific approaches seek to become "considerate readers" of Matthew's Gospel, readers who try to bridge the cultural distance between themselves and the Gospel so that they will understand it on its own terms. The means for doing this are varied but often involve comparative analysis of societies similar to those that formed contexts for Jesus and for the author of Matthew's Gospel.

Postcolonial Criticism

The discipline that has come to be called postcolonial biblical criticism did not come to the fore until the last few years of the twentieth century, but it quickly achieved recognition as an important new approach to biblical studies. In broad terms, postcolonial criticism might be categorized as a subset of what is called "ideological criticism," a field that gained respect within the guild of biblical studies after the popularity of literary approaches brought a new interest in the role that readers play in interpretation. A multitude of ideological approaches emerged that sought to explore how biblical writings might be interpreted when they are read from particular ideological perspectives. Marxist criticism, Jungian criticism, "womanist criticism" (interpreting texts from the perspective of African-American women), and many other specific types of ideological criticism seek to put forward interpretations that other scholars may miss due to the limitations of their own, usually unacknowledged, ideological perspectives. Postcolonial criticism offers interpretations from the perspective of marginalized and oppressed people of the earth, especially those in Asia, Africa, or Latin America. The term derives from the fact that the perspectives represented are those of people who were recently "colonized" by a dominant "imperial" power. In studies of Matthew, postcolonial critics seek to recover "silenced voices" in the history and culture of Gospel interpretation and in the Gospel itself. The process of doing this often involves contesting presuppositions and either exposing or accenting the political implications of dominant interpretations of the Gospel. For example, postcolonial critics seek to articulate the view that Matthew's Gospel takes toward imperial power (the Roman Empire) and toward those who were subordinated and dominated by that power. A key question concerns whether Matthew's Gospel offers a legitimation of imperialism that must be actively resisted and overcome by critics committed to social change or whether Matthew's Gospel provides a counterperspective that seeks to undermine oppressive institutions.

↓

1

The Historical-Critical Method and the Gospel of Matthew

DONALD A. HAGNER AND STEPHEN E. YOUNG

*T*HESE ARE CHALLENGING TIMES IN WHICH TO PRACTICE THE historical-critical method (HCM). While for roughly two hundred years within academic circles it was *the approach* to interpreting the New Testament (NT), over the past three or four decades academics have begun to embrace a plurality of methods. Indeed, some new methods arose largely *in reaction* to perceived deficiencies of the HCM. Accordingly, in what follows, we outline an approach to the HCM that includes a rationale for its continued use.

THE HISTORICAL-CRITICAL METHOD IN THE CONTEXT OF CURRENT SCHOLARSHIP

To place our discussion in perspective, an important clarification is needed from the outset: the HCM is not a single, monolithic approach, nor has it been so in the past. More than a single method, the HCM is an array of disciplines sometimes practiced in conjunction with each other, and sometimes separately. Furthermore, the HCM has been practiced for centuries by a vast array of interpreters, most of whom incorporated into their practice nuances and perspectives of their own. At times, revisions to the HCM have amounted to whole *new disciplines* being incorporated into its practice (e.g., form criticism in the 1920s, redaction criticism in the 1950s, and semantics and linguistics roughly from the 1970s onward). In these ways, to a greater or lesser extent, each generation of interpreters has adapted its practice of the HCM to its new insights. In sum, being already diverse as a result of its many constitutive disciplines, the HCM has also changed and adapted over time, in a manner similar to any other area of learning.

Several implications follow:

1. Certain aspects of the HCM that are currently the target of disapproval represent only a segment of scholarship and are not intrinsic to the method itself. It follows that in rejecting these elements or emphases, one is therefore not justified in rejecting the HCM as a whole.[1] For example, one often hears that the HCM is concerned only with "the world behind the text" and should be replaced by methods that enable one to engage the text and give attention to its impact in the act of reading ("the world in front of the text").[2] It is true that the HCM is concerned with the world behind the text, but not necessarily to the exclusion of other interests. It is important to note that when the HCM attends to the world behind the text, this is generally not an end in itself but a means toward the end of understanding the text from that perspective.

2. Some aspects of the manner in which the HCM has been practiced are today rightly rejected as representing the presuppositions of a different day and age. The idea, for example, of a purely objective and detached scholarship, though common not many decades ago, has clearly run its course. Practice of the HCM today must begin with the recognition that all interpretation is contextual. Even the questions one chooses to bring to the text are determined in part by one's life experience, and they, in turn, will determine in part the outcome of one's interpretation.

3. The strength of the HCM lies in enabling the interpreter to understand ancient texts, and this presupposes the interpreter's aim to study these texts as *ancient* texts. Interpreters who wish, for example, to sever an

---

[1] On the need for a more balanced perspective in evaluating past practices in biblical criticism, see A. C. Thiselton, "New Testament Interpretation in Historical Perspective," in *Hearing the New Testament: Strategies for Interpretation*, ed. J. B. Green (Grand Rapids: Eerdmans, 1995), 10–36.

[2] Following P. Ricoeur, it is common to distinguish between "the world behind the text," or the situation of the author, the first readers, and the process that led to the production of the text, "the world of the text" itself, and "the world in front of the text," how the text engages and transforms the reader; see P. Ricoeur's *Hermeneutics and the Human Sciences* (Cambridge: Cambridge University Press, 1981), 142–44, and *Essays on Biblical Interpretation* (Philadelphia: Fortress, 1980), 98–104.

ancient text's tie to the past, focusing solely on its impact on communities of readers in the present, will not be well served by the HCM. For those who share the conviction that understanding what an ancient text *means* involves understanding what it *meant*, the HCM remains indispensable.

4. Finally, the diversity of the HCM also implies that what is offered in this chapter is only *a* model. Not all those who practice the HCM would agree with the emphases given here, and some would include other elements. According to the present model, the HCM exists primarily to facilitate *arriving at the meaning of NT texts in their original contexts.* The disciplines and methods that together constitute the HCM serve either to establish the form of a text or to illumine a particular facet of a text within its ancient contexts, whether literary, historical, social, or any other context. Regardless of what other methods we may apply, without an understanding of these contexts our collective insight into the meaning of NT texts would be greatly impoverished. Together with acknowledging past and present weaknesses in its application, our own generation must reenvision the practice of the HCM in light of current insights regarding such things as the nature and sources of meaning, the pervasive influence of prejudices and presuppositions, and the impact of interpretations on current social issues. In this process those components of the HCM that constitute its essential raison d'être must be identified and retained as invaluable to the study of the NT. The main body of this chapter is dedicated to presenting each of these components.

Text as Communicative Event

Defining the purpose of the HCM as arriving at the *meaning* of NT texts in their original contexts involves one of the most controversial issues in contemporary philosophy. There is much ongoing debate not only over the definition of meaning itself,[3] but also over where meanings reside in the act of reading and whether one can set boundaries for

---

[3] Thiselton discusses referential, semantic, ideational, functional, and de facto theories. See A. C. Thiselton, "Meaning," in *A Dictionary of Biblical Interpretation*, ed. R. J. Coggins and J. L. Houlden (London: SCM, 1990), 435–38.

these meanings.[4] We have space here only to lay a brief general ground-work with regard to this discussion and then to focus on a key aspect of the HCM: that of the relationship between author and meaning.

In general terms, the HCM locates meaning primarily in the *language of texts*, but as conditioned by the *intention of the authors* (both of these understood not in isolation, but as informed by a variety of *contexts*). In addition, it takes into account the impact of the *original* or *intended readers* on the meaning of texts – not only in terms of what they might have understood given their own contexts (so that one could say that in this model readers function *as* a context), but also in terms of how the authors might have shaped their communication in light of their knowledge of, and relationship with, the recipients.[5]

In sum, while the HCM locates the meaning of a text in a combination of the language of text, the authors, the readers, and various contexts, it clearly gives a central place to the role of the author. This approach to meaning has been criticized on the grounds that the intentions of an author can be elusive. There is some truth to this criticism, especially if by arriving at the "meaning intended by the author" one implies thinking the thoughts of the author or getting into the author's mind. This approach is less problematic, however, if one approaches texts as *communicative events*. Essential to a communicative event is the idea of choice at every step, which for all the Gospel writers entailed, for example, the choice of words, of grammatical constructions, of a genre of writing, and of sources and their use. These choices at every juncture are what make it possible for each evangelist to communicate one *meaning* over another and to provide insight into his intention as an author. It is thus appropriate to seek the meaning of each Gospel in terms of what each evangelist intended to communicate, rather than what each Gospel means in isolation, because while authors make choices, texts do not.[6]

---

[4] For an introduction to these issues (with bibliography), see J. J. E. Gracia, "Meaning," in *Dictionary for Theological Interpretation of the Bible*, ed. K. J. Vanhoozer (Grand Rapids: Baker Academic, 2005), 492–99.

[5] On language vs. textuality, and the complex relationship between text, author, reader, and various contexts, see J. J. E. Gracia, *A Theory of Textuality* (Albany: State University of New York Press, 1995).

[6] See further D. A. Hagner, "The Place of Exegesis in the Postmodern World," in *History and Exegesis: New Testament Essays in Honor of Dr. E. Earle Ellis for His 80th Birthday*, ed. S.-W. A. Son (London: T&T Clark, 2006), 292–308, here pp. 302–7. For an in-depth defense of the concept of the author in terms of texts as communicative events,

This understanding of Gospels as communicative events undergirds the entire approach to the HCM as presented in this chapter. A number of methods and disciplines that form part of the HCM seek to understand the implications for meaning of each choice made by the evangelists, for example, whether to write in one genre or another, or whether to follow or diverge from a source. All this is not meant to imply that by identifying the meaning intended by the author the meaning of a text is exhausted, but only that the meaning intended by the author should take precedence over other meanings when seeking to understand a text *in its original context* – which is the goal of the HCM.

The Interpreter as Cultural Broker

The HCM is a means of *placing the interpreter imaginatively within the world in which a text came into existence*, with the goal of better understanding the meaning of the text from that perspective. Viewed in these terms, the role of the practitioner of the HCM can be likened in many ways to that of the cultural broker. Cultural brokers are individuals who are so familiar with the ways of two (or more) cultures that they can become a bridge between them, facilitating understanding and communication. Usually cultural brokers are familiar with one of the cultures from birth, and they instinctively know how things "work" in that culture from having been immersed in it. The second culture usually requires more intentional learning. In like manner, the NT critic as a cultural broker will not only know the NT, but will also study everything that may convey information about the ancient cultures surrounding it.

A helpful image often used in hermeneutical theory is that of the "horizon," or everything that an individual can see from any given vantage point, within the limits set by his or her situation. In traditional modern historiography it was assumed that one could set aside one's own horizon and by placing oneself imaginatively in a historical situation, take on the horizon of that time and place. We have lately come to realize that this is impossible. Rather, in reading an ancient text, understanding of that text will take place when one's present horizon becomes

see K. J. Vanhoozer, *Is There a Meaning in This Text?* (Grand Rapids: Zondervan, 1998), 197–280.

fused with the horizon presupposed by the text. This implies that the text is not interrogated, as it were, from a distance. In order for true understanding to take place one must *enter into conversation* with the text, allowing it to exert influence on one's prejudices and presuppositions, that is, to reshape one's horizon.[7]

This idea that one enters into a *conversation* with ancient texts is central to another image that is helpful in defining the role of the NT critic as a cultural broker – the "hermeneutical circle." The basic idea behind the hermeneutical circle is that one can only understand the whole in reference to the parts and the parts in reference to the whole.[8] When seeking to understand an ancient text, words and phrases have meaning only when viewed in relation to other words and phrases, to the argument as a whole, to the thought of the author, to the situation in which the author wrote, and so on. One cannot gain insight into the whole, however, without assigning meaning to the parts. In this sense, then, understanding will always be provisional, in that one may need to revise a prior understanding of the parts based on a fuller understanding of the whole, which in turn will lead to a new revision of one's understanding of the whole, in an ongoing circle. The hermeneutical circle also involves the ongoing impact of interpreter on text and text on interpreter. When one approaches an ancient text for the first time, the prejudices and presuppositions that form part of one's present horizon will dictate certain aspects of one's understanding of the text. Presuppositional myopia, however, need not remain terminal. Some measure of true understanding of the text in its own context can take place even on the first reading so that the text will reshape certain elements of one's horizon. In this sense, then, the text has influenced the reader. When returning for another reading of the same text, one is no longer the same person as when one approached it for the first time. One's horizon has shifted somewhat, becoming more aligned with the horizon of the text. The second reading will involve fewer of one's own prejudices and presuppositions, and more of those implied by the text. This in turn will result in the text having an even greater impact

---

[7] This discussion of deriving modern meaning from ancient texts is written in conversation with some points in H.-G. Gadamer, *Truth and Method*, 2nd rev. ed. (New York: Crossroad, 1990), 302–7. For a helpful discussion of "horizon," see A. C. Thiselton, *The Two Horizons* (Exeter: Paternoster, 1980).

[8] Thiselton provides a good introduction to the place of the hermeneutical circle in the history of the discipline in *New Horizons in Hermeneutics* (Grand Rapids: Zondervan, 1992).

in the second reading than it did in the first. Over time, and as the result of conversing with many products of an ancient culture, one's horizon is shaped so as to perceive reality increasingly from the latter's perspective.

Cultural brokers serve as models for NT critics not only in enabling communication and facilitating understanding across cultures, but also to the extent that they serve as catalysts for social change. Cultural brokers are currently employed in Europe and North America in such diverse fields as folkloristics, anthropology, international business, diplomacy, tourism, and the arts. Of special interest to us here, however, is that they are also increasingly filling roles in fields such as health care, social services, and education, where they are called on to address the issue of the imbalance of power in the relationship between service providers (doctors, social workers, teachers) and those they serve (patients, clients, students). Addressing imbalances of power should also be part of the role of the NT interpreter, as those who practice feminist criticism and various forms of liberation theology (among others) have forcefully and increasingly brought to our attention over the past several decades.[9] When feminist critics argue that NT texts do not support the misogynistic use to which they are often put, or when liberation theologians emphasize the presence of a preferential option for the poor in NT texts, biblical criticism is working as it should. Insights such as these can be powerful tools in the hands of NT critics who, as cultural brokers, seek to bring about change in the wider society.[10]

---

[9] A classic statement of feminist theology is E. Schüssler Fiorenza's *In Memory of Her* (New York: Crossroad, 1983), and see the chapter entitled "Feminist Criticism and the Gospel of Matthew" by E. Wainwright in the present volume. Liberation theology was born in Latin America, and its classic statement from that perspective is G. Gutierrez, *A Theology of Liberation* (Maryknoll: Orbis, 1973), though this was preceded by the lesser-known work by R. Alves, *A Theology of Human Hope* (Washington, DC: Corpus Books, 1969); see C. R. Padilla, "Evangelical Theology in Latin American Contexts," in *The Cambridge Companion to Evangelical Theology*, ed. T. Larsen and D. J. Treier (Cambridge: Cambridge University Press, 2007), 259–73, here p. 264. Liberation theology has since found expression around the world, in numerous contexts where people suffer oppression; for representative articles, see C. Rowland, ed., *The Cambridge Companion to Liberation Theology*, 2nd ed. (Cambridge: Cambridge University Press, 2007).

[10] The reality in the West, unfortunately, has tended to be otherwise; these insights serve as "a severe indictment of traditional Western scholarship, for having failed to see the challenge the Bible raises to those in power" (Barton, *Nature of Biblical Criticism*, 161). D. Patte provides a helpful "androcritical model" that can be pursued by white European-American male critics, who have drawn much criticism for their tendency to ignore, and thus further contribute to, the problem of imbalances of power. See D. Patte, *Ethics of Biblical Interpretation* (Louisville: Westminster John Knox, 1995).

NT critics who can function as cultural brokers for the ancient NT world are shaped and grown by all the preceding factors. These critics will be sufficiently familiar with the complexities of both cultures they represent to avoid making facile comparisons and superficial applications across cultures. Their respect for both cultures will keep them from treating the NT as a source of maxims to be applied woodenly in today's world. Ideally these critics will not be dogmatic about the meaning of the NT texts, recognizing the provisional results of their own interpretation, and will have a receptive attitude to insights provided by other critics who begin the task of interpretation from a different ideological viewpoint or sociocultural background. Finally, the task of these critics will not be limited to enabling communication, but will also extend to addressing issues arising from imbalances of power and redressing wrongs that have been occasioned by an incomplete understanding, or a *mis*understanding, of the NT message.

The HCM and the NT as the Church's Book

Before proceeding to an overview of the various disciplines included in the HCM, one more topic deserves attention: one of the criticisms leveled at the HCM from certain quarters is that it is inimical to the Christian faith. Addressing this question brings us once again to consider the issue of presuppositions. The HCM *itself* is not inimical to faith, but there has been no lack of critics who have chosen to apply the HCM based on *presuppositions* that are inimical to faith. Some, for example, have approached the NT with the preunderstanding that there is no transcendent reality and that therefore miracles and divine revelation belong to the realm of myth, or with the presupposition that human reason is autonomous and can master a fully objective world. In short, many scholars who employ the HCM have approached the NT guided by Enlightenment presuppositions. It should come as no surprise that these scholars have often arrived at conclusions that are inimical to faith.

There is no direct connection, however, between the HCM and the presuppositions of the Enlightenment. J. Barton has argued that the origins of the HCM are not to be traced to the Enlightenment, as is commonly assumed in the English-speaking West, but to the Reformation, as is commonly held in Germany. A critical approach to Scripture, in Barton's words, "is linked with the Reformation insistence on the authority of the Bible, read freely, over the Church." Barton continues, "Christian believers, according to Reformation principles, have the right to ask whether the Bible really means what the Church says it means. In that sentence lies the whole development of biblical criticism in germ."[11] It follows that one need not blindly adhere to Enlightenment presuppositions in embarking on the critical study of biblical texts.

Practicing the HCM from within the church, and without adhering to Enlightenment presuppositions, can lead to results that are positive for faith, as the authors of this chapter have experienced in their own work.[12] To mention only some of our significant presuppositions, we assume that God has worked decisively in history through his son Jesus Christ; that the cross was the focal point of that event; that the cross not only effected a change in the human condition before God but also conveyed a radical message about the nature of God himself; and that the inclusion of four Gospels within the NT canon implies that there is value not only in the historical witness of the evangelists to this event but also in their distinctive interpretations of it for faith. This is the context out of which the authors of this chapter apply the HCM to the Gospels, and in so doing we have found our faith strengthened rather than destroyed.

Having provided a rationale for the continued use of the HCM, as well as some general guidelines for the spirit in which it might be applied, we now turn to a brief examination of what each of its constitutive disciplines or methods contributes to the study of the NT.

Source Criticism

Source criticism is dedicated to identifying, reconstructing, and describing sources contained within NT documents. Applied to the Gospels, source criticism has dealt primarily with what is known as the Synoptic Problem: how one is to account for the extensive agreements between Matthew, Mark, and Luke (the "Synoptics").

---

[11] J. Barton, "Historical-Critical Approaches," in *The Cambridge Companion to Biblical Interpretation*, ed. J. Barton (Cambridge: Cambridge University Press, 1998), 9–20, here p. 16.

[12] See further Hagner, "Exegesis in the Postmodern World," though written in conversation with postmodernism rather than Enlightenment presuppositions.

If it were simply a matter of explaining the Synoptics' similarity in content, one could appeal to a common dependence on oral tradition, and one would not have a Synoptic Problem. The "problem" arises with how to explain the similarities that go beyond content to include ordering, wording, and other elements. For example, while many agreements in order might conceivably lead back to oral performances, when both Matthew and Mark break off their narrative of the ministry of Jesus at precisely the same place and go back to an account of John the Baptist's activity (Matt. 14:3–12/Mark 6:17–29), this stretches the viability of oral tradition as an explanation. An even more compelling example is offered by the parenthetical remark shared by Matthew and Mark, "let the reader understand" (Matt. 24:15/Mark 13:14) – here we are dealing clearly with a word from a writer to his reading audience. That it is found in two separate writings indicates clearly that one depends at least indirectly on the written form of the other. This type of agreement has led most scholars to posit some kind of literary relationship among the Synoptics.

Currently the most widely held solution to the Synoptic Problem is the Two-Source Hypothesis: Mark wrote first and was used independently as a source by Matthew and Luke. Matthew and Luke also used a second source for the material they hold in common that is not found in Mark. This second source, now lost, is the "Sayings Source" or "Q" (which stands for the German word *Quelle* or "source"). Many treatments add additional levels of complexity: Matthew and Luke had access to slightly different forms of Q (Q^M and Q^L), slightly different forms of Mark ($Mark^M$ and $Mark^L$), as well as their own "Special Sources" (M and L). Still, apart from such fine-tuning, the designation "Two-Source Hypothesis" reflects that in the final analysis Matthew and Luke used two main sources: Mark and Q. The main weakness of this hypothesis is that it rests in large part on the conjectured existence of Q, a document that is otherwise unmentioned and unknown. Nevertheless, the Two-Source Hypothesis has remained the dominant explanation for the Synoptic Problem for more than a century and a half.[13]

---

[13] Classic expositions of the Two-Source Hypothesis include W. Sanday, ed., *Studies in the Synoptic Problem by Members of the University of Oxford* (Oxford: Clarendon, 1911); J. C. Hawkins, *Horae Synopticae* (Oxford: Clarendon, 1909); B. H. Streeter, *The Four Gospels*, 2nd rev. ed. (London: Macmillan, 1930). Recent major defenses include F. Neirynck, *Duality in Mark*, BETL 31 (Leuven: Leuven University Press, 1972); *Minor Agreements of Matthew and Luke against Mark with a Cumulative List*, BETL 37 (Leuven: Leuven

The Two-Source Hypothesis, however, is not the only one currently vying for acceptance. W. R. Farmer (1921–2000) recently revived the "Griesbach Hypothesis" that was popularized by J. Griesbach (1745–1812) at the end of the eighteenth century. According to this hypothesis, Matthew wrote first. Second came Luke, who used Matthew and a considerable amount of material from other sources. Mark wrote last, mostly conflating Matthew and Luke, but also contributing a small amount of additional material (hence this is also known as the "Two-Gospel Hypothesis," in that Mark used Matthew and Luke).[14] While Farmer's work has brought about a welcome reconsideration of the Synoptic Problem, most scholars hold that the Griesbach Hypothesis raises more questions than it answers.

The complexity of the Synoptic Problem and the various hypotheses that have been offered go well beyond what one can gain from the brief sketch given previously.[15] A student of the Gospels has much to gain from wrestling personally with the evidence in the Gospels themselves and from weighing the various scholarly arguments against each other. One must take a position on the interrelationships among the Gospels in order to fully engage in their study. Especially when it comes to the practice of redaction criticism, to be covered later, one's findings will differ radically depending on which of the solutions to the Synoptic Problem one takes as a starting point.

Genre and Form Criticism

The basic insight to be gained from genre and form criticism is that not all writings are intended to be read, or are read, in the same way. The

University Press, 1974); C. M. Tuckett, *The Revival of the Griesbach Hypothesis*, SNTSMS 44 (Cambridge: Cambridge University Press, 1983).

[14] Among W. R. Farmer's works see especially *The Synoptic Problem: A Critical Analysis* (Dillsboro: Western North Carolina Press, 1976) and "The Two-Gospel Hypothesis: The Statement of the Hypothesis," in *The Interrelations of the Gospels*, ed. D. L. Dungan, BETL 95 (Leuven: Leuven University Press, 1990), 125–56; Farmer also edited a volume on what impact the acceptance of the Two-Gospel Hypothesis might have on NT studies: *New Synoptic Studies* (Macon: Mercer University Press, 1983).

[15] See further the surveys (with bibliography) by C. M. Tuckett, "Synoptic Problem," in *ABD* 6 (1992): 263–70; R. H. Stein, "Synoptic Problem," in *Dictionary of Jesus and the Gospels*, ed. J. B. Green, S. McKnight, and I. H. Marshall (Downers Grove: InterVarsity, 1992), 784–92; B. Reicke and D. B. Peabody, "Synoptic Problem," in *DBI* 2 (1999): 517–24.

genre of a whole work, or a large section of a work, carries with it certain expectations as to how it is to be understood. Genre functions something like an implicit contract between the writer and the reader. One does not write or read a love letter the same as a medical prescription, or a science-fiction novel the same as a biography. Likewise, smaller units within a written work alert one by their literary form that they are to be read differently than material with other forms.[16] When one encounters a metaphor in a text, one subconsciously recognizes that the author did not intend for the words to be read literally and seeks for an appropriate figurative meaning. To do otherwise would be a blunder at the level of form and would result in misunderstanding.

The ability to distinguish genre and form is indispensable for the accurate understanding of ancient documents such as the Gospels. The problem is that while we can naturally identify most genres and forms of twenty-first-century literature, our lack of familiarity with ancient literature may lead us to misinterpret the Gospels by reading them in ways other than intended. This is why form and genre criticism are indispensable parts of the HCM.

GENRE CRITICISM. The discipline of genre criticism seeks to identify the genre of the Gospels as a whole to provide guidance on how they are to be read.[17] A genre can be loosely defined as a set of texts that share a certain family resemblance. Elements that are usually taken into consideration for determining this family resemblance include external features such as structure, length, and use of sources, and internal features such as the intention of the author, subject matter, and style. On the basis of these features and others, a majority of scholars today categorize the Gospels as a subtype of ancient Greco-Roman biography or *bios*.[18]

---

[16] One could view genre and form as synonymous; in the present treatment, genre applies to whole works such as Gospels and epistles or to large segments within them, while form applies to smaller units of discourse such as individual pericopes or sayings.

[17] From the 1920s through the 1960s the Gospels were commonly regarded as without parallel in ancient literature, constituting a genre unto themselves. This was based largely on the form-critical assessment of the Gospels as *Kleinliteratur*, or unsophisticated collections of oral traditions in which authorial creativity played no role. As noted previously, with redaction criticism came the recognition of the creative role of the evangelists, implying that the Gospels were literature in their own right. This brought renewed efforts by genre critics over the past four decades to identify the Gospels' genre by comparing them to other ancient texts.

[18] This majority has not reached consensus; D. E. Aune lists ten authors who have variously argued over the last few decades that the Gospels fit within the genre of Hellenistic

There are implications that follow from this categorization. R. A. Burridge notes, for example, that it implies a christological hermeneutic: "Since the Gospels are portraits of a person, they must be interpreted with a biographical focus upon their subject, Jesus of Nazareth."[19] This in turn implies that (a) if the main concern in interpretation is to arrive at what the Gospels say about Jesus, what they can tell us, for example, about the history of the early Christian communities or about the reality of Christian experience should not distract from that aim; (b) there is no truth to the claim that the early church had no interest in the person of the earthly Jesus; otherwise they would not have written Gospels but only discourses of the risen Christ, along Gnostic lines; and (c) one can expect variability in content among the Gospels, arising from the evangelists' selectivity in their use of historical sources, but also a limit to the evangelists' creativity, since the Gospels were written about a historical person within the lifetime of people who were his contemporaries.[20] Burridge has dedicated an entire volume to exploring how the recognition of the Gospels as a subtype of ancient *bios* should impact their use as sources of ethical instruction. He prefaces his treatment with the claim that "the biographical genre of the Gospels suggests that we need to look at the whole narrative of Jesus' life and death, and include his deeds, actions and example alongside his teachings and words to determine his ethics."[21] This is a welcome contribution to the discussion on ethics, in that it provides a corrective to an approach that relies almost exclusively on Jesus's sayings (especially those contained in the Sermon on the Mount). Not everyone will agree with Burridge on every point, but his work provides

---

romance or popular fiction, Old Testament biographical narratives, the Jewish novel, Greek tragedy, and "apocalyptic historical monograph" (*The Westminster Dictionary of New Testament and Early Christian Literature and Rhetoric* [Louisville: Westminster John Knox, 2003], 206).

[19] R. A. Burridge, "Gospel as Genre," in *Encyclopedia of the Historical Jesus*, ed. C. A. Evans (New York: Routledge, 2008), 232–36, quote from p. 234.

[20] Burridge, "Gospel as Genre," 234–35; R. A. Burridge, *What Are the Gospels?*, 2nd rev. ed., BRS (Grand Rapids: Eerdmans, 2004 [1st ed. 1992]), 247–50. Authors who have been instrumental in the growing recognition of the Gospels as *bioi* include R. A. Burridge, C. H. Talbert (*What Is a Gospel?* [Philadelphia: Fortress, 1977]), and D. E. Aune (*The New Testament in Its Literary Environment*, LEC 8 [Philadelphia: Westminster, 1987]), vindicating the earlier claim of C. W. Votaw in "The Gospels and Contemporary Biographies," *AJT* 19 (1915): 45–73, 217–49 (reprinted as *The Gospels and Contemporary Biographies in the Greco-Roman World*, FBBS 27 [Philadelphia: Fortress, 1970]).

[21] R. A. Burridge, *Imitating Jesus* (Grand Rapids: Eerdmans, 2007), quote taken from p. 32.

a good example of how one's understanding of the genre of the Gospels can and should influence one's interpretation.

Before moving on to consider form criticism, we must note that genre and genre criticism do not have to do only with complete texts such as the Gospels, but also with discrete portions within them. Depending on one's perspective regarding the genre of Mark 13, for example, one might choose to read it in light of criteria used in interpreting apocalyptic literature (as its common designation "the Markan Apocalypse" would imply). Or perhaps one might study not only Mark 13 but also John 13–17 in light of criteria used to interpret testamentary literature, a genre with which both passages show an affinity. Constraints of space do not allow us to further develop this line of investigation; suffice it to say that genre criticism is very useful for studying not only each Gospel as a whole, but also segments within the Gospels.

FORM CRITICISM.   *Form criticism* has traditionally been concerned with three tasks: (1) classifying the material in the Synoptics according to form; (2) recovering the original form of this material while still in its oral stage (as well as tracing when possible its subsequent changes);[22] and (3) identifying the life situation (*Sitz im Leben*) in which the material was created.[23] The second and third of these tasks are problematic.[24] To put it briefly, in carrying out the second task form critics tended to treat form as a prescriptive rather than a descriptive category. Having classified oral Jesus tradition into various ideal forms according to what they perceived

---

[22] In some studies tracing the development within the Jesus tradition is treated separately as "Tradition Criticism."

[23] The three classic form-critical works are K. L. Schmidt, *Der Rahmen der Geschichte Jesu* (Berlin: Trowitzsch, 1919); M. Dibelius, *From Tradition to Gospel*, LTT (Cambridge: James Clarke, 1971 [1st German ed. 1919]); and R. Bultmann, *The History of the Synoptic Tradition*, 3rd ed. (Oxford: Blackwell, 1972 [1st German ed. 1921]), to which one might add V. Taylor, *The Formation of the Gospel Tradition*, 2nd ed. (London: Macmillan, 1935 [1st ed. 1933]). On what follows, see C. A. Evans, "Source, Form and Redaction Criticism," 27–32; Evans, "Form Criticism," in *Encyclopedia of the Historical Jesus*, 204–8; S. H. Travis, "Form Criticism," in *New Testament Interpretation: Essays on Principles and Methods*, ed. I. H. Marshall (Grand Rapids: Eerdmans, 1977), 153–64, here pp. 157–60; for a thorough discussion, see E. Güttgemanns, *Candid Questions Concerning Gospel Form Criticism*, PTMS 26 (Pittsburgh: Pickwick, 1979). A good introduction to form criticism is E. V. McKnight, *What Is Form Criticism?*, GBS (Philadelphia: Fortress, 1969).

[24] For a brief critique of the (ab)uses of form criticism, see Evans, "Source, Form and Redaction Criticism," 27–30.

as their function, they then treated these forms as criteria for what Jesus could or could not have said. Certain forms could (supposedly) only be used within certain contexts; if in carrying out the third task form critics located these contexts within the life of the early church, then the material in question could not have originated with Jesus. In Germany especially (and to a much lesser extent in England), the origin of much of the Jesus tradition in the Gospels was thus, on a very questionable basis, attributed not to Jesus but to the church. This whole enterprise was carried out not only with a rather unsophisticated understanding of how oral tradition actually worked in antiquity,[25] but also with a misplaced confidence in the interpreter's ability to reconstruct the life situation of the early church. While the goals of these form-critical tasks remain valuable, the application of the method needs to be revisited to incorporate a more informed understanding of the inner workings of oral tradition in the time leading up to the Gospels, and its results should be offered more in the form of suggestions than absolutes, to better reflect their hypothetical nature.

There are other contributions of form criticism that are more important for our purposes. The discipline's basic insight into the relevance of form for understanding the Jesus tradition is indispensable for interpreting the Gospels. Similar to what we saw regarding genre, people respond to different forms in different ways: an (often) unconscious agreement exists between the speaker and the hearer, or between the writer and the reader, that a certain form of speech will include certain components and be structured in a certain way, and will elicit a certain type of response.

Much work has been done along these lines on the parables in the Gospels, both because of their importance within the Synoptic tradition and because of their power to provoke the reader to respond.[26]

---

[25] Both Bultmann and Dibelius spoke of "laws of [oral] tradition" as if they had rigorously established how oral tradition worked, but their premises remained largely unexamined. One of their central presuppositions, e.g., was that oral tradition developed from simple to complex, but E. P. Sanders has shown that in the synoptic tradition there is movement *both* from the simple to the complex *and* from the complex to the simple. See E. P. Sanders, *The Tendencies of the Synoptic Tradition*, SNTSMS 9 (Cambridge: Cambridge University Press, 1969). For further critique of form criticism, see B. Gerhardsson, *The Reliability of the Gospel Tradition* (Peabody: Hendrickson, 2001).

[26] In addition to parables, examples of forms in the Gospels include pronouncement stories, stories about Jesus, proverbs, miracle stories, controversy stories, and Passion

Scholars have come to recognize that parables do not function primarily to convey propositional truth or to illustrate teachings, but rather to create a world into which hearers are invited, where their vision of reality is transformed.[27] Some parables work, for example, by surprising the reader by their strangeness or by the unexpected twist of their outcome. Such parables encourage the reader to identify with the characters they portray and then speak directly to the reader-turned-character, presenting the reader with the need to make a commitment and thus to act. In this manner the relationship between parables and readers extends well beyond the conveyance and appropriation of factual information, achieved via the readers' intellectual grasp of the parable's "punch line." Along these lines, A. C. Thiselton suggests that Jesus's purpose in using parables instead of direct discourse "may well be *to prevent premature understanding without inner change.*"[28] Not only are parables used for a purpose other than the communication of intellectual truth, they are a means of avoiding this communication, unless it is accompanied by what is more important, a change in the hearer.[29]

This observation concerning the purpose of parables is but a brief example taken from much important work done on the parables over the past three or four decades.[30] Important to stress here is that, as illustrated by this example, the "parable" as an identifiable form within the Gospels is illumined by certain unique interpretive approaches that do not necessarily apply to other forms.

Narrative, among others. For a helpful comparative chart of the forms identified by Taylor, Bultmann, and Dibelius, see *Westminster Dictionary of New Testament and Early Christian Literature and Rhetoric,* 188–89.

[27] See Thiselton, *On Hermeneutics,* 417–40, 465–88.

[28] Thiselton, *On Hermeneutics,* 517; italics in the original.

[29] This approach to form criticism works well with reader-response criticism, with the latter's emphasis on the active role of communities of readers in constructing the meaning of the text. One must apply reader-response criticism with care, however, as Thiselton cautions, "the notion that biblical texts might not have the capacity to transform readers 'from beyond', but merely invoke 'constructions' drawn from the hitherto undiscovered inner resources of the reading community, does not cohere readily or well with Christian theology" (*On Hermeneutics,* 524, and see also pp. 397–521; cf. also Thiselton, *New Horizons in Hermeneutics*).

[30] See, e.g., J. D. Crossan, *In Parables* (New York: Harper & Row, 1973); P. Ricoeur, "Biblical Hermeneutics," *Semeia* 4 (1975): 27–148; W. R. Herzog, II, *Parables as Subversive Speech* (Louisville: Westminster John Knox, 1994); R. Etchells, *A Reading of the Parables of Jesus* (London: Darton, Longman and Todd, 1998).

Redaction Criticism

Redaction criticism is concerned with the final stage of the formation of the Gospels, and focuses on the evangelists' editorial work in using their sources. The aim of redaction criticism is "the detection of the evangelists' creative contribution in all its aspects to the Christian tradition which they transmit."[31] Prior to the advent of redaction criticism, form criticism had portrayed the evangelists as nothing more than "scissors-and-paste" editors. The work of the earliest redaction critics – G. Bornkamm on Matthew, H. Conzelmann on Luke-Acts, and W. Marxsen on Mark[32] – pointed out the inadequacy of this portrayal. These scholars showed that the evangelists were authors and theologians in their own right. While in the past scholars tended to harmonize the message of the four canonical Gospels (especially of the Synoptics), redaction criticism has considerably enriched our understanding by establishing that they contain four distinct portrayals of Jesus.

Redaction criticism has been practiced with two main emphases. In Germany the method arose primarily as a historical discipline, focusing on what has become known as the "world behind the text." Practiced in this way, redaction criticism is concerned with "the origin and settings of traditions, on the conditions of their development and on the historical circumstances that best explained their final editing."[33] It is thus especially important that one remain alert to the change in perspective

---

[31] On what follows see S. S. Smalley, "Redaction Criticism," in *New Testament Interpretation*, ed. I. H. Marshall (Grand Rapids: Eerdmans, 1977), 181–95, quote from p. 181; also Evans, "Source, Form and Redaction Criticism," 17–45; D. R. Catchpole, "Source, Form and Redaction Criticism of the New Testament," in *Handbook to Exegesis of the NT*, ed. S. E. Porter (Leiden: Brill, 1997), 167–88. N. Perrin's *What Is Redaction Criticism?*, GBS (Philadelphia: Fortress, 1969), remains valuable, though unfortunately Perrin tends to create an opposition between redactional work and historical reliability, as if one necessarily precluded the other.

[32] English translations of their seminal works can be found in G. Bornkamm, G. Barth, and H. J. Held, *Tradition and Interpretation in Matthew*, NTL (Philadelphia: Westminster, 1963); H. Conzelmann, *The Theology of St. Luke* (London: Faber, 1960); W. Marxsen, *Mark the Evangelist: Studies on the Redaction History of the Gospel* (Nashville: Abingdon, 1969).

[33] J. R. Donahue, "Redaction Criticism: Has the *Hauptstrasse* Become a *Sackgasse?*," in *The New Literary Criticism and the New Testament*, ed. E. V. McKnight and E. S. Malbon, JSNTSS 109 (Sheffield: JSOT Press, 1994), 27–57, quote from p. 34. For a brief critique of some misuses of redaction criticism as a historical discipline, see Smalley, "Redaction Criticism," 187.

implied in moving from one life situation to another. The material in the Gospels involves three different life situations: that of Jesus, that of the postresurrection church, and that of each evangelist and his community. Words spoken by Jesus during his ministry may have had one meaning in that context, accrued newer and deeper meaning after the resurrection, and then been given a special meaning or been interpreted and applied to a specific situation within an evangelist's community. Redaction criticism facilitates learning about all three of these life situations so that one can understand the text of the Gospels in their light.[34]

In the United States redaction criticism took a different direction, being practiced "primarily as an exercise in literary criticism where the emphasis was on the final product as a unitary composition with concern for the overarching themes and motifs and for the structure of the whole and of the individual parts."[35] In taking this approach, one identifies the material any given evangelist has chosen to include or leave out from his sources in composing his narrative, and considers how he may have modified, expanded, or abbreviated the material.[36] This aspect of redaction-critical work is most straightforward when examining how Matthew and Luke used Mark. It is more problematic when used to study how Matthew and Luke used Q, or how Mark used his own sources, as this involves sources that are no longer extant.[37] (Here one must clarify that a major pitfall to avoid is to assume that the theology of an evangelist is equal to the sum of the changes he effected on the materials at his disposal. The theology of each evangelist may be represented also within the material each adopted unchanged from his sources.) One also studies

---

[34] See further D. A. Hagner, "Interpreting the Gospels: The Landscape and the Quest," *JETS* 24 (1981): 23–37, here pp. 26–32.

[35] Donahue, "Redaction Criticism," 34.

[36] Not all the evangelists' changes to their sources were necessarily theologically motivated; e.g., G. Stanton has argued that Luke changed his sources at times for stylistic rather than theological purposes. See G. Stanton, *Jesus of Nazareth in New Testament Preaching*, SNTSMS 27 (Cambridge: Cambridge University Press, 1974), 31–66.

[37] This presupposes the priority of Mark, the reigning majority solution to the Synoptic Problem. Studying Mark's use of his sources, or Matthew and Luke's use of Q, is problematic in that one must rely on the document(s) under consideration to reconstruct the source(s) and then make statements about the use of the source(s) in said document(s); all this involves an element of circular reasoning that is by necessity rather speculative.

how each evangelist has arranged the material in his Gospel, both at the level of brief pericopes and short narratives[38] and at the level of the Gospel as a whole. Special attention is given to material that is viewed as the creation of the evangelists, such as introductions to pericopes and editorial summaries, as they may represent important repositories of the evangelists' theology. At each step one must pause to consider each part of a Gospel in light of the whole and the whole in light of each part – a good example of the hermeneutical circle as mentioned previously. Overall, redaction criticism practiced in this way provides insight not only into how each evangelist understood the material at his disposal, but also into how he interpreted the material in his own unique way for his readers. As J. Donahue has noted, redaction criticism as a literary enterprise was a precursor to many of the literary approaches that later became popular in interpreting the NT.[39] With its attention to the creative work of the evangelists and its focus on the finished form of the text, it is well suited to be practiced in conjunction with newer literary methods such as narrative criticism.[40]

Historical/Cultural Background Studies

The HCM also involves focusing on specific cultural or historical issues that arise in reading any given Gospel narrative. Understanding certain narratives or sayings will demand familiarity with the place of table fellowship in Jewish antiquity; others will require a grasp of gender roles; still others will require the interpreter to know something about Jewish purity laws, the various Jewish parties, or the details of the Roman administration of Palestine. Encyclopedia and dictionary articles are a useful entry point to specific topics such as these, not only because

---

[38] Indispensable for redaction-critical work at the level of pericopes is a Greek synopsis that arranges them in parallel columns; the most widely used is K. Aland, ed., *Synopsis quattuor Evangeliorum*, 15th ed. (Stuttgart: Deutsche Bibelgesellschaft, 2001), also available in a Greek-English edition.

[39] Donahue, "Redaction Criticism," 34.

[40] On narrative criticism see M. A. Powell, *What Is Narrative Criticism?*, GBS (Minneapolis: Fortress, 1990); *The Bible and Modern Literary Criticism* (Westport: Greenwood, 1992); and his chapter on "Literary Approaches and the Gospel of Matthew" in this volume.

of the content of the articles but also because of their bibliographies, which serve as guides for further research.[41] Here we encounter again the hermeneutical circle: the study of each particular historical or cultural item will inform one's understanding of the history and culture of the period as a whole, and vice versa. It is important to stress here the value of a wide-ranging knowledge of the history and culture of Gospel times as a whole: one may be blind to the importance of specific topics that could inform one's reading of the Gospels unless one is already familiar to a certain extent with the history and culture in which they were immersed.

Of all the steps within the HCM, historical and cultural studies are especially open to enrichment from other approaches such as those represented in the remainder of this volume, and many who practice the HCM incorporate these other approaches as a matter of course. Social-scientific approaches to interpretation, for example (especially those based on sociology and cultural anthropology), have become indispensable in seeking to understand the social and cultural forces operative in NT texts.[42] Historical Jesus studies also shed much valuable light on the history and culture of the world of the Gospels, especially as practiced by those engaged in the "Third Quest." These scholars rightly seek to understand the words and actions of Jesus within the context of first-century Judaism, and in so doing shed much light on the particular combination of religious, social, economic, and political forces that shaped the latter.[43] Postcolonial and feminist criticism are valuable sources for new insights into the culture of NT times (both within and behind the text), especially in relation to issues of oppression, marginalization, and deprivation, but also more generally in relation to such areas as imbalances of power,

---

[41] See especially C. A. Evans and S. E. Porter, eds, *Dictionary of New Testament Background* (Downers Grove: InterVarsity Press, 2000); *Dictionary of Jesus and the Gospels; Anchor Bible Dictionary; Encyclopedia of the Historical Jesus.*

[42] S. C. Barton, "Historical Criticism and Social-Scientific Perspectives in New Testament Study," in *Hearing the New Testament,* ed. J. B. Green (Grand Rapids: Eerdmans, 1995), 61–89, esp. pp. 67–69; see further the chapter by B. Malina in the present volume entitled "Social-Scientific Approaches and the Gospel of Matthew."

[43] See R. Morton, "Quest of the Historical Jesus," in *Encyclopedia of the Historical Jesus,* ed. C. A. Evans (New York: Routledge, 2008), 472–79, here 476–78, and the article by Evans entitled "Historical Jesus Studies and the Gospel of Matthew" in the present volume.

expectations associated with gender, and social dynamics having to do with class and economic standing.[44]

HISTORICAL-CRITICAL METHOD: INTERPRETATION
OF MATTHEW 27:57–28:15

We might argue that Matthew 27:57–28:20 makes up a single large unit.[45] But certainly the four or five smaller units that compose 27:57–28:15 cohere nicely: 27:57–61 reports the burial of Jesus; 27:62–66 provides a narrative concerning the posting of a guard at the tomb; 28:1–7 details the announcement of the resurrection to the women at the tomb, while 28:8–10 gives an account of the appearance of the risen Jesus to the women; finally 28:11–15 tells of a story concocted by the Jewish authorities to explain the missing body. We will take up these sections one by one.

MATTHEW 27:57–61. This passage follows immediately on the crucifixion narrative. The genre, continuing from the previous verses, is historical narration. Accepting the Two-Source Hypothesis (Mark and Q) here and in the following exegesis, we note that Matthew's pericope is only half as long as Mark's. Matthew (with Luke) omits Mark's account of Pilate's question about whether Jesus was already dead (Mark 15:45) as essentially unimportant material.[46] Matthew is concerned not with establishing the reality of the death of Jesus, against claims that he had only swooned on the cross, but rather with the claims that the body had been stolen by

---

[44] See Segovia, "Postcolonial Criticism and the Gospel of Matthew" in the present volume and Wainwright, "Feminist Criticism and the Gospel of Matthew" in the present volume.

[45] See C. H. Giblin, "Structural and Thematic Correlation in the Matthean Burial-Resurrection Narrative (Matt. xxvii. 57–xxviii.20)" *NTS* 21 (1974–75): 406–20, who detects a chiastic structure in this material. But see the critique of D. Senior, "Matthew's Account of the Burial of Jesus (Mt 27:57–61)," in *The Four Gospels 1992*, ed. F. Segbroeck, C. M. Tuckett, G. Van Belle, and J. Verheyden, BETL 100 (Leuven: Leuven University Press, 1992), 1433–48.

[46] The present pericope has a number of minor agreements between Matthew and Luke against Mark, encouraging some to think of a dependence of Luke on Matthew. But these agreements can readily be explained through independent editing on the part of Matthew and Luke, and the possible influence of oral tradition. See, e.g., C. M. Tuckett, "On the Relationship between Matthew and Luke," *NTS* 30 (1984): 138–39.

the disciples (thus 27:62–66 and 28:11–15). The security of the tomb may also be in view in Matthew's addition of "large" (*megan*) before the word "stone" (27:60). The possibility of the tomb being mistaken is ruled out by the fact that the custody of the body is given to a disciple of Jesus,[47] the wealthy and influential Joseph of Arimathea – unknown to us except from this Synoptic pericope and John 19:38 – and that he buries the body in a new tomb he owned. Matthew alters Mark's description of Joseph as "one awaiting the kingdom of God" to "who had himself become a disciple of Jesus" (27:57; cf. John 19:38: "who was a disciple of Jesus, but secretly, for fear of the Jews"), thereby assuming the association between the kingdom and discipleship to Jesus.[48] Matthew refers to Joseph only as "a rich man" (27:57; possibly an allusion to Isa. 53:9b), omitting Mark's reference to him as being a "prominent member of the Council [i.e. Sanhedrin]" (Mark 15:43), perhaps not wanting to associate him with the enemies of Jesus (cf. Luke's remark in Luke 23:51, "who had not consented to their purpose and deed").

Matthew's simple opening words, "When it was evening" (cf. Mark's reference to "the day of preparation, that is, the day before the Sabbath," 15:42), indirectly point to the urgent necessity of removing the dead body from the cross, in obedience to Deut. 21:22–23, where it is said that a criminal's body "must not remain on the tree overnight; you must bury him the same day."[49] Pilate, who seems to have known of Joseph and who would have been happy not to tread further on Jewish sensitivities, accedes to Joseph's request.[50] This concession is historically likely, given Matthew's emphasis on Pilate as wanting to indicate his innocence in the whole matter (27:24; cf. the reported dream of Pilate's wife in 27:19). By his request, Joseph keeps Jesus from being buried in a common grave with the thieves who had been crucified with him, although often bodies

---

[47] So too against the possibility of a mistaken tomb, Matthew follows Mark in mentioning the presence of Mary Magdalene and "the other Mary" sitting opposite the tomb (27:61).

[48] We may compare Joseph with Nicodemus, another leader of the Jews who became a disciple of Jesus and who would also become involved in the burial of Jesus (John 3:1, 7:50, 19:39).

[49] See too Josephus, *Jewish War* 4.5.2; cf. Philo, *Flacc.* 10.83: "I have known cases when on the eve of a holiday . . . people who have been crucified have been taken down and their bodies delivered to their kinsfolk."

[50] It is unlikely that the *Gospel of Peter* 3–5, 23–24, is historically correct that the body of Jesus was under the custody of Herod and the Jews, and that Pilate had to ask Herod's permission to turn the body over to Joseph.

were left hanging on their crosses where they decayed or became carrion for vultures.[51]

Joseph in an act of devotion wrapped the body in "clean (*katharos*) linen" (the Synoptic tradition knows nothing of the account in John 19:39 about Nicodemus bringing spices to anoint the body), customary in honorable burials, and then placed it "in his new tomb" (cf. John 19:41), a cavelike tomb carved out of a limestone hillside[52] (27:60). This was apparently a family tomb recently prepared,[53] perhaps with the imminent death of a family member in mind. Matthew's addition of the word "new" underscores that the tomb had not yet been used, and again this fact counteracts the possibility of a later confusion of bodies. The tomb was sealed with a "large stone" rolled into place along a track (cf. 28:2; Mark 16:4). Thus although crucified as a common criminal and therefore regarded by the Jews as cursed by God (Deut. 21:23), Jesus was nevertheless buried honorably in the tomb of a rich man.

The two women, Mary[54] Magdalene and "the other Mary," probably Mary the mother of James and Joseph (27:56),[55] had watched the crucifixion of Jesus, and undoubtedly also the deposition and the removal of the body to Joseph's tomb where, Matthew now records, they were sitting, "opposite the tomb (here for the first time *taphos* rather than *mnēmeion*, although there appears to be no difference in meaning between the two words)" (27:61), perhaps in a prayer vigil.[56] These words replace and abbreviate Mark's "they were watching where it [the body] was laid" (Mark 15:47), but function in the same way, that is, to provide evidence against any inference that the two women eventually went to the wrong tomb on the dawn of Sunday (28:1).

This narrative, and especially the final verse, prepares by design for the resurrection appearance to the same women in 28:1–10. The sequence

---

[51] For helpful discussion of Roman and Jewish attitudes to the bodies of the crucified, see R. Brown, *The Death of the Messiah* (New York: Doubleday, 1994), 2:1207–11.

[52] This sort of tomb, containing shelves and niches, was not uncommon in first-century Palestine; see *m. B. Bat.* 6:8.

[53] *Gospel of Peter* 6.24, probably dependent on Matthew, says that the sepulcher was called "the Garden of Joseph."

[54] The better manuscripts read "Mariam" (Miriam), the Hebraic spelling.

[55] Matthew's reference to only two of the three women is probably due to the influence of Mark 15:47.

[56] The sitting posture of the women may indicate mourning (cf. Ps. 137:1; *Gospel of Peter* 7.27); cf. the frequent idiom of "sitting in sackcloth and ashes."

of death–burial–resurrection constitutes the very heart of the kerygma of the early church. Before we come to the climax of the story, however, Matthew adds a brief narrative found nowhere else in the Gospels.

MATTHEW 27:62–66. As M material, not found in the other Synoptics (or John), this pericope and its companion in 28:11–15 are by rule historically suspect.[57] The fact, however, that this narrative is found only in Matthew says nothing about its historicity, positive or negative. It is of course hypothetically possible that Matthew simply made up the story, but such a negative conclusion about the historicity of the narrative is unnecessary if we allow that Matthew writes retrospectively and with his usual degree of freedom in the retelling of tradition at his disposal.[58]

Unless one rules out a priori, and without evidence, that Jesus ever alluded to his future resurrection, it is likely that a report of some such anticipated resurrection would have reached the ears of the Jewish authorities. And whatever they made of this report, it is perfectly understandable that they would have wanted to prevent Jesus's disciples from stealing the body[59] and then making the claim that Jesus had in fact risen from the dead (see 27:64). Having done their utmost to suppress this budding messianic movement by instigating the murder of its leader, the last thing they wanted to allow was any pretension that he had risen from the dead.

It is clear that the passage is apologetic and polemical in nature, but again that says nothing about it being unhistorical. The claim that Matthew created the story out of his imagination, for apologetic purposes, raises such questions as why there is not more abundant creation

---

[57] In defense of the historicity of the passage, see G. M. Lee, "The Guard at the Tomb," *Theology* 72 (1969): 169–75; D. Wenham, "The Resurrection Narratives in Matthew's Gospel," *TynB* 24 (1973): 21–54; and W. L. Craig, "The Guard at the Tomb," *NTS* 30 (1984): 273–81.

[58] Pace Luz's overly strong conclusion, leaning on H. S. Reimarus and D. F. Strauss: "There is no way to salvage the historicity of Matt 27:62–66 and 28:11–15." U. Luz, *Matthew 21–28*, Hermeneia (Minneapolis: Fortress, 2005), 587. Brown, who does not accept the historicity of the story, is more cautious: "Absolute negative statements (e.g., the account has no historical basis) most often go beyond the kind of evidence available to biblical scholars." *The Death of the Messiah*, 2:1312.

[59] Body stealing was not unknown in the ancient world. See B. M. Metzger, "The Nazareth Inscription Once Again," in *Jesus und Paulus*, ed. E. E. Ellis and E. Grässer (Göttingen: Vandenhoeck & Ruprecht, 1975), 221–38.

of material and why it is not made to accomplish its purpose more effectively.[60] Compared to the resurrection narrative of the *Gospel of Peter*, Matthew seems restrained and historically responsible.[61] Furthermore, the Jews could have easily denied the existence of the guard, if there had been none, and the Christians would have had no need to invent the idea of sleeping guards when Matthew's account already indicated that the guards were quite immobilized.[62]

"On the next day," further identified as the day "after the preparation [i.e. for the Sabbath]," the Jewish authorities went to Pilate with their request. That this occurred on the sabbath and involved the chief priests and the Pharisees (an odd linking of Jesus's adversaries that is also made by Matthew in 21:45) points to the urgency of this extraordinary event. The hasty, informal gathering of these Jewish authorities need not be thought of as indicating an official meeting of the Sanhedrin.

There is no small irony that in the same sentence (27:63) the Jewish authorities address Pilate as *kyrios* ("lord," albeit in the sense of "sir") and refer to Jesus as *planos* ("deceiver"). Although we cannot be certain of what they had heard, the Jewish authorities probably understood the prophecy of Jesus that "after three days I will rise" as little as did the disciples. Furthermore, although the Pharisees believed in an eschatological resurrection of the dead, they certainly did not believe that Jesus would rise from the dead. Matthew uses two different formulas, "after three days" and, more typically, "on the third day" (16:21, 17:23, 20:19). Fitting the present statement more closely is the use of the Jonah analogy in Jesus's words to scribes and Pharisees earlier in the narrative, where

---

[60]   There is a parallel narrative in the *Gospel of Peter* 28–33 that could witness to an independent historical tradition, but is more probably an elaboration of the Matthean story: "They [the scribes, Pharisees and elders] were afraid and came to Pilate, entreating him and saying, 'Give us soldiers that we may guard his sepulchre for three days, lest his disciples come and steal him away and the people suppose that he is risen from the dead, and do us harm.' And Pilate gave them Petronius the centurion with soldiers to guard the sepulchre, and all who were there together rolled a large stone and laid it against the door to the sepulchre to exclude the centurion and the soldiers, and they put on it seven seals, pitched a tent there and kept watch." Quoted from *The Apocryphal Jesus: Legends of the Early Church*, ed. J. K. Elliott (Oxford: Oxford University Press, 1996), 71.

[61]   N. T. Wright also argues against the story being a creation of Matthew *ex nihilo*. See N. T. Wright, *The Resurrection of the Son of God* (Minneapolis: Fortress, 2003), 636–40.

[62]   This is the argument of Craig, "The Guard at the Tomb," 278f. He shows that we have implausibility upon implausibility if the story is regarded as a Christian creation.

Jesus presents as a sign that he will be in the heart of the earth for three days and nights, just as Jonah was in the belly of the whale for three days and nights (Matt. 12:38–40, 26:61). It is doubtful that the Jewish authorities had any clear idea of what Jesus had foretold or what he meant by it. Matthew uses formulaic language and he may give more precision to their knowledge of Jesus's prediction than they actually had. More important to them is what words of this kind might inspire the disciples to do. In accord with their limited understanding, they ask for a guard to be posted "until the third day," which reckoning from the day of the request would give them a measure of extra protection.

The fear of the Jewish authorities that the disciples might steal the body of Jesus[63] is the reason they ask for the tomb to be made secure (not to prevent the resurrection!). Ironically, it is this fear that is later manufactured into the fatuous claim that is then used to explain the empty tomb (28:13). Further irony is found in the description of the claim "he has been raised from the dead" (27:64) as representing a "deception worst than the first," while those very words would become the heart of the kerygma of the early church, which galvanized the Mediterranean world in a way that the actual ministry of Jesus could not.

Although Pilate's response could be interpreted as meaning "you have a guard [which you may use]," more probably *echete* is to be understood as "take a guard [which I will provide for you]."[64] The word for guard is *koustōdian* (here and in 28:11), a Latin loanword, and the soldiers (*stratiōtai*, a word commonly used for Roman soldiers; cf. 27:27) who are sent are answerable to Pilate, as we see later in the narrative (28:12, 14). The Jewish authorities would not have needed to get Pilate's permission to post soldiers of their own temple guard. Pilate is happy enough to grant the request of the Jewish authorities, perhaps in his own way, fearing the unrest that might be caused if the body were stolen. The tomb had already been closed by the great stone rolled into place on the day before (27:60), but now it would be officially sealed (*sphragizō*, 27:66) with wax seals (cf. Dan. 6:17). It is worth noting that the tactic of the Jewish authorities was not exactly foolproof since by the time the guard sealed the tomb, it would have already been unguarded for a night and part of the following

---

[63] A number of later textual witnesses add *nyktos*, "by night," through the influence of 28:13.

[64] For this sense of the verb, see BDAG.

day. It seems improbable that if Matthew were inventing the story, he would have allowed such a gap. At the least he would have recorded that the soldiers checked to see if the body was there before they sealed the tomb.

MATTHEW 28:1–7. The account of the resurrection of Jesus will of necessity be reinterpreted as something other than historical by those whose worldview will not allow for the transcendent or miraculous within history. In a strict sense, it is true that a historian is unable to deal with causation from outside the system. This is why the HCM must be tempered or modified, for it will be of little use if our method rules out a priori what the text wants to relate. There is still much, however, that a historian can do, despite the limitations that come with the subject.[65]

The time notice here, *ōpse de sabbaton* (lit. evening of the sabbath), is to be taken as "after the Sabbath," as can be seen from the following words: "toward the dawn of the first day of the week," that is, early Sunday morning. Mary Magdalene and "the other Mary" (the mother of James and Joseph; cf. 27:56) come "to see [*theōrēsai*] the sepulcher." Mark (16:1) has three women (Salome is the third) who come to anoint Jesus's body with spices. Matthew thus freely recasts his Markan source; any significance to the changes he makes is difficult to determine. Matthew's apocalyptically tinged account of the earthquake and descent of an angel from heaven who rolls aside the stone and sits on it replaces the wondering of the women about how they will gain access to the tomb (Mark 16: 3–4). Matthew's narrative thus avoids having an open tomb without witnesses before the arrival of the women.

The issue of how the women expected to be able to enter the tomb if there really had been a guard posted is often raised as a major obstacle to the historicity of the story. But the women are not governed by such practical considerations. Rather, they are driven by their devotion, and if they knew of the guard perhaps hoped against hope that they could persuade them to be allowed to enter the tomb.[66] The other evangelists

---

[65] Our present, increasingly postmodern, culture may exhibit more openness to the possibility of the genuinely miraculous, but it brings with it its own set of problems.

[66] C. S. Keener points out that the guards would hardly have been worried about the women somehow "stealing the body under their noses," as if by some sleight of hand. See C. S. Keener, *A Commentary on the Gospel of Matthew* (Grand Rapids: Eerdmans, 1999), 697.

may not have known of the story or, at least, having decided not to include it, obviously had no need in their narratives to address the problem the guards would have been to the women fulfilling their purpose.

The angel in Matthew's narrative, described as having the appearance of "lightning" (cf. Dan. 10:6) and raiment "white as snow" (cf. 17:2), is far more impressive than Mark's "man" in a white robe who sits inside the tomb (to be understood as an angel, as also the two men "in dazzling apparel" in Luke 24:4). The earthquake is conceivably an aftershock of the one recorded in 27:51, unless the evangelist has added it to call attention to the unusual event he now records.

The guards posted at the tomb were "shaken" at the visage that appeared before them. Matthew enjoys the irony in the fact that they "became as dead men," perhaps having fainted from their fear, while the dead man they were supposed to be guarding had become alive and had exited the empty tomb. Matthew does not have the women immediately enter the tomb, as in Mark. They are first addressed by the angel and then invited by him to come inside to see the place where the body of Jesus had been placed on late Friday afternoon.

The angel addresses the women with the words "Do not be afraid," which replace Mark's "Do not be amazed." To the angel's words, Matthew adds, "I know," namely, "that you seek Jesus the crucified one," omitting Mark's descriptor, "the Nazarene." The substantive perfect participle, "the crucified one," serves nearly as a title here, as the key and distinguishing character for the newly risen one. In 28:6 Matthew puts the words drawn from Mark, "he is not here," first in the sentence to stress the reality of the empty tomb. Then comes the joyful announcement, "He has risen," to which Matthew adds, "as he said," in order to stress the fulfillment of Jesus's own prediction (Matt. 16:21, 17:23, 20:19). The angel invites the women to "come, see the place where he lay"[67] – a slight rewriting of Mark. To the command to go and tell the disciples, Matthew adds *tachys* ("quickly"). In a Gospel where Peter is so important, Matthew's omission of "and to Peter" is surprising. (Peter's forgiveness for denying

---

[67] The majority of manuscripts supply the subject *ho kyrios*, "the Lord," (A C D L W, families 1 and 13, and the Textus Receptus, while 1424 and a few other manuscripts have *to sōma tou kyriou*, "the body of the Lord," and Phi has *ho iesous*, "Jesus." For the shorter reading, to be preferred here, are Aleph, B, Theta, 33, and a few other witnesses.

his Lord is taken for granted in 28:16.) Whereas the message to be relayed to them in Mark is "he is going before you to Galilee," in Matthew it is the good news itself "that he has risen from the dead" (28:7).[68] The passive form of the verb here (as also in 28:6) could possibly be a true passive, pointing to divine agency: God has raised him. Matthew follows Mark in the next words, "there you will see him," only preceding them with his favored *idou*, "Look!" Matthew changes the next Markan words, "as he said" (used already in another connection in 28:5), into words from the angel, preceded by another *idou*: "Look, I have told you." Matthew's added logion in 28:10 makes "as he said" redundant at this point.

The considerable restraint of Matthew's resurrection account should be noted. No attempt is made to describe the event itself or the risen Jesus (contrast the account in the *Gospel of Peter*). Indeed, more attention is given to the glory attending the appearance of the angel (28:3). The fact that the evangelist does not describe the resurrection itself or the risen Jesus has caused some commentators to wrongly conclude that the resurrection as an event within history is therefore of little consequence to the evangelist. On the contrary, the lack of such a description and the lack of reported witnesses to the event increase one's sense of the historical reliability of the account. To treat something as a holy mystery of which one is reluctant to speak and which is in any event beyond the capability of language should not be taken as denial of its reality, as if only the message and not the fact mattered.

MATTHEW 28:8–10. The women go "quickly," as they were told to do by the angel. That they were marked by "fear," Matthew undoubtedly gets from the end of Mark 16:8. But whereas the latter notes specifically that "they said nothing to anyone," Matthew gives no such impression. Rather, "they ran to tell his disciples." From this point onward we no longer have access to the Markan source possibly used by Matthew.[69]

---

[68] The surprising omission of *apo tōn nekrōn*, "from the dead," in D is probably through the influence of 28:6.

[69] It seems probable to us that Mark did not end with 16:8 – although that is far from impossible – but that the original ending of the Gospel was lost very early on and that the endings of Mark known in the relatively late manuscript tradition were attempts to compensate for this loss by supplying an appropriate ending. It remains a possibility that Matthew continues to be dependent on Mark for parts of the rest of his Gospel, but where and to what extent can only be a matter of speculation.

In contrast to the present ending of Mark's Gospel, which describes the women as trembling and astonished, Matthew notes the "fear and great joy [*charas megalēs*]" of the women (28:8). They show not a shred of doubt concerning the angel's report (contrast 28:17). But on their way to tell the disciples the astounding news,[70] they are encountered by the risen Jesus himself. Matthew does introduce this statement with his common marker of the noteworthy, *idou*, "Look," but otherwise presents his report in a rather matter-of-fact manner. The verb "met" (*hypentēsen*) is the regular word used in everyday meetings. Jesus says but the one word *chairete*, "Hail!," the ordinary greeting used in that culture. (BDAG suggests "Good morning!") Nothing is said of the reaction of the women except for their grasping the feet of Jesus and worshiping him (28:9). To grasp the feet of a person was to express one's obeisance and homage, usually to a ruler or a king. The verb *prosekynēsan*, "to worship" (lit. "to bow down in obeisance"), occurs also in 28:17, and also in reference to Jesus in 4:9–10, 14:33, and 28:17. The women worship Jesus not so much because he is alive again, but rather because of who he is and because his resurrection is the vindication of the things he said and did during his ministry. Understandably the women were also fearful. Jesus therefore says to them, "Fear not" (28:10), thus repeating the words the angel first spoke to them (28:5).

The women thus become the first to actually see the risen Jesus. In that culture and that time, the testimony of women was not regarded as reliable. It is virtually impossible that an account spun out of thin air by the evangelist would have made women the first witnesses of the resurrection and the bearers of the news to the disciples. Against the standards of his time, Matthew's record validates the importance and role of the women as witnesses.

The women are told by Jesus, as they had been by the angel (28:7), to go and tell the disciples – here *tois adelphois mou*, "my brothers" – not that Jesus has risen, as in 28:7, but that they are to go to Galilee, where they will see Jesus (*me ōpsontai* "they will see me," with a slight emphasis

---

70 At the beginning of 28:9, the majority of later manuscripts (A C L, family 1) and the Textus Receptus have the words *hos de eporeuonto apaggeilai tois mathētais autou*, "but as they were going to report to his disciples" (omitted by aleph B D W, theta family, 13, 33, and a few other witnesses). The words could have been accidentally omitted by homoioteleuton or could be added as a natural expansion through the influence of the preceding verse.

on the pronoun). When they see him they will know that he has risen from the dead. The reference to the disciples here as "my brothers" seems unusual, although Jesus uses the word this way in 12:48–50 (cf. 25:40). It may well be the case that there is a note of forgiveness in the use of the word here, coming as it does after the abandonment of Jesus by the disciples in the hour of crisis (26:56).

This passage provides an obvious high point in Matthew's narrative and prepares for the climactic, final passage of the Gospel, 28:16–20, with the appearance of Jesus to the eleven disciples and the giving of the great commission to them to "make disciples of all nations" (28:19). In these two passages Matthew's Christology reaches its culmination. The Jesus of Matthew, who has shown sovereign power in his deeds and unparalleled authority in his teaching, and who has pointed repeatedly to himself as uniquely related to God and as playing a unique role in God's purposes, now appears in the resurrection glory, announcing that "all authority in heaven and on earth has been given to me" (28:18). These two passages easily belong together, but the connection is interrupted by the necessity of concluding the story of the guards, which itself may have originally been a unity with 27:62–66.

MATTHEW 28:11–15. In 28:3 Matthew noted that at the sight of the majestic angel the guards who had been assigned to keep the tomb secure (27:66) "trembled and became like dead men." Resuming the story of the guards, Matthew notes that while the women were on the way to tell the news to the disciples – something Matthew lets drop from the narrative so that we never do read of them giving their message to the disciples – so too, some of the guards make their own report to the chief priests in the city, the ones to whom they were responsible for their mission, telling them (28:11, *apēggeilan*) "everything that happened" (*hapanta ta genomena*). The chief priests and elders (the two groups are regularly mentioned together in the Passion Narrative as the enemies of Jesus) meet together, in turn, to consider their strategy in light of the guards' report. Matthew does not tarry to indicate what their response to the report itself concerning the appearance of the angel and the empty tomb might have been.

The problem for the Jewish authorities was the apparently undeniable reality of the empty tomb – the absent body – and how to explain it. The guards are bribed with a rather large sum of money (*argyria hikana*) in a narrative that is reminiscent of the chief priests' bribing of Judas (26:15, *triakonta argyria*). They are told to spread the story that "his disciples came by night and stole him away while we were asleep." There is no little humor in this, of course, on several counts: if they were asleep, they confessed themselves as incompetent to an extreme; if they were asleep, how did they know what happened; how possibly could the stone have been rolled away without waking any of the guards? More implausibility follows in the claim that "if it comes to the governor's ears" – how could it eventually not? – the Jewish authorities would cover (*peisomen*, "conciliate") for the guards and keep them out of trouble. That is, they would of course keep the bribery a secret, but they would also offer no complaint to Pilate for the incompetence of the guards – exactly what they would have done, of course, if the body had actually been stolen!

The guards were happy enough not to have been punished for what had happened, to take the money, and to do as they were told, no doubt hoping for the best. It is sometimes argued that the guards would never have admitted that they had been sleeping on their watch because the penalty for this would have been death. But this does not seem always to have been the case (cf. Tacitus, Histories 5:22). In this case it is quite conceivable that since Pilate had not instigated the mission, he would have been willing not to impose a penalty on the guards if the Jewish authorities did not wish to.[71]

Matthew concludes his account with the note that "this story (*ho logos*) has been spread among Jews to this day" (28:15). The anarthrous reference to "Jews" (*ioudaioi*) here is the only time in the Gospel the word is used negatively to refer to those who do not believe in Jesus or his resurrection. At the same time, this statement is the final and climactic point in Matthew's rather long and consistent polemic against the unbelieving Jews and the Jewish authorities who repeatedly oppose Jesus. This strand of the Gospel undoubtedly reflects the hostility between the synagogue and the church in the evangelist's day, in particular the tension felt by Matthew's Jewish Christian readers vis-à-vis the Jewish community.

---

[71] So Brown, *The Death of the Messiah*, 2:1311.

Thus in Matthew's day, decades after the resurrection, a common explanation of the claim that Christ rose from the dead, at least among Jews who did not accept the Christian message, was that the body had been stolen by the disciples. Several decades after Matthew, the claim is seen again in Justin Martyr (Dial. 108.2). This explanation of course has surfaced throughout history – and not only among Jews – as one convenient, if improbable, way of explaining the inexplicable.

2

↓

Literary Approaches and the Gospel of Matthew

MARK ALLAN POWELL

*L*ITERARY CRITICISM OF THE GOSPELS IS A BROAD FIELD THAT encompasses a variety of approaches derived from the modern study of fiction and other works of narrative literature. This does *not* mean that literary critics regard the Gospels as works of fiction or that they lack appreciation for the historical witness of the Gospels. It does mean that literary critics focus more intentionally on the art of storytelling and on the manner in which the Gospels engage their readers than do most other academic approaches to the New Testament. Scholars use literary approaches to answer *certain* questions about the Gospels (e.g., "what accounts for this story affecting its readers in particular ways?"). They recognize that literary approaches do not shed much light on *other* questions (e.g., "did what is reported here actually happen?"). Accordingly, there is a strong tendency for scholars who use literary approaches to view those methods as supplemental, as one way of sometimes studying the Gospels rather than as the only way of ever studying the Gospels.

The Bible is written literature and so, strictly speaking, all methods for studying it could be called "literary approaches." All exegetical methods involve reading and reflecting on literary texts. In practical terms, however, *literary* approaches are usually contrasted with *historical* ones based on the primary focus of the scholar's interest. It has sometimes been said that historical approaches treat the Bible as though it were a window – the main interest is not in the written literature itself but in what it reveals about the world it portrays. Thus, historical scholars read Matthew's Gospel to learn about Jesus, his followers, and the early Christians who preserved the traditions contained in this Gospel. By contrast, literary approaches are said to treat the Bible as though it were a mirror – the main interest is in what readers see and experience relative to their own lives and their own world. Thus, literary critics study Matthew's Gospel to determine how readers might be affected or transformed by this book. The window/mirror analogy is not perfect but may be helpful for gaining an initial understanding of how these different spheres of inquiry operate.

Literary methods tend to approach the Bible from the perspective of readers rather than from the perspective of authors.[1] Historical criticism invariably does the latter, by focusing on such questions as "Who wrote this book? When, where, and under what circumstances? What sources did the author have at his disposal and how did he use those sources?" Literary criticism, by contrast, looks at the work that has been produced and asks, "For whom will this book be meaningful? What will it mean to those people, and why will it mean this? What features or dynamics of the work determine the effects that it is likely to have on its readers?"

LITERARY APPROACHES TO THE GOSPELS

We will now attempt to describe what literary critics actually do when they study the Gospels. First, we will consider some of the practical points that often come up when a Gospel text is analyzed with different literary approaches.[2] Next, we will describe some of the theoretical concerns that drive literary critics and motivate them to use these different approaches the way that they do.

Principles and Procedures of Modern Literary Analysis

Gospel scholars who employ literary approaches have not developed unique methods for studying the Gospels as distinctive, ancient books. Rather, they have borrowed methods originally developed for the study

---

[1] This tends to be true of most approaches employed in modern literary criticism. There are, however, author-oriented schools of literary criticism, for which E. D. Hirsch continues to be the most visible apologist. See, e.g., his *The Aims of Interpretation* (Chicago: University of Chicago Press, 1976).

[2] The two primary works that detail these principles and procedures are M. A. Powell, *What Is Narrative Criticism?*, GBS (Minneapolis: Fortress, 1990), and J. L. Resseguie, *Narrative Criticism of the New Testament: An Introduction* (Grand Rapids: Baker Academic, 2005).

of modern secular literature (especially novels) and have sought to apply those methods (with some modification) to the Gospels.[3] It is generally believed that the Gospels have enough features in common with the modern narrative that allow for such transposition of categories to work.

One prominent example of such a critical investigation would be *plot analysis*.[4] For more than two centuries, literary critics have been commenting on the plots of various novels, plays, and other literary works, but until quite recently our four Gospels were not accorded that sort of attention. Biblical scholars tended to view the Gospels as compilations of pericopes rather than as coherent narratives that might evince a single plot line from beginning to end. This has now changed, and it is common for scholars who use literary approaches to discuss "the plot of the Gospel of Matthew" (or of any of the Gospels) in terms similar to those used for describing contemporary short stories. Secular scholars have done an enormous amount of work in the area of plot analysis, classifying different sorts of plots (tragic, comic, etc.) and identifying key features that contribute to plot development. Gospel scholars have sought to determine whether and to what degree such insights apply to the Gospels.

In general, it has been determined that the basic plot line for each of our Gospels is driven by *conflict* (as opposed, for instance, to being driven by character development – none of our Gospels is, first and foremost, a tale of Jesus's growth as a character, tracing his expanding consciousness and personal transformation). Accordingly, *conflict analysis* has played a big role in literary approaches to the Gospels: scholars seek to determine what elements of conflict are present in each episode and how what happens in each episode relates to the development and resolution of

---

[3] The number of "secular" resources upon which Gospel scholars draw is vast. A representative sampling of the most influential would include W. Booth, *The Rhetoric of Fiction*, 2nd ed. (Chicago: University of Chicago Press, 1983); S. Chatman, *Story and Discourse: Narrative Structure in Fiction and Film* (Ithaca, NY: Cornell University Press, 1978); P. J. Rabinowitz, *Before Reading: Narrative Conventions and the Politics of Interpretation* (Ithaca: Cornell University Press, 1987). For a more comprehensive (though now somewhat dated) list, see M. A. Powell, with the assistance of C. G. Gray and M. C. Curtis, *The Bible and Modern Literary Criticism: A Critical Assessment and Annotated Bibliography* (New York: Greenwood, 1992).

[4] See, especially, Powell, *What Is Narrative Criticism?*, 35–50; Resseguie, *Narrative Criticism*, 197–240; and the works listed by Resseguie on pp. 269–70.

conflict in the story as a whole.[5] The nature or character of a conflict may sometimes be described in terms of *threats* that characters or other elements in the story pose to one another. As conflict develops in the narrative, its nature may change – a new threat may be added or an existing one removed. Or, the essence of the conflict may remain the same with changes only in its intensity. Conflict that is left unresolved in the narrative tends to impinge most directly on the reader (i.e., the reader feels invited to mull over such conflict and to wonder how comparable conflicts might be resolved in the world outside the story).[6]

Literary critics sometimes say that every narrative may be understood in terms of "story" and "discourse." *Story* refers to what the narrative is about: the events, characters, and settings that make up its plot. *Discourse* refers to how the narrative is told: the way in which the events, characters, and settings are presented to the reader.[7]

EVENTS. The events of which a narrative is composed are simply those things that happen in the various episodes that make up the story. For purposes of plot analysis, events are sometimes classified as kernels and satellites.[8] Kernel events are those that are integral to the narrative: the event could not be deleted without destroying the logic of the plot. By contrast, satellite events are not crucial to the narrative; they function to fill out the story line as determined by the kernel events.[9]

The discourse aspect of a narrative concerns the manner in which events are reported. The basic events that make up a story can be related in significantly different ways to yield diverse narratives (this often happens with our three Synoptic Gospels). Thus, scholars seek to explicate how the author has chosen to incorporate individual events

---

[5] See three books by J. D. Kingsbury: *Matthew as Story*, 2nd ed. (Minneapolis: Fortress, 1988); *Conflict in Mark: Jesus, Authorities, Disciples* (Minneapolis: Fortress, 1989); *Conflict in Luke: Jesus, Authorities, Disciples* (Minneapolis: Fortress, 1991).

[6] Both the notion of defining conflict in terms of "threats" and the proposition concerning unresolved conflict presented here derive from Powell, *What Is Narrative Criticism?*, 43.

[7] The nomenclature is from Chatman, *Story and Discourse*.

[8] The concept derives from R. Barthes, but it was popularized by way of Chatman (*Story and Discourse*, 53–56). The terms "kernel" and "satellite" are Chatman's translation of Barthes' *noyau* and *catalyse*.

[9] For application of this concept to Matthew, see F. J. Matera, "The Plot of Matthew's Gospel," *CBQ* 49 (1987): 233–35.

into the narrative. They seek to identify such rhetorical techniques as foreshadowing, suspense, irony, symbolism, and the use of various narrative patterns (framing, step progression, concentric patterns, etc.).[10] Particular questions arise concerning *order* (the place which the narration of each event occupies in the sequence of events in the narrative), *duration* (the length of time accorded to each event in the narrative relative to the duration of other events in the narrative), and *frequency* (the number of times each event is narrated or referenced in the narrative).[11]

Literary critics also examine events in terms of *causal connections*. The point is to determine links between a given event and other events in terms of cause and effect. Three categories are used: *possibility* (event makes the occurrence of another event possible); *probability* (the event makes the occurrence of another event more likely); and *contingency* (the event makes the occurrence of another event necessary).[12] This sort of analysis has led scholars to see closer connections between the episodes of our Gospels than had been recognized previously. Further, the Gospels (especially Luke) display a tendency to turn causality on its head by identifying future, yet-to-be-reported events as the *cause* for which present or past events are the *effect*. In other words, things sometimes happen not because something else *has* occurred, but because something else *is going to* occur; a predetermined future makes events in the present "necessary" (Luke 24:26; cf. 9:22; 13:33; 17:25; 24:7).[13]

CHARACTERS. The characters who feature in a narrative are simply the people in the story (or sometimes, though not in our Gospels, animals or other entities that are personified). Literary critics usually describe characters in terms of the traits and point of view that might be ascribed to them. Traits may be defined as "persistent personal qualities that

---

[10] For bibliographical lists of Gospels studies concerned with these various aspects of narrative rhetoric. see Powell et al., *Bible and Modern Literary Criticism* (in which the bibliographical items most relevant to any specific aspect of literary criticism may be accessed via the index); Resseguie, *Narrative Criticism*, 259–62.

[11] G. Genette, *Narrative Discourse: An Essay in Method* (Ithaca, NY: Cornell University Press, 1975).

[12] See R. W. Funk, *The Poetics of Biblical Narrative* (Sonoma, CA: Polebridge, 1988), 52–58.

[13] This notion of "teleological plot" was first advanced in M. A. Powell, "The Plot and Sub-plots of Matthew's Gospel," *NTS* 38 (1992): 187–204. It draws on a concept of "backward" and "forward" causality presented in S. Rimmon-Kenan, *Narrative Fiction: Contemporary Poetics* (London: Routledge, 1983), 18.

describe the character involved" (e.g., Sherlock Holmes is "perceptive"; Ebenezer Scrooge is "stingy").[14] Point of view refers to "the norms, values, and general world view that govern the way a character looks at things and renders judgments upon them."[15] Divergence in point of view and incompatibility of traits between characters often form the basis for the development of conflict.[16]

Characters are classified with regard to various criteria. First, *round characters*, who evince inconsistent traits or a somewhat unpredictable point of view, may be contrasted with *flat characters*, who exhibit consistent traits and a predictable point of view. Likewise, *dynamic characters*, who show development or change in their basic profile (traits and point of view) over the course of the narrative, may be contrasted with *static characters*, who do not.[17] Most Gospel studies have identified Jesus in the Gospel of Matthew as a round but somewhat static character. He can be harsh and angry, but he is also gentle and consoling. Still, Jesus is not portrayed as becoming a decidedly different person as the narrative progresses: the reader's perception of Jesus may evolve and grow, but there is no sense that this is because Jesus himself is changing.

Literary critics often speak of *character groups*, various characters who evince such consistency of traits and point of view that they are essentially treated as a single character throughout the narrative. For example, the disciples of Jesus in the Gospels often function as a group of people who act and think alike. When a Gospel reports that "the disciples said . . . ," the reader is not expected to think that they spoke in unison, but that whatever was said represented the viewpoint of all (as though they were a single character). Likewise, literary study of Matthew has revealed that this Gospel presents the religious leaders of Israel as a character group: the

[14] On characters and characterization, see Powell, *What Is Narrative Criticism?*, 51–67; Resseguie, *Narrative Criticism*, 121–66; and the works listed in Resseguie, 265–68.

[15] B. Uspensky, *A Poetics of Composition: The Structure of the Artistic Text and Typology of a Compositional Form* (Berkeley: University of California Press, 1973). See also Resseguie, *Narrative Criticism*, 167–96, and the works cited on pp. 268–69.

[16] On this, see especially M. A. Powell, "The Plot to Kill Jesus from Three Different Perspectives: Point of View in Matthew," in *Society of Biblical Literature 1990 Seminar Papers*, ed. D. J. Lull (Atlanta: Scholars Press, 1990), 603–13.

[17] On such classifications of "character types," see M. H. Abrams, *A Glossary of Literary Terms*, 7th ed. (Fort Worth: Harcourt Brace College Publishers, 1999); E. M. Forster, *Aspects of the Novel* (New York: Harcourt Brace Jovanovich, 1927); W. H. and C. Hugh Holman, *A Handbook to Literature*, 8th ed. (Upper Saddle River, NJ: Prentice Hall, 1999).

Pharisees, Sadducees, chief priests, scribes, and elders who feature in this narrative function in the plot as a single character. Matthew recognizes superficial differences between them (e.g., Sadducees do not believe in resurrection, Matt. 22:23), but such differences are outweighed by the fact that all these diverse religious leaders seem to have the same basic character traits, as well as the same outlook and motives (point of view). Further, they all have the same function in the conflict-driven plot of this Gospel: they are, above all, the implacable opponents of Jesus.[18]

Readers often relate to characters in a story in one of the following ways: *empathy* (the reader identifies with the character – realistically or ideal- istically – and experiences the story from that character's point of view); *sympathy* (the reader may or may not identify with the character, but feels favorably disposed toward the character); and *antipathy* (the reader may or may not identify with the character, but feels unfavorably disposed toward the character).[19] Such perceptions are impossible to predict, but readers often feel sympathy for characters for whom the protagonist feels sympathy, and antipathy for characters for whom the protagonist feels antipathy.

In terms of the discourse aspect of narrative, literary critics try to describe the method of *characterization* that the author uses to portray the characters and present them to the reader. One straightforward tech- nique involves simply *telling* the reader outright what characters are like (in terms of traits or point of view). Matthew's Gospel does this when it says that Joseph, the earthly father of Jesus, is "a righteous man." Thus, the reader has no doubt that "righteous" is one of Joseph's traits and that Joseph will typically evaluate things from a point of view of righteous- ness. More often, however, characterization is accomplished by *showing* readers what characters are like (as opposed to telling them outright). The narrative describes the actions, speech, thoughts, or beliefs of the various characters and, perhaps, indicates how a particular character or character group is understood from the point of view of *other* charac- ters in the story.[20] For example, Matthew's Gospel never tells the reader

---

[18] This well-established point was first made in J. D. Kingsbury, "The Developing Conflict between Jesus and the Jewish Leaders in Matthew's Gospel: A Literary-Critical Study," *CBQ* 49 (1987): 57–73.

[19] Powell, *What Is Narrative Criticism?*, 56–58. The important distinction between realistic and idealistic empathy was first offered here.

[20] Booth, *Rhetoric of Fiction*, 3–20.

outright that the Pharisees are hypocrites, but it does portray them as acting in ways that the reader might consider to be hypocritical, and it also makes clear that Jesus thinks they are hypocrites.

Characterization is said to occur on four different *planes of expression*: the *spatial–temporal plane* (actions of the characters in space and time); the *phraseological plane* (speech, including thoughts if they are verbalized as speech); the *psychological plane* (inside views of the character's motives), and the *ideological plane* (norms, values, and general world view ascribed to the character).[21] *Incongruity* may occur when the author provides conflicting characterization: a character's own self-description may differ from the perception of that character attributed to others; or, a character's speech may present the character differently than the character's actions. (In Matthew 2, Herod says he wants to worship Jesus, but then tries to kill him.) The reader must decide which level of characterization is more reliable.[22]

SETTINGS. The settings of a story include the spatial, temporal, and social features that define the environment in which characters interact and events take place.[23] Spatial settings include the physical environment (geographical and architectural locations), as well as the "props" and "furniture" (articles of clothing, modes of transportation, etc.) that make up this environment. Temporal settings include the broad sweep or concept of time assumed by the narrative ("monumental time") as well as the chronological and typological references to time, as it is measured by the characters in the story ("mortal time").[24] Examples of monumental time would be the periods indicated by such expressions as "the days of Noah," "this generation," or "in those days"; examples of mortal time would be "year," "day," "night," "sabbath." Social settings include political institutions, class structure, economic systems, social customs, and the general cultural context assumed to be operative in the narrative

---

[21] Uspensky, *Poetics of Composition*.

[22] For an extended example of such analysis applicable to Matthew, see M. A. Powell, "Characterization on the Phraseological Plane in the Gospel of Matthew," in *Treasures New and Old: Essays on the Gospel of Matthew*, ed. D. R. Bauer and M. A. Powell (Atlanta: Scholars Press, 1996), 161–77.

[23] See Powell, *What Is Narrative Criticism?*, 69–83; Resseguie, *Narrative Criticism*, 87–120; and the works listed by Resseguie on pp. 262–65.

[24] P. Ricoeur, *Time and Narrative*, 3 vols. (Chicago: University of Chicago Press, 1984–88).

(e.g., the social institution of slavery is part of the social setting for Uncle Tom's Cabin; the Roman occupation of Palestine is part of the social setting for all four New Testament Gospels).

Settings may possess symbolic connotations. In the Gospel of Matthew, "the wilderness" (3:1, 3; 4:1; 11:7) connotes a place of testing (since Israel was tested during wilderness wanderings subsequent to the exodus). The "sea" seems to be a place of danger (Matt. 8:24, 32; 14:26; 18:6) and "night" is often a time for watchfulness and preparation (Matt. 24:43; cf. 26:34); in John's Gospel, by contrast, night seems to connote secrecy (John 3:2; 19:39; also Matt. 2:14) or even a time of obscurity and ineptitude (John 9:4; 11:10). Settings may also be set in opposition to each other – "day and night"; "land and sea"; "heaven and earth" – and when this happens certain specific settings may gain significance as boundaries or bridges that connect such oppositions. Evening or dawn may be a boundary between day and night; a beach, a boat, or an island may be a boundary between land and sea; a mountain may be a boundary between heaven and earth.

Scholars interested in the discourse aspect of narrative will inquire as to how the author or narrator of the story describes settings for the reader. For example, settings may be described with either an abundance or a paucity of detail. When the latter is the case (as in our Gospels), it might be said that the story leaves much to the reader's imagination or, on the contrary, that the reader is simply assumed to know a good deal about the settings so as to need little description.

Dynamics of the Reading Experience

When Bible scholars began adopting literary approaches to the Gospels in the 1980s, they focused first on literary *method*, analyzing the narrative texts of the Gospels in light of categories such as those described earlier. The next move, however, was to adopt aspects of literary *theory*, and in the 1990s it became common for Gospel scholars to discuss biblical books in light of what literary theorists have to say regarding how readers "make meaning" out of texts. In general, most theorists of that period viewed literary texts as "raw materials" out of which diverse meanings could be crafted. The author of a text is of course responsible for supplying this raw material and, so, has a definitive role in determining what the text is going to mean. But the author's role is not final: readers are the ones who ultimately decide what texts mean, and they do so by constructing meaning from the raw materials that the author has provided. They are guided by the author's intentions, but they are not constrained by those intentions; sometimes, readers construct meaning from texts that transcend or defy what the author probably had in mind. Whereas author-oriented historical criticism would typically have described such a phenomenon as "misunderstanding the text," reader-oriented literary criticism does not necessarily construe the matter that way.

Much of this discussion begins with recognizing the reality of *polyvalence* or multiple meanings. Virtually all stories do, in fact, come to mean different things to different people. How do we account for this? At least four different but overlapping factors seem to contribute to such divergence in interpretation.[25]

SOCIAL LOCATION. The social location of a reader refers to such identifying characteristics as age, gender, nationality, race, health, career, social class, and marital status. Readers who share certain aspects of social location tend to understand texts in similar ways that can be distinguished from understandings produced by readers of a different social location.

READING STRATEGY. The manner in which a text is received affects the way in which it is understood. For example, if a text is heard out loud, it might be understood differently than if it is read silently. If a section of a text is read as an isolated pericope, it might be understood differently than if it is encountered as an episode in a longer work. If a book like Matthew's Gospel is read as a part of a larger book ("the New Testament" or "the Bible"), it might be understood differently than if it is read as a freestanding work.

EMPATHY CHOICE. Readers often experience stories differently because they identify (realistically or idealistically) with different characters in the story and interpret what transpires in the narrative from different

---

[25] These were first proposed and described at length in a book that draws upon Matthew's Gospel for its primary illustrations. See M. A. Powell, *Chasing the Eastern Star: Adventures in Biblical Reader-Response Criticism* (Louisville: Westminster John Knox, 2001), esp. 13–27.

perspectives. The story of Jesus's encounter with a Canaanite woman in Matthew 15:21–29 may be experienced from the woman's perspective (how did she feel about her encounter with Jesus?), from the perspective of the disciples who witnessed that event (what did they learn from it?), or from the perspective of Jesus himself (what did he take away from this event – did it affect his future life and ministry?).

CONCEPTION OF "MEANING." Diverse interpretations of a text's meaning are determined at a basic level by different philosophical constructs of what constitutes "meaning." Some readers are prone to construe meaning as a cognitive message that the author seeks to pass on to them (e.g., the "point" or "moral" of the story); others are more inclined to identify meaning with an affective or emotive response produced in them through the experience of receiving the text (e.g., the meaning of a story might be that it "invokes laughter" or "inspires worship" or "promotes repentance").

This discussion may provide an example of what was meant earlier when we said that literary approaches tend to approach the Gospels from the perspective of readers rather than from the perspective of authors. Author-oriented historical criticism does not deny polyvalence completely: it is, of course, possible that the author of Matthew's Gospel could have intended to make multiple points in a single passage or story; he may even have intended for a story to have the capacity to work differently for different readers.[26] Still, when historical critics approach texts from this angle, seeking to determine what meaning the author intended to convey, the range of possible meanings that are discerned tends to be fairly limited. When literary critics seek to determine what a text might mean to readers in different social locations, or to readers who receive the text in a variety of ways, or to readers who make different empathy choices, or to readers who have different conceptions of what constitutes "meaning," and so on, the range of possible meanings attributable to the text expands significantly.

---

[26] See R. T. France, "The Formula Quotations of Matthew 2 and the Problems of Communication," NTS 27 (1981): 233–51. France suggests that Matthew wrote his Gospel with the intention of communicating different (though compatible) messages to readers whose educational backgrounds or perceptive capacities varied.

Varieties of Reader-Oriented Literary Approaches

Scholars who employ literary approaches in the interpretation of the Gospels do so in diverse ways and for diverse ends. In general, the differences owe to variant conceptions of *which readers* are the focus of the interpreter's inquiry.

READER-RESPONSE CRITICISM. The field of literary study known as reader-response criticism envisions interpreting texts from the perspective of *unspecified readers.* Accordingly, it is a catchall term for any sort of literary method that approaches any text from the perspective of any reader (however that "reader" might be defined). Historically, reader-response criticism arose in the latter half of the twentieth century as a reaction against interpretation that was excessively author-oriented. At first, it seemed sufficient to insist that texts be understood from a reader's perspective rather than from an author's perspective. But before long, all sorts of questions arose: shouldn't texts be understood from the perspective of an *informed* or *competent* reader (as opposed to an ignorant or incompetent one)? Shouldn't they be understood from the perspective of a *first-time reader* (as opposed to someone who has read the story repeatedly and knows its ending from the start)? These and many similar questions led to a proliferation of reader-response criticisms – many different literary approaches that sought to interpret texts from the perspectives of readers who met certain qualifications or could be defined in terms of certain particular criteria.[27] By the end of the twentieth century, "reader-response criticism" had become virtually synonymous with "modern literary criticism" since almost all literary critics sought to interpret texts from a reader's perspective, in one sense or another. Still,

---

[27] On the development of reader-response criticism and its importance for biblical studies, see E. V. McKnight, *The Bible and the Reader: An Introduction to Literary Criticism* (Philadelphia: Fortress, 1985); *Postmodern Use of the Bible: The Emergence of Reader-Oriented Criticism* (Nashville: Abingdon, 1988); S. D. Moore, *Literary Criticism and the Gospels: The Theoretical Challenge* (New Haven: Yale, 1989). R. Fowler first sought to apply reader response to the Gospel of Mark with his *Let the Reader Understand: Reader-Response Criticism and the Gospel of Mark* (Harrisburg: Trinity Press International, 1996; originally published in 1991). I followed a few years later with an application to the Gospel of Matthew (Powell, *Chasing the Eastern Star*).

even though the various types of modern literary criticism were almost all varieties of reader-response criticism, it was not uncommon for proponents of one approach to identify *their* preferred method as (true) "reader-response criticism" in distinction from other approaches, which they would designate by other names. Thus, the semantics can be very confusing, and even in Gospel studies the term "reader-response criticism" is used to mean different things. Sometimes, the term is employed in a broad sense to include virtually everything that we are discussing in this chapter; other times it is used in a more narrow sense to designate some specific approach. Thus, what is described in the subsequent sections as "ideological criticism" is sometimes called "reader-response criticism," or (more often) what is described as "postmodern criticism" is sometimes called "reader-response criticism."[28]

RHETORICAL CRITICISM. In Gospel studies, the field identified as rhetorical criticism usually focuses on how a text would have been understood by its original readers, the actual historical people for whom the book was written. Rhetorical critics often attempt to reconstruct the community in which a book was produced, and then they analyze how the rhetoric of the work would have proved effective for people in that particular context (in accord with principles of rhetoric that were known and practiced within such an environment). Accordingly, rhetorical criticism is something of a "hybrid methodology," and it is usually classed as a variety of historical criticism rather than as a type of literary criticism. It can probably be placed in either category, for it employs literary techniques for historical ends.[29]

WIRKUNGSGESCHICHTE. The approach known as *wirkungsgeschichte* or "history of influence criticism" focuses on how texts have been

---

[28] Thus, "narrative criticism" can be distinguished from "reader-response criticism" if the latter term is roughly synonymous with "ideological criticism" or "postmodern criticism" (and this is the case in Powell, *What Is Narrative Criticism?*; and Resseguie, *Narrative Criticism*). Or, "narrative criticism" can be presented as one of several types of reader-response criticism, if the latter term is taken in its broader sense (and that is what is recommended in Powell, *Chasing the Eastern Star*, as well as in this current study).

[29] A classic literary study of a Gospel that uses rhetorical criticism is V. K. Robbins, *Jesus the Teacher: A Socio-Rhetorical Interpretation of Mark* (Philadelphia: Fortress, 1984).

understood by actual readers throughout history.[30] Scholars who practice this approach compile as much data as they can regarding the diverse
interpretations that have been ascribed to various texts. They are interested not only in academic or theological interpretations (e.g., those
evident in biblical commentaries) but also in popular and secular understandings: how the text has been preached and how it has impacted
art, music, legends, and the like. For example, the story of the magi
in Matthew 2 came to be elaborated in both ecclesiastical festivals and
secular dramas: the magi were identified as kings, they were accorded
names (Caspar, Melchior, and Balthazaar), and their gifts to Christ were
ascribed various symbolic meanings.[31] Literary critics are interested in
what such elaborations say about the capacity for the story to capti-
vate audiences and to generate meaning beyond the limitations of its
initial content.[32] In itself, however, *wirkungsgeschichte* constitutes more
of a "research field" than a "method of interpretation": it is to literary
criticism what archaeology is to historical studies.

IDEOLOGICAL CRITICISM. The wide variety of approaches that might
be included under the umbrella-term "ideological criticism" seek to interpret texts from the perspective of readers who occupy a specific social
location.[33] Thus, a Marxist critic may seek to interpret Matthew from
the perspective of Marxist ideology: the author of Matthew's Gospel was
obviously not a Marxist, but a critic may still inquire as to what meaning
this Gospel will have to readers who are Marxists. It is sometimes said
that all biblical interpreters are ideological critics since it is impossible
for any interpreter to divest him or herself of ideological presuppositions

---

[30] This approach is especially associated with the work of Ulrich Luz, as represented in
his three-volume commentary on Matthew: *Matthew 1–7, Matthew 8–20, and Matthew
21–28*, trans. W. C. Linss and J. E. Crouch, Hermeneia (Minneapolis: Augsburg Fortress,
1989–2005).

[31] See R. C. Trexler, *The Journey of the Magi: Meanings in History of a Christian Story*
(Princeton: Princeton University, 1997).

[32] See Powell, *Chasing the Eastern Star*, 131–84, 190–96.

[33] For example, see some of the essays in C. H. Felder, ed., *Stony the Road We Trod:
African American Biblical Interpretation* (Minneapolis: Augsburg Fortress, 1991); M. F.
Foskett and J. K.-J. Kuan, eds, *Ways of Being, Ways of Reading: Asian American Biblical
Interpretation* (St. Louis: Chalice, 2007); F. F. Segovia and M. A. Tolbert, eds, *Reading
From This Place, Vol. 1: Social Location and Biblical Interpretation in the United States*
(Minneapolis: Augsburg Fortress, 1995); *Reading From This Place, Vol. 2: Social Location
and Biblical Interpretation in Global Perspective* (Minneapolis: Augsburg Fortress, 2000).

and perspectives that affect interpretation. While this may be true, not everyone applies their ideological stance to texts in ways that are explicit and deliberate. There is a difference between (a) a redaction critic who happens to be a Lutheran, being inevitably influenced by his confessional perspective when he attempts to discern the historical intentions of the author of Matthew's Gospel, and (b) a Lutheran theologian articulating what Matthew's Gospel might mean to Lutherans today when it is interpreted from a perspective that assumes principles of Lutheran theology. The latter approach may or may not use literary-critical methodology, but its legitimation derives from principles of literary theory: if texts can legitimately mean different things to different people, and if they can have legitimate meanings that transcend the historical intentions of their authors (e.g., when the readers belong to a context unknown to that author), then it may be appropriate to define the meaning of a text for a particular subgroup of readers who belong to such an unanticipated context.

The most popular variety of ideological criticism in academic circles has been *feminist criticism*, a field sufficiently diverse as to defy classification under any particular heading. There are, for example, feminist form critics and feminist redaction critics who would not want their work to be viewed as a variety of explicit ideological criticism or as a subset of literary approaches. Some feminist critics, however, *do* view their task in terms analogous to what was just described for a hypothetical Lutheran earlier: they seek to discern the meaning of a text when it is read from the perspective of feminism, without any supposition that this is a meaning the author would have anticipated (or even endorsed).

POSTMODERN CRITICISM. Scholars who identify themselves as practitioners of postmodern interpretation focus on meaning that could be ascribed to texts by *any reader in any context*. Thus, appreciation for polyvalence leads to an essential denial of what other scholars might call "misinterpretation." Postmodern critics take the notion that texts can mean different things to different people to its logical extreme; hypothetically, texts can mean anything to anybody. Therefore, all claims to have discerned the meaning of a text are contextual and must be regarded as *a* particular meaning that the text has for certain readers in certain contexts. Accordingly, any attempt to establish certain interpretations as normative or preferred is viewed with suspicion. Postmodern critics often practice an interpretive strategy called *deconstruction,* through which they seek to demonstrate the instability of the text and of all proposed interpretations of it. For example, a postmodern critic might deconstruct a traditional understanding of a text by exposing its dependence on certain contextually derived presuppositions. Postmodern critics often claim that interpretation reveals more about interpreters than it does about the texts they seek to interpret. Nevertheless, the process of interpretation need not be abandoned. It may be continued in a chastened way: postmodern critics "play" with texts, interpreting them in ways that they find interesting. They do not imagine that they will arrive at an absolute understanding of truth, but by interpreting texts in dialogue with other interpreters, they hope to discover things about themselves and about other interpreters.[34]

NARRATIVE CRITICISM. The field of narrative criticism focuses on meaning that may be ascribed to a text's implied reader, interpreting the work from the perspective of readers who receive the text in the manner that appears to be expected of them.[35] We will say more about this in a moment, but first let us note that narrative criticism is by far the most widely practiced of all literary approaches currently employed in Gospel studies. It has no exact counterpart in the secular field, but draws heavily (and eclectically) from fields called New Criticism and narratology.[36] In biblical studies, narrative criticism has become something of a "baseline" approach for almost all literary studies of the Gospels. Even scholars who ultimately want to interpret the text in accord with some other literary scheme usually start with a narrative-critical analysis in order to (a) lay a foundation on which they can build with supplemental insights or

---

[34] See A. K. M. Adam, *What Is Postmodern Biblical Criticism?*, GBS (Minneapolis: Fortress, 1995); S. D. Moore, *Poststructuralism and the New Testament: Derrida and Foucault at the Foot of the Cross* (Minneapolis: Fortress, 1994); D. Seeley, *Deconstructing the New Testament,* BIS 5. (Leiden: Brill, 1994).

[35] The concept of an implied reader is derived mainly from W. Iser, *The Implied Reader: Patterns of Communication in Prose Fiction from Bunyan to Beckett* (Baltimore: Johns Hopkins University, 1974); *The Act of Reading: A Theory of Aesthetic Response* (Baltimore: Johns Hopkins University, 1978). Many Gospel scholars employ the concept as modified by Booth, *Rhetoric of Fiction,* and/or Rabinowitz, *Before Reading.*

[36] For description and bibliography pertinent to these fields of literary criticism, see Powell et al., *Bible and Modern Literary Criticism.*

(b) define the accepted or traditional literary understanding, which they might subsequently hope to contest or challenge. Either way, narrative criticism has become foundational to almost all literary studies of the Gospels, and so it is the approach to which we shall devote the most attention.

The *implied reader* is *the reader presupposed by the text.* This is a heuristic concept: an implied reader is an imaginary person who is to be envisioned as always responding to the text with whatever knowledge, understanding, action, or emotion is called for. Or, to put it differently, the implied reader of any given text might be described as the reader that the author appears to have had in mind when producing that text. In relying on such a concept, narrative criticism recognizes that reading is a process that engages the imagination. For example, if readers incidentally hear how a story turns out before they finish reading it, they may pretend not to know the ending in order to allow the story to affect them the way it would if they did not possess that knowledge. At the very least, they will probably realize that reading the text in light of such knowledge could compromise their reading experience. It would strike most people as ridiculous for a student to claim that "The Tell-Tale Heart" by Edgar Allan Poe is not a suspenseful story and then to defend that thesis by saying, "I did not find it suspenseful because I read the ending first and knew how it was going to turn out." The point for most people in discussing whether a story is suspenseful would be to ask, "Is this story likely to prove suspenseful for people who read it in the way that it was expected to be read?" Or, in literary terms, "Would it be suspenseful for its *implied reader?*"

How Gospel Scholars Use Narrative Criticism

The goal of narrative criticism is to discern the meaning of a text from the perspective of its implied reader. This goal is usually fulfilled by describing a range of what are called "expected responses" or ways in which an implied reader might be expected to respond. To discern this range of meanings, interpreters need to do three things:

1. *Receive the text in the manner the author assumed it would be received.* For a Shakespearean play, this might mean seeing the work performed on stage (as opposed to reading a script). For

a Gospel, it means (at least) reading the entire work all the way through from beginning to end. Some scholars would say that, ideally, it means reading it straight through at a single sitting or *hearing* the Gospel read out loud from beginning to end. Such modes of reception are not always practical, but narrative critics will at least ask, "What would the text mean to someone who did receive it in such a fashion?"

2. *Know everything that the reader is expected to know – but no more than this.* The reader of Matthew's Gospel is expected to know the Old Testament and certain things about the Roman world, but Matthew's reader is probably not expected to know the material from the other Gospels or doctrinal propositions from later Christianity. To discern the expected impact of Matthew's Gospel on its implied reader, narrative critics must strive to obtain knowledge that is assumed for the story and they must "bracket out" knowledge that would not be assumed for the story. The question sometimes becomes, "What would the text mean to someone who did not know certain things that we know today?"

3. *Believe everything the reader is expected to believe – but nothing other than this.* The reader of any one of our four Gospels is assumed to hold certain beliefs and values that may or may not coincide with beliefs or values of modern readers today (e.g., the reader may be expected to believe that demons are literal beings; that ghosts actually exist; that slavery is an acceptable social institution; or that women are intrinsically inferior to men). To determine the response expected of an implied reader, modern readers must ask, "How would a reader with these assumed beliefs and values respond to this story?"

In practice, then, narrative criticism allows for discernment of what I call "polyvalence within perimeters."[37] In essence, my proposal is that diverse interpretations of texts or responses to texts may be classified as "expected" or "unexpected" readings, and that such a classification may be made without prejudice regarding the value of the reading

[37] M. A. Powell, *What Do They Hear? Bridging the Gap between Pulpit and Pew* (Louisville: Abingdon, 2007); cf. Powell, *Chasing the Eastern Star*, 8, 71. Actually, in those published works, I call the phenomenon "polyvalence within parameters." Helpful critics have since corrected my vocabulary (a *parameter* is a single basis for comparison; *perimeters* are plural boundaries within which something might be found).

in question. An *expected reading* is one that seems to be invited by signals within the text itself (as discernible through narrative criticism). An *unexpected reading* is one that is produced when factors extrinsic to the text cause the reader to resist or ignore the text's signals. In terms of narrative criticism, an *expected reading* would be one compatible with the response of a text's implied reader, while an *unexpected reading* would be one that is incompatible with the response of a text's implied reader.

This may be illustrated as follows: imagine four different people reading the story of the passion of Christ recorded in Matthew 26–27. They respond emotionally to the narrative:

- Reader One is *inspired* by the story because it presents Jesus as a man of integrity who is willing to die nobly for his convictions.
- Reader Two is *traumatized* by the story because it reveals the depth of human depravity on the part of those who denounce, betray, and torture an innocent man.
- Reader Three is *comforted* by the story because it portrays Jesus's death as an atoning sacrifice through which God offers forgiveness and mercy to the undeserving.
- Reader Four is *delighted* by the story because it reports the gruesome execution of a meddlesome busybody who tried to tell everyone else how they should live.[38]

Narrative critics would classify the first three responses as *expected readings* – though very different from each other, they all respond to cues within the text (and so exemplify *polyvalent* responses). But narrative critics would classify the fourth response as an *unexpected reading* – it responds to the story in a way that the narrative does not solicit or invite. Such a response would probably be arrived at by a reader who approaches the story with beliefs and values quite different from those attributable to the story's implied reader. The classification of Reading Four as "unexpected," however, does not in itself convey any value judgment as to its validity. Obviously, this particular unexpected reading might be deemed "perverse" or wrong in some ethical sense, but such a judgment transcends what can be determined through exegetical or literary analysis as such. In any case, Reading Four cannot be simply dismissed as a

---

[38] This illustration and the commentary on it that follows are taken from Powell, *Chasing the Eastern Star*, 60.

"misinterpretation" on the grounds that it is not what the historical author of Matthew's Gospel intended. We cannot be certain which of the *other* readings that author would have intended. All three of them? Only one? Which one? Or something else entirely? We cannot know for certain what the historical author intended – he is not available for comment. Still, those first three readings exemplify "polyvalence within perimeters" in that though different from each other, they lie within the bounds of what might be attributed to the text's implied reader.

Why Gospel Scholars Use Narrative Criticism

Narrative criticism is used by scholars with different hermeneutical goals. Indeed, it is often used by scholars who pursue interpretive goals typically associated with author-oriented criticism. Scholars have come to realize that narrative criticism, in and of itself, is not a "reader-oriented method" or an "author-oriented method." It is probably best described as a *text-oriented method* in that it approaches the text from the perspective of a hypothetical reader who must be reconstructed from what is found in the text.

To state the matter more comprehensively, narrative criticism views each Gospel as a communication between an implied author and an implied reader. An *implied author* is *the author of the work as he or she can be reconstructed from the text.* In the secular study of modern literature, a distinction between the implied author of a book and the actual author who wrote the work can be significant. The actual author might give interviews or appear on television discussing the book and stating what his or her intentions were in writing it. Students in an academic setting may be asked to bracket out such information and concentrate only on impressions they would form regarding authorial intent *from the work itself*: what do the literary features of this book suggest the author wanted to accomplish?

Such concerns are of less moment in Gospel studies because we possess very little information concerning the actual persons who wrote these books. Almost all of our suppositions concerning the author of Matthew's Gospel are in fact derived from the work itself; thus, the "implied author of Matthew's Gospel" discernible through narrative criticism offers about as close a picture of the real author of that book as we are likely to obtain. The "intention of the implied author" discernible through narrative criticism may be taken as an index of the intention of the actual author sought through historical criticism. To get from one to the other requires only a minor leap of logic, namely, an assumption that the effects that the literary features of the book suggest it is intended to have on people were used knowingly, that is, that the historical author intended his book to work the way that it actually does work.

The bottom line is that, today, narrative criticism is generally viewed as a text-oriented method of interpretation employed by scholars who have diverse hermeneutical goals:

- *An author-oriented hermeneutic.* Narrative criticism seeks to determine how readers are expected to respond to the story, but historically minded critics often assume that such expectations reflect the historical intentions of the author. Thus, narrative criticism may be used to supplement or confirm the insights of redaction criticism. This approach to interpretation is often, though not always, accompanied by a confessional posture that grants authoritative status to authorial intent: acceptance of the Bible as Scripture means that people are called to believe whatever message the author intended to convey.

- *A text-oriented hermeneutic.* Some interpreters are interested in using narrative criticism for its own sake, ascribing normative value to the meaning that would be expected of an implied reader and declaring other (unexpected) readings to be intrinsically invalid. Determining how readers are expected to respond to biblical stories is thus viewed as a complete exegetical process. This perspective often seems to be informed by a confessional posture that recognizes the expected response to Scripture as the divinely ordained one. Thus, authoritative status is granted to the exegetically discerned anticipated response of implied readers rather than to the exegetically defined intention of a historical author (i.e., authoritative or normative meaning equals "what the biblical book means for people who receive it in a manner expected of them" rather than "what the author of the book intended for it to mean to people").

- *A reader-oriented hermeneutic.* Many interpreters use narrative criticism as a base method to guide them in discerning and understanding disparate and polyvalent responses. By gaining a general idea of how readers are expected to respond to a story, interpreters are able to identify more readily the points at which individuals or communities adopt variant reading strategies and they are able to probe the processes that determine these. Authoritative status may or may not be granted to what is deemed to be the expected reading. In either case, this reading strategy enables dialogical interpretation, such as might be favored by many postmodern or ideological critics.

LITERARY CRITICISM AND THE GOSPEL OF MATTHEW: AN OVERVIEW

We will now draw on narrative criticism to describe a few aspects of how Matthew's Gospel would be understood or received by its implied reader. The data intrinsic to such a description would be utilized by most literary approaches to Matthew, albeit in different ways and to different ends.

Defining Matthew's Implied Reader

Matthew's implied reader is expected to read the entire narrative from beginning to end, allowing the story to unfold as though reading it for the first time. In terms of knowledge, Matthew's implied reader is expected (1) to know everything that is revealed within the narrative[39] (e.g., to remember what is said at one point in the narrative and to make the appropriate connection when something similar is said later) and (2) to know everything that would have been regarded as "common knowledge" within the world that produced this book[40] (e.g., the implied reader knows that "the holy city" [27:53] is Jerusalem, and that when Jesus falls on his face in Gethsemane [26:39] he is not being clumsy but has assumed a posture appropriate for prayer). In terms of beliefs and values, Matthew's implied reader is expected (1) to accept the system of beliefs and values espoused within the narrative; this would include, for example, believing that the world is ruled by God (who guides people through dreams, prophets, and divinely inspired scripture) and that the world is infested with demons who serve Satan, a powerful supernatural being opposed to God, and (2) to accept the system of beliefs and values

---

[39] I call this "knowledge of the story setting"; see Powell, *Chasing the Eastern Star*, 87–89.
[40] I call this "knowledge of the discourse setting"; see Powell, *Chasing the Eastern Star*, 89–106.

that would have been typical for the setting in which the narrative was produced (e.g., that it would normally be shameful for a woman to become pregnant without having had relations with her husband).

All expectations of an implied reader apply to the "story world" of the narrative – *not to the actual world outside the story*. Historical criticism may claim that the actual author of this book expected his readers to believe certain things about the actual world in which they live (that it is ruled by God, etc.). Literary critics do not deny this, but it is not the focus of their concern: they simply state that the implied reader of this narrative is expected to recognize that certain things hold true *for the world of this story*. The implied reader of George Orwell's *Animal Farm* is expected to recognize that in the world of *that* story, animals can talk. The implied reader of Matthew's Gospel is expected to recognize that in *this* story, God rules a world that has been infested by demons.

The significance of this (hopefully) noncontroversial point becomes evident when we continue to identify beliefs and values that the implied reader of Matthew's Gospel is probably expected to hold. As indicated earlier, narrative critics may claim that Matthew's implied reader is expected to regard slavery as an acceptable social institution, or to believe that ghosts are real and dangerous beings, or to think that the dominion of men over women is divinely ordained (and therefore good), or any number of other things that many readers today would have trouble accepting. The point for literary criticism is not that modern readers should feel compelled to believe such things about the real world in which they live (the world outside the story); the point is simply that the story Matthew tells should be interpreted in light of the value system that its readers are assumed to possess. This point becomes especially significant when the narrative seems to *challenge* the beliefs and values that its readers are assumed to possess: Jesus's words to Peter regarding forgiveness (Matt. 18:22) will only be shocking to a reader who believed Peter's offer to forgive someone seven times was extraordinarily generous (Matt. 18:21). Likewise, a modern reader might be inclined to think the Canaanite woman in Matthew 15:21–29 is "assertive" or "bold" when she shouts after Jesus in public (Matt. 15:21–29), but narrative critics would be more interested in asking how Matthew's *implied* reader would be assumed to evaluate that behavior. The answer is that the implied reader is probably expected to regard the woman as incredibly obnoxious. But, then, the real question becomes, how would a reader who thought the woman was behaving in a way that was incredibly obnoxious be affected by what follows, when Jesus praises the obnoxious woman for her "great faith"?

Major Characters of Matthew's Narrative

Characters are especially important to Matthew's narrative and the implied reader is expected to regard certain characters in particular ways. Jesus is obviously the most significant character, the protagonist, and he is portrayed as the authoritative Son of God whose words and actions are definitively true. His point of view is established as normative for the narrative, such that the implied reader is never expected to question the validity of his perspective.[41] The disciples of Jesus, however, represent a character group that is considerably less reliable than Jesus himself. They are people of little faith (6:30; 8:26; 14:31; 16:8; 17:19–20) who often disappoint Jesus (16:5–12; 22–23; 19:13–14; 20:20–28; 26:56, 69–74). Thus, they are the best examples of "round characters" in this narrative and may serve as the most likely candidates for reader empathy. Some episodes portray them as loyal, obedient, or even as insightful, while others portray them as fearful, self-serving, dense, or just plain irresponsible. The most consistent element of their characterization may be that they are always presented as "favored by Jesus," as persons whom he has chosen to belong to him and as persons who, according to him, are destined for great things (4:19; 10:5–23; 12:49; 19:28).[42]

The most interesting character group in this narrative, however, is the amorphous collection of parties that we may describe with the umbrella term "religious leaders of Israel." This group (composed of Pharisees,

---

[41] J. D. Kingsbury, "The Figure of Jesus in Matthew's Story: A Literary-Critical Probe," *JSNT* 21 (1984): 3–36; "The Figure of Jesus in Matthew's Story: A Rejoinder to David Hill," *JSNT* 25 (1985): 61–81. Cf. D. B. Howell, *Matthew's Inclusive Story: A Study in the Narrative Rhetoric of the First Gospel,* JSNTSS 42 (Sheffield: JSOT Press, 1990).

[42] See Kingsbury, *Matthew as Story,* 13–17, 129–46; Powell, "Characterization on the Phraseological Plane," 169–71. For somewhat different views, cf. J. K. Brown, *The Disciples in Narrative Perspective: The Portrayal and Function of the Matthean Disciples,* AcBib 9 (Atlanta: Society of Biblical Literature, 2002); W. Carter, *Matthew: Storyteller, Interpreter, Evangelist* (Peabody, MA: Hendrickson, 1996), 242–58.

Sadducees, scribes, priests, elders) is depicted as unilaterally opposed to Jesus and, indeed, as unwittingly opposed to God. In a nutshell, they are "evil" (9:4; 12:34, 39, 45; 16:4; 22:18), allied with Satan, the evil one (13:19, 38–39). Matthew's reader is not expected to think they are opposed to Jesus because they misunderstand him or fail to identify him for who he is. Rather, they are opposed to him precisely because he is God's Son and they have rebelled against God (21:33–45). They are a "brood of vipers" (3:7; 12:34; 23:33) or children of hell (23:15). Jesus declares that they will be sentenced to hell (23:33; cf. 5:20) and he makes no attempt to minister to them (not even to call them to repentance), any more than he would try to minister to the demons he exorcizes. In one terribly revealing passage, he counsels his disciples to "leave them alone" (15:14). They are to be regarded as "plants that the heavenly Father did not plant" (15:13), as people who were placed in this world by the devil rather than by God (see 13:24–30; 36–43), and the only positive thing that can be said about them is that they will be uprooted in time.[43]

In considering such a portrayal, we should remember that expectations of an implied reader apply to a story world only. It is a sad fact of history that Matthew's Gospel has been interpreted in ways that support anti-Semitism, and the Gospel's presentation of the religious leaders of Israel no doubt contributed to that. While such problems need to be addressed theologically, the immediate concern for narrative criticism is to identify the anticipated effect of such characterization on the implied reader. In literary terms, the religious leaders are flat characters, and the literary function of flat characters is never to present a realistic depiction of people in the world outside the story. The literary function of flat characters is to provide personification of values. Stories that employ flat characters typically do so in order to comment on the values that those characters are made to embody. In this case, Matthew's implied reader is expected to recognize that what the religious leaders do in this story is what *evil* does: evil condemns the guiltless (12:7), blasphemes the Holy Spirit (12:31), neglects the weightier matters of the law (23:23), and so on. The religious leaders of Israel "stand for evil" in this story, and even if we question the

---

[43] Kingsbury, "Developing Conflict"; *Matthew as Story*, 17–24, 115–28; Powell, *What Is Narrative Criticism?*, 58–67.

Gospel author's choice of telling the story in such a way, we can recognize how the story is expected to affect its implied reader.[44] Thus, Matthew's implied reader is not expected to draw historical conclusions regarding scribes and Pharisees who inhabit the world outside this story. Rather, Matthew's implied reader is expected to come to a deeper understanding of the nature of evil: it tends to be hypocritical, masquerading as good (23:27–28); it involves unwitting self-deception, failing to recognize its own duplicity (15:14; 23:16–22); it perverts what would be good, ignoring motives or outcomes (6:2, 5, 16).

Basic Plot Lines

The plot of Matthew's Gospel is primarily conflict driven and may be understood as a complex of interwoven "plot lines."[45] One such plot line concerns the conflict between Jesus and his disciples: Jesus is often disappointed by the disciples' failures, and they persistently resist his attempts to bring them in line with his point of view. What is perhaps most compelling (and surprising) about this plot line is that Jesus appears to lose the conflict: he does not succeed in forming the disciples into the people he thinks they should be. Indeed, the reader imagines that "the worst thing that could happen" with regard to this particular plot line would be if the disciples were to reject Jesus altogether and completely desert him. This is precisely what *does* happen when the story reaches its climax (Matt. 26:56, 69–75).

Another major plot line in the story concerns the conflict between Jesus and the religious leaders of Israel. This conflict is somewhat defined in

---

[44] The point here is *not* to let the author "off the hook" for telling a story that (whatever his intention) lent itself very easily to anti-Semitic interpretation. The point is simply that critique of the ethical choices implied by an author's decisions regarding how to tell a story is a separate enterprise from the literary task of simply discerning how the story is expected to work. Persons who use narrative criticism may eventually want to offer such a critique, but the method of narrative criticism, in and of itself, is *descriptive* (with regard to how stories are expected to work) rather than *evaluative* (with regard to whether or not a story ought to be told in a particular way).

[45] See, especially, M. A. Powell, "The Plot and Subplots of Matthew's Gospel," *NTS* 38 (1992): 187–204. In this article, I acknowledge important work by R. Edwards, F. Matera, and especially J. D. Kingsbury. I now regret the use of the word "subplots" – it is better to speak simply of "interwoven plot lines."

terms of two threats that the leaders pose to Jesus: they want to turn the people of Israel against him and they want to destroy him, that is, have him put to death. Again, the reader imagines that the worst possible outcome for this conflict would be for these threats to succeed. And, again, this is precisely what *does* happen when the Gospel story reaches its climax in Matthew's passion narrative: the people do turn against Jesus and he is killed (27:15–26).

But there is more to this story than the interactions of Jesus with his disciples and the religious leaders of Israel. As a backdrop to those story lines, there is another major plot line involving an almost hidden conflict, namely the conflict between God and Satan – and *this* conflict is actually definitive for everything else in the world of this story. This background conflict is also resolved in Matthew's passion narrative, but unlike the other conflicts, it is resolved positively. When Jesus dies on the cross, he fulfills the will of God (cf. 26:39, 42) and defeats the will of Satan (cf. 16:21–23). Ironically, then, Jesus must "lose" his conflicts with the religious leaders and with his own disciples in order for the greater conflict between God and Satan to be resolved favorably. Thus, the reader learns something else about evil, namely that God triumphs over evil, even when evil succeeds at doing its worst.

LITERARY APPROACHES: INTERPRETATION OF MATTHEW 27:57–28:15

In some respects, the account of Jesus's burial and resurrection serves as the conclusion to Matthew's Gospel and is absolutely integral to all that has gone before it. In another, important sense, however, it serves as a new beginning, as the foundation narrative for a story yet to be told. We will examine a few aspects of the passage that would be particularly significant to scholars using literary approaches,[46] and then we will offer some concluding comments regarding how this episode fits with the overall plot line of Matthew's narrative as delineated earlier.

---

[46] See especially K. H. Reeves, *The Resurrection Narrative in Matthew: A Literary-Critical Examination* (Lewiston, NY: Mellen Press, 1993); cf. J. P. Heil, *The Death and Resurrection of Jesus: A Narrative-Critical Reading of Matthew 26–28* (Minneapolis: Fortress, 1991).

Literary Observations on the Text

The episode consists of four discernible scenes: the burial of Jesus, the setting of a guard at the tomb, the resurrection of Jesus and his subsequent commissioning of the women, and the report of the guard.

THE BURIAL OF JESUS (27:57–61). The designation of Joseph of Arimathea as "a rich man" reminds the reader immediately of the story in Matthew 19:16–26, but the further indication that Joseph is also "a disciple of Jesus" (27:57 NRSV) or, more accurately, "a person who has been discipled or instructed by Jesus" creates immediate tension for the implied reader. Joseph is not a former rich man – he has not sold his possessions and given his money to the poor – and yet he appears to be presented here as a person who is faithful to Jesus. This is puzzling for Matthew's implied reader, who knows that, in this story, it is impossible for any human being who is rich to have a life that is ruled by God (i.e., to enter the basilea [kingdom or rule] of heaven, 19:24). Accordingly, Joseph must be regarded as a walking miracle. It may be humanly impossible for a rich man to be faithful to Jesus, but what is impossible for humans is possible with God (19:26).

The most striking aspect of Joseph's unlikely appearance, however, is that he functions as a stand-in for Jesus's absent disciples and, accordingly, serves as a faithful foil to expose the depth of those disciples' unfaithfulness. Matthew's reader is expected to recall that after John the Baptist was murdered by Roman authorities, his disciples came for the body and provided their master with a decent burial (14:12). Why wouldn't Jesus's disciples do the same? It was bad enough that Jesus's disciples fled when Jesus was arrested (26:56) and that Peter subsequently denied Jesus (26:69–75), but *this* lapse – their failure to see to his burial – emphasizes their apostasy even more.

Finally, the mention of the women in this passage highlights the faithlessness of the disciples even more. Previously, Matthew has told us that many women, including the ones mentioned here, were present at the crucifixion, watching from a distance.[47] That reference cast into stark

---

[47] The reader would be expected to know that women who were friends or family of the condemned could not be present at the execution site itself, where they would be subject to abuse by the soldiers. Thus, the "distance" implies no moderation of

relief the fact that the male disciples were *not* present, nor even watching to see what would become of their master. The reference now to the women watching the tomb picks up that thread and carries it forward: the women are *witnesses*, while the male disciples, whom Jesus empowered to be apostles (10:1–2), are not.

THE SETTING OF THE GUARD (27:62–66). The religious leaders of Israel enter the story now. Specifically, the "chief priests and Pharisees," who in this story are representatives of a united front of powerful Jewish leaders opposed to Jesus,[48] are brought into collusion with Pilate, the Roman governor, who grants their request to place a guard at the tomb. In Matthew's story, both political and religious leaders are evil perpetrators of injustice and, notably, whenever they come together it is always for death. Early in the story, the political ruler manipulates religious leaders in a conspiracy to kill Jesus (2:3–6); later, the religious leaders manipulate the political authority in service of their own plot to have Jesus put to death (26:3–5; 27:1–2, 11–26). Now, the two forces combine in an attempt to preserve that death (or, at least, to prevent any rumor of life).

The leaders' request is ironic in several ways. First, they characterize others with terminology applicable to themselves. They call Jesus a "deceiver" (27:63, *planos*, NRSV "impostor") though, in the story, they themselves are the ones who have acted deceptively (22:15). They also slander Jesus's disciples as persons who would spread false reports about Jesus's resurrection (claiming it had occurred, when they knew it had not); but as the story continues, the leaders themselves will turn out to be the ones who spread false reports about that resurrection (claiming it did not occur, when they knew that it had).

In making their request for a guard, the leaders also ironically acknowledge the foolishness of what they have done and the negative consequences that it will have for them. They say that if Jesus's disciples begin proclaiming his resurrection, "the last (deception) will be worse than

---

their devotion. They are doing what they can in a desperate situation: when it is not possible to be close to Jesus physically, they nevertheless "keep watch" (as he has commended his followers to do when he is absent from them [24:42–44].

[48] The combination "chief priests and Pharisees" is also in 21:45; cf. "Pharisees and Sadducees" (3:11; 16:1, 11, 12;); "scribes and Pharisees" (5:20; 12:38; 15:1; 23:2, 13, 15, 23, 27, 29); "chief priests and scribes" (2:4; 20:18; 21:15); "chief priests and elders" (21:23; 26:3; 27:1, 3, 12, 20; 28:12); "elders and chief priests and scribes" (16:21; 27:41).

the first" (27:64). This wording closely parallels what Jesus said earlier in 12:45, such that the leaders now liken themselves to a man who is temporarily relieved of one unclean spirit only to end up possessed by many more. Basically, the leaders are depicted here as acknowledging that if Jesus is said to be risen, they will be worse off than if they had never had him crucified in the first place. And the reader cannot help but imagine that if a *false* report of resurrection would render their situation worse than it had been before, how much more might a *true* report of a resurrection render that situation intolerable.

The rationale for the leaders' request is also ironic in that it attributes a loyalty to Jesus's disciples that the reader knows is lacking. The disciples have abdicated responsibility for Jesus's body, not even bothering to recover it or to bury it or even to witness the burial. It hardly seems likely that they would now come to take the body from the tomb and courageously (if deceptively) proclaim him as risen. The leaders' depiction of the disciples is so far off the mark that it serves to remind the reader of just how uncommitted to Jesus those disciples truly are.

Finally, the leaders' mention of Jesus's prediction that after three days he would rise strikes the reader as incredibly ironic since that prediction was offered, repeatedly, to the *disciples* (16:21; 17:23; 20:19; cf. 17:9; 26:32).[49] The enemies of Jesus remember what Jesus said (27:63) and act on it, but Jesus's own disciples do not. There is no indication here, or in what follows, that the disciples were waiting and counting the days to see a fulfillment of what Jesus had told them would happen.

THE RESURRECTION AND COMMISSIONING OF THE WOMEN (28:1–11). The account of the empty tomb that follows includes numerous aspects that we can only touch on here. The appearance of an "angel of the Lord" leaves no doubt that God is directing these affairs. Matthew's story of Jesus began with events in which angels were actively involved (1:20; 2:13–14; 19; 4:11), but the insertion of God into human affairs continues now in an amplified sense. Previously, God's angel appeared to humans in dreams and guided them through that medium. Now the angel of the Lord is physically active on earth (moving the stone) and is visibly

---

[49] One might wonder how the religious leaders knew of the prediction. Reeves suggests that the reader is to assume they understood the "sign of Jonah" reference in 12:40. See *Resurrection Narrative*, 48–49.

present to all onlookers – even to the guards, who become "like dead men" (an ironic fate for those entrusted to guard the dead). And now God's angel speaks directly to people without mediation (e.g., through dreams or a prophet).

The earthquake (28:2) recalls what happened at the moment of Jesus's death (27:51–54) – indeed, on that occasion, tombs were also opened and the dead were also raised.[50] Thus, even though Matthew's narrative presents the resurrection of Jesus as "a new beginning," it also portrays the death, burial, and resurrection of Jesus as a single eschatological drama. The resurrection is both the culmination of what has happened and the start of something entirely new.

The role of the women in this part of the story, however, is what commends our greatest attention. The narrative has prepared the reader for their importance by twice noting their presence and participation in this drama: they have witnessed the crucifixion of Jesus and his entombment; now they witness his resurrection and are commissioned to proclaim the news of his resurrection. They respond with eager obedience and with "fear and great joy." Then, they encounter Jesus himself; they worship him and are commissioned by him to go and tell his "brothers" to go to Galilee where they will see him. We should note, in passing, that Jesus's desire for the disciples to be recovered – and, indeed his reference to them as "my brothers" (28:10; cf. 12:46–50) – conveys a strong sense of his faithfulness to these errant disciples in a way that contrasts sharply with their faithlessness to him. Clearly, they are to be forgiven for their apostasy, welcomed back, and restored to positions of leadership (see 28:16–20).

But it is the women who are portrayed as ideal followers of Jesus (and, so, as foils for the absent male disciples). In this regard, it may be important to point out that Matthew's implied reader is *not* expected to think the women have come to the tomb to anoint Jesus's dead body with spices. That information, which is sometimes read into the story, actually comes from Mark 16:1. It is extraneous data that readers of Matthew must "bracket out" if they want to discern how the reader of Matthew's Gospel

---

[50] Interestingly, they do not actually come out of their tombs until *after* Jesus has been raised. See D. D. Hutton, "The Resurrection of the Holy Ones (Mt 27:51b–53). A Study of the Theology of the Matthean Passion Narrative," Th.D. dissertation, Harvard University, 1970.

is expected to understand *this* Gospel's story.[51] But if the women have not come to anoint Jesus's body, why are they there? The reader might imagine that they have simply come to mourn, but their appearance at dawn on the third day suggests that they have *probably* come to see the resurrection that Jesus announced would occur (16:21; 17:23; 20:19; that the women were present when these predictions were made is apparent from 20:20–28; 27:55–56). These women have watched everything closely up to now, marking the time, and as soon as the momentous third day dawns they arrive at the tomb to see what will happen next. Their vigilance is rewarded and they become witnesses, first, to the empty tomb and, then, to the risen Lord himself. It was probably common knowledge in the setting where this narrative was produced that the "Christian gospel" was essentially a witness to three things – the death, burial, and resurrection of Jesus Christ (the three things that Paul, for example, identifies as being "of first importance" in 1 Cor. 15:3–4). In Matthew's narrative, the women become witnesses to these three things; indeed, they become the *only* witnesses to these three things (i.e., to all three).

The response of the women, "fear and great joy," represents an ideal combination of elements. Fear in Matthew's Gospel is essentially a negative quality that has potential for positive results: on its own, fear is debilitating (e.g., 14:30–33) but it is sometimes appropriate (10:28) and can motivate worship (17:6) or even a confession of faith (27:54). Joy, by contrast, is typically a positive quality (2:10; 13:44; 25:21, 24) that has potential for negative results: on its own, joy can signify faith that is superficial and unlikely to endure (13:20–21). The mixture of fear and joy, then, allows for a paradoxical compatibility to the benefit of both elements: joy is what turns fear into worship; fear is what prevents joy from being shallow.

So, now, these ideal disciples and witnesses to the three key events of the Christian gospel (the death, burial, and resurrection of Jesus) are commissioned by an angel, and then by Jesus himself, to regain Jesus's disciples for him. These women become the first people to worship the risen Lord and the first to proclaim the gospel that is to be taken to the

---

[51] See Reeves, *Resurrection Narrative*, 50. A similar point could be made even more strongly from the perspective of redaction criticism: the historical author of Matthew's Gospel has deliberately omitted this information because he does not want his readers to think that this was the women's reason for coming to the tomb.

world (cf. 24:14). Such primacy in worship and mission gives them the role in the church that had originally been offered to Peter (16:18–19). The apostasy of Jesus's male disciples is forgiven, but it costs them the legacy that they might have had. Jesus wills for his church to be founded by women, grounded in *their* proclamation of the gospel, and marked forever by their experience of "fear and great joy." Accordingly, the so-called Great Commission with which the Gospel concludes is actually presented as a secondary commission. The unfaithful men cannot be sent to make disciples of all nations until after the faithful women first make disciples of them. Indeed, their calling to preach the gospel is made conditional on their ability to receive the gospel as proclaimed by women. To put it bluntly, if men are not able to accept women's proclamation of the gospel and submit themselves to it, there will be no mission to the nations (at least none carried out by men) and there will be no church (at least no church that includes male believers). The church of Jesus Christ is founded by women, but it may also include men – if the women follow Christ's direction to include men and if the men are willing to accept their inclusion on precisely those terms.[52]

We may be prompted to consider, however, *why* the narrative would develop in this way? Does it represent some kind of first-century femi-nist misanthropy? Is the intention to exalt the godliness of women at the expense of men? I don't think so. Matthew's Gospel presupposes a patri-archal mindset, a view that understands the social superiority of men over women not as the result of unfortunate prejudices but as intrinsic reality. Men have power and women do not: that is just the way things are. The implied reader is expected to accept the essential legitimacy of such gender roles without imagining that anything so basic to human society could or should ever be different. Thus, feminism, as such, remains a foreign perspective, but Matthew's implied readers are expected to have

---

[52] This section of the chapter is taken from my book, *Chasing the Eastern Star*, 128–30, which in turn drew upon M. A. Powell, "Matthew," in *Harper-Collins Bible Commen-tary*, rev. ed., ed. J. L. Mays and B. R. Gaventa (San Francisco: HarperSanFrancisco, 2000). Readers may want to compare and contrast my discussion of these matters with what is offered in J. Kopas, "Jesus and Women in Matthew," *TTod* 47 (1990): 13–21; E. S. Malbon, "Fallible Followers: Women and Men in the Gospel of Matthew," *Semeia* 28 (1983): 29–48; T. Mattila, "Naming the Nameless: Gender and Discipleship in Matthew's Passion Narrative," in *Characterization in the Gospels: Reconceiving Narrative Criticism*, ed. D. Rhoads and K. Syreeni, JSNTSS 184 (Sheffield: Sheffield Academic Press, 1999), 153–79; and of course E. M. Wainwright's chapter on feminist criticism in this book.

their evaluation of gender roles critiqued and challenged *within* the basic patriarchal mindset that is presumed for this story world. The critique comes generally through the claim that *God prefers the powerless to the powerful.* The first will be last, and the last first (19:36; 20:16). The one who is least is the greatest of all (20:26–27). Thus, women are not exalted as founders of the church and exemplars of faith because they should be considered "equals" with men. They are so exalted precisely because they are not equals. In this Gospel's vision of the future, women may be the greatest in the kingdom even if, there, the men are still the ones on the thrones (19:28).

This Gospel *assumes* that its implied reader will evince a patriarchal mindset that regards men as intrinsically more powerful than women. It seeks to develop or transform this assumed perspective not by challenging the mindset itself but *by questioning the positive evaluation of power.* At the beginning of the story, Matthew's implied reader is assumed to believe that men are greater than women because men are more powerful than women. By the end of the story, Matthew's implied reader is expected to have come to believe that women are greater than men because men are more powerful than women. Women are greater than men in the same sense that children are greater than adults (18:1–4). This is not feminism, which typically seeks to empower women and sometimes seeks to debunk stereotypical gender roles altogether. But it is a critique of patriarchy *from within,* a critique that the implied author foists on the implied reader without any sure resolution of where it might lead or what could happen as a result. Indeed, we might note that it is potentially a critique of feminism as well, a challenge to the basic assumption that *the acquisition (or maintenance) of power is a good thing.* The point of view of this narrative is that power (understood as "the capacity to manipulate, dominate, or control others") is antithetical to God's purposes; those who neither seek nor possess such power are favored and preferred by God.

THE REPORT OF THE GUARD (28:11–15). This concluding scene for our selected passage recounts how the guard at the tomb report what has happened to Jesus's enemies, who respond by bribing the guard (on this compare 26:15; 27:3) to spread a false rumor about Jesus's disciples having stolen the body while they slept. The reader is expected to note that the movement of the guards leaving the tomb to tell Jesus's enemies what has happened parallels the movement of the women leaving the tomb to tell his disciples what has occurred. Likewise, the guards' commission to spread the false rumor about the theft of Jesus's body parallels the disciples' commission to baptize and teach all nations, given by Jesus in the next few verses (28:16–20).[53]

This episode contributes to Matthew's characterization of the religious leader of Israel and brings to a conclusion the plot line that traces the conflict between Jesus and those leaders. Two matters are especially significant.

First, the episode reveals that the religious leaders are absolutely recalcitrant and exposes the depth of their evil obstinacy and hypocrisy (cf. 13:14–15). They perpetrate the very sort of deception that they attribute to others; *they* become the "impostors" (cf. 27:62) and they do so in an unconscionable manner that lacks any pretense of righteous rationale. Twice in this narrative, the religious leaders have actually requested a sign from Jesus, implying (duplicitously) that they would believe in him if only a proper sign were given (12:38; 16:1). Now, they reject the sign he promised (12:40; cf. 16:4); knowing full well that Jesus has risen from the dead, they do not repent, but redouble their efforts to oppose him by spreading a teaching that they know to be untrue.

Second, the episode reveals that the religious leaders are successful. The narrator speaks directly to the reader to say that the false report denying Jesus's resurrection has been believed among the Jews "to this day" (28:15). We indicated earlier that the conflict between Jesus and the religious leaders in Matthew's story can be defined in terms of two threats that those leaders pose to Jesus: they threaten to turn the Jewish people against him and they threaten to kill him. In the climactic passion narrative, both threats succeed. Now, the reader is expected to realize that the resurrection of Jesus has not undone the success of the first threat: even though Jesus has risen from the dead, the religious leaders of Israel continue to turn the people against him. In like manner, I would argue that the second threat is not undone by the resurrection either. Some

---

[53] This parallel is amplified by Matthew's use of the verb *didaskō* ("teach") in 28:15. By indicating that the guards do as they were "taught," Matthew styles the false rumor regarding the theft of Jesus's body as a "teaching" of the religious leaders (cf. 16:12). See Reeves, *Resurrection Narrative*, 64.

scholars have suggested that the leaders' plot to kill Jesus fails because Jesus does not stay dead. I think this trivializes the consequences of the crucifixion as presented in this narrative. Although there is some sense in which Jesus will be present with his followers to the end of the age (28:20), there is also a very real sense in which he will no longer be with them (see 26:11). The leaders wanted to remove Jesus from the scene, and they have done so. He will no longer be doing the things that brought him into conflict with them: teaching in Galilee, healing in synagogues, overturning tables in the temple, and so on. Indeed, Matthew's implied reader is expected to realize that the crucifixion of Jesus has ushered in an era in which fasting replaces feasting as a sign of the kingdom (9:15). The bridegroom has been taken away, and only the parousia – *not* the resurrection – will change that (26:29). We may also note, tangentially, that the next scene in Matthew's story will make clear that the resurrection has also not undone the causes of Jesus's conflict with his disciples. The "little faith" that has marked that conflict throughout the narrative has not vanished with the resurrection: the problem of their "little faith" or doubt continues (28:17).

In short, this scene reveals that the forces of evil are both unconscionable and powerful. Jesus is risen, but evil continues unabated. The fact of his resurrection does not persuade the forces of evil to repent, nor does it seem to reduce the effectiveness of their opposition to him. This would seem like an odd way for Matthew to end his story, but we should remember two things: (1) this is not quite the ending; there is still another scene, which features Jesus commissioning his followers to make disciples of all nations and promising them his eternal presence and (2) this part of the story is less an "ending" than it is "a new beginning." This particular scene identifies the context for "the story yet to be told," the context in which the commission given in the next scene will have to be carried out. Jesus's disciples – doubters still – will have to conduct their mission in a world where evil remains both unconscionable and incredibly powerful. The "story yet to be told" will be an account of sheep being sent into the midst of wolves (10:16), of faithful people being flogged in synagogues and dragged before Gentiles (10:17–18), of family members betraying one another (10:21), and of disciples being hated for bearing Jesus's name (10:22). And yet it will be a story of fear *and* great joy (28:8), of doubt *and* worship (28:17), for both those who are made disciples and those who make them will be people who know that Jesus is risen.

Overall Contribution to Narrative Themes and Effect on the Overall Plot

A literary analysis of Matthew 27:57–28:15 emphasizes ways in which this passage contributes to the story that unfolds in Matthew's narrative as a whole. Much more could be said, but we have noted a few particular themes.

THE FAITHLESSNESS OF JESUS'S FALLIBLE DISCIPLES AS CON-TRASTED WITH HIS FAITHFULNESS TO THEM. This is a persistent theme developed throughout Matthew's narrative, as the disciples repeat-edly disappoint Jesus (16:5–12, 22–23; 19:13–14; 20:20–28; 26:56, 69–74) and yet he identifies himself with them and characterizes them in terms that their own words or deeds would not appear to justify (4:19; 10:5–23; 12:49; 19:28). Here, the disciples' failure to remain with Jesus is highlighted by way of contrast with the faithful actions of Joseph and the women, as well as by the religious leaders' ironic presumption that his disci-ples would be more loyal to him (albeit in a duplicitous way) than they actually are. The faithfulness of Jesus to his flawed disciples is brought out by his identification of them as his brothers and by the double commission to the women to tell the disciples they are to be restored (28:7, 10).

THE DIVINE PREFERENCE FOR THE POWERLESS OVER THE POWER-FUL. This is also a persistent theme throughout the narrative, prevalent in the teaching of Jesus (5:5; 18:4; 19:14, 30; 20:16; 20:26; 23:11–12) and in narrative portrayals of characters who possess power, wisdom, or wealth as typically opposed to God (2:1–18; 14:1–12; 26:3–5, 57–68; 27:1–2, 11–43; cf. 11:25–26; 20:25). Here, the theme is carried forward through the exalta-tion of women as exemplars of faithfulness, as witnesses to Jesus's death, burial, and resurrection, and as forbears of the new community that is to be founded on the basis of their testimony.

THE POWER AND PERSISTENCE OF EVIL. This is also a major theme in Matthew's apocalyptic tale, a story in which characters may be classed as "good" or "evil," or as "righteous" or "unrighteous" (5:45). The story world of this narrative may be likened to a field in which wheat (people who belong to God) and weeds (people put there by the devil) must grow side by side until the harvest (13:24–30, 36–43). Here, we learn that the resurrection of Jesus has not altered this basic state of affairs: evil continues unabated, with great success.

All things considered, a literary analysis of this passage reveals that Matthew's account of Jesus's burial and resurrection serves not only as an epilogue to the main story that has just been told, but also as "a new beginning" for a story yet to be told. The main story concerned God's plan to send Jesus as one who "would save his people from their sins" (1:21). This is accomplished with Jesus's crucifixion, when he gives his life as a ransom for many (20:28) and pours out his blood for the forgiveness of sins (26:28). Now, the resurrection of Jesus begins a new story. Some things are the same: the forces of evil continue to be powerful (28:15) and the disciples of Jesus continue to doubt (28:17). But behind the scenes, something is now fundamentally different: Jesus has saved his people from their sins and he is risen from the dead. Thus, he can initiate a new mission, one that invokes a new name (28:19; cf. 1:21, 23), one that is grounded in his universal authority (28:18) and sustained by his abiding presence (28:20).

Summary: How the Analysis Might Be Utilized

This analysis of Matthew 27:57–28:15 draws on narrative criticism to describe how Matthew's implied reader would be expected to understand the story. Most literary approaches to the Gospel would utilize aspects of such analysis, though they might do so in diverse ways. Some historically minded scholars would view such an approach as offering a possible index to the actual intentions of the book's historical author. Some "text-centered critics" would claim that narrative analysis itself provides the "correct interpretation" of the passage, the meaning that should be accepted as normative. Some "reader-oriented critics" might view the "meaning expected of an implied reader" as more of a basis for comparison with interpretations that legitimately understand the passage from perspectives the implied reader would not have been assumed to evince. And some postmodern critics would view *any* description of "how readers are expected to understand texts" as illusory constructs of critics who unwittingly try to establish their own experiences with the text as normative. Literary approaches are varied and they are employed by scholars for many different reasons and in service of many different ends.

3

↓

Feminist Criticism and the Gospel of Matthew

ELAINE M. WAINWRIGHT

*M*ANY HAVE UNDERTAKEN TO WRITE A COMPREHENSIVE account of the development of feminist biblical criticism generally and of feminist New Testament studies in particular.[1] In this chapter, it seemed good to me, having followed these things closely from the beginning, to give an account of how this particular hermeneutical approach has been manifest in Matthean studies. Similarly, however, to the way in which the Lucan "orderly account" (Luke 1:1) remained in dialogue with many other undertakings, so too will this exploration of what is unique to Matthean feminist interpretation have as its dialogue partner the past twenty-five years of feminist New Testament and Gospel criticism.

Twenty-five years is a significant marker for this study as 1983 saw the appearance of *In Memory of Her*, Elisabeth Schüssler Fiorenza's

---

[1] For a sample only, see several articles in A. Y. Collins, ed., *Feminist Perspectives on Biblical Scholarship* (Chico: Scholars, 1985); J. C. Anderson, "Feminist Criticism: The Dancing Daughter," in *Mark and Method: New Approaches in Biblical Studies*, ed. J. C. Anderson and S. Moore (Minneapolis: Fortress, 1992), 103–34; the articles in E. Schüssler Fiorenza, ed., *Searching the Scriptures: Volume One: A Feminist Introduction* (New York: Crossroad, 1993), which are not all necessarily from a historical perspective but which together provide an overview of feminist New Testament criticism up to the early 1990s; E. Castelli, "Heteroglossia, Hermeneutics, and History: A Review Essay of Recent Feminist Studies of Early Christianity," *JFSR* 10.2 (1994): 73–98; and more recently, K. O'Brien Wicker, A. S. Miller, and M. W. Dube, eds, *Feminist New Testament Studies: Global and Future Perspectives* (New York: Palgrave Macmillan, 2005), which brings the history of New Testament feminist studies up to the present and sets out the issues that will continue to confront the discipline into the future.

groundbreaking reconstruction of early Christian origins and her pro-
vision of a theoretical framework for feminist New Testament studies
that would impact the discipline for the subsequent quarter century.[2]
It was also the year in which the first specific feminist study of
Matthew appeared, namely Janice Capel Anderson's "Matthew: Gender and Reading," which was the opening article in an edition of
Semeia entitled *The Bible and Feminist Hermeneutics*, edited by Mary
Ann Tolbert.[3] Both these studies model what has developed in feminist New Testament interpretation. First each author explores feminism as a hermeneutic, perspective, ideology, or worldview that informs
every aspect of her interpretive project. Neither, however, claims to
develop an explicitly feminist biblical methodology but rather to bring
her feminist hermeneutical principles to bear on the biblical methodologies used and hence to shape them in significant ways – in the
case of Schüssler Fiorenza, her chosen methodology in *In Memory
of Her* was historical criticism,[4] while for Anderson it was the then
new literary criticism. This particular combination of hermeneutics
and hermeneutically informed methodologies enabled each to undertake her interpretive work: a feminist theological reconstruction of
early Christian origins and a gendered reading of the Gospel of
Matthew.

A historical survey of Matthean feminist scholarship characterizes
the first major section of this chapter. A contemporary feminist-critical
reading lens is then brought to a reading of Matthew 27:57–28:15, a task
that constitutes the second section of this chapter.

---

[2] E. Schüssler Fiorenza, *In Memory of Her: A Feminist Theological Reconstruction of
Christian Origins* (New York: Crossroad, 1983).

[3] J. C. Anderson, "Matthew: Gender and Reading," *Semeia* 28 (1983): 3–27. This article
also heads the more recent collection of feminist studies of the Gospel of Matthew edited
by A.-J. Levine, *A Feminist Companion to Matthew* (Sheffield: Sheffield Academic Press,
2001), 25–51.

[4] Schüssler Fiorenza, *In Memory of Her*, does entitle one of her theoretical chapters
"Toward a Feminist Critical Method," 41–67, but within that and her subsequent
chapter on a feminist model of historical reconstruction, she addresses ways of being
attentive to the silences in androcentric historiography and theology and of developing what she calls a sociological-theological model for reconstruction of early
Christian origins so that historical approaches are informed by her feminist-critical
perspective.

FEMINIST INTERPRETATIONS OF THE GOSPEL OF MATTHEW

Uncovering Androcentrism and Patriarchy within the Global Context of Empire

"Pervasive androcentrism" was the phrase used to characterize the Gospel of Matthew in 1983 by Anderson. She recognized that the Matthean text was written from an androcentric perspective and that it embodied "patriarchal assumptions."[5] She went on to detail briefly the androcentrism of the language and assumptions of the text in relation to both divine and human characterization: men are assumed to be central to the story as in the counting of the four or five thousand men besides the women and children (Matt. 14:21, 15:38); and G*d[6] and Jesus are generally characterized by male images and metaphors, predominantly that of father for G*d. She also notes the patriarchal family structures that are assumed or encoded in the text.

The two terms, *androcentrism* and *patriarchy*, which have been central to feminist biblical criticism, entered the field from feminist-critical theory. Schüssler Fiorenza discussed their impact on the New Testament in detail in 1983. As a result of androcentrism or a male-centered perspective, Matthew's Gospel names women "only when their presence has become a problem or when they are 'exceptional,' but it does not mention women in so-called normal situations."[7] The absence of women from texts does not, therefore, necessarily point to their absence from history. Schüssler Fiorenza goes on to draw out the implications of such

---

[5] Anderson, "Gender and Reading," 7.

[6] One of the ways in which Schüssler Fiorenza has proposed to interrupt too easy a familiarity with our naming of the divine is to write that name as G*d (see E. Schüssler Fiorenza, *Jesus: Miriam's Child, Sophia's Prophet: Critical Issues in Feminist Christology* [New York: Continuum, 1994], 191, n. 3). On the G*d image in Matthew, see J. Sheffield, "The Father in the Gospel of Matthew" in Levine, *Feminist Companion*, 52–69, and E. M. Wainwright, "From Antiochean to Antipodean Naming of Divinity," in *God Down Under: Theology in the Antipodes*, ed. W. W. Han Lamb and I. Barns, ATFS 10 (Adelaide: Australian Theological Forum Press, 2003), 87–117. Schüssler Fiorenza also summarizes her recommendation of "thinking twice" as she has extended it to "wo/men as inclusive of men, s/he as inclusive of he, and fe/male as inclusive of male." See "The Power of the Word: Charting Critical Global Feminist Biblical Studies," in Wicker, Miller, and Dube, *Feminist New Testament Studies*, 45.

[7] Schüssler Fiorenza, *In Memory of Her*, 44.

language use for feminist-critical interpretation, namely that it "must understand and translate New Testament androcentric language on the whole as inclusive of women, until proven otherwise."[8] "Disciple," for instance, must be considered to be inclusive of women, as feminist interpretation has demonstrated.[9] The androcentrism evident in the language of the Gospels also influenced the choice of traditions and sources so that stories of women may not have been included in the written text with the same frequency as similar stories of men.[10] Such choices do not necessarily reflect the actual historical context of men and women but the androcentric perspective of those compiling written narratives.[11] Feminist interpretation seeks to uncover such androcentrism in relation to the text of Matthew's Gospel, its translation and interpretation, and the historical reconstruction of the community.

Patriarchy, in contrast to androcentrism, is not only an ideology or social construction but has been defined in a variety of ways within feminist-critical theory and biblical interpretation to demonstrate that it is "a sociopolitical system and social structure of graded subjugations and oppressions."[12] Later Schüssler Fiorenza coined the term *kyriarchy* in order to make clear that this system is not characterized simply by the power of men over women, but that graded subjugations render the power relationships much more complex. Gender functions at all levels of such an intricate web of power.[13]

---

[8] Schüssler Fiorenza, *In Memory of Her*, 45.

[9] See E. M. Wainwright, *Towards a Feminist Critical Reading of the Gospel According to Matthew*, BZNW 60 (Berlin: de Gruyter, 1991), 330–39.

[10] For an example, see E. M. Wainwright, "'Your Faith Has Made You Well': Jesus, Women and Healing in the Gospel of Matthew," in *Transformative Encounters: Jesus and Women Re-viewed*, ed. I. R. Kitzberger (Leiden: Brill, 2000), 231–32.

[11] Authors, in antiquity, are more likely to have been men as they had greater access to and control over the resources needed for such writing. I have demonstrated, however, that women were very actively engaged in the oral shaping of the Jesus tradition in the Matthean community. See E. M. Wainwright, *Towards a Feminist Critical Reading*, 339–52, and *Shall We Look for Another? A Feminist Rereading of the Matthean Jesus* (Maryknoll: Orbis, 1998), 39–40. The data are not available, however, to distinguish the oral and written phases of such traditioning.

[12] E. Schüssler Fiorenza, *Bread Not Stone: The Challenge of Feminist Biblical Interpretation* (Boston: Beacon Press, 1984), 5.

[13] Schüssler Fiorenza explores the nuances of this terminology and the system it represents in *But She Said: Feminist Practices of Biblical Interpretation* (Boston: Beacon, 1992), 8, 105–18. The need for such nuancing became evident as women of color and indigenous women from many different contexts entered biblical studies, bringing their critique of the power dynamics in the field, including the dominant voices of white

That the Matthean text encodes patriarchal structures and reflects androcentric ideologies is evident from the patrilineage of Jesus with which the Matthean author opens the Gospel story. Anderson analyzes this in her 1987 article, "Mary's Difference: Gender and Patriarchy in the Birth Narratives."[14] Her feminist perspective enables her to recognize that while "a male ideology and its associated patriarchal institutions" are encoded within the text of Matthew 1–2, these are "not stable."[15] The female characters – Tamar, Rahab, Ruth, the "wife of Uriah," and Mary – introduce ambiguity into the text: they "may be defined and controlled by a divine male Patriarch" or "they may have an independent integrity beyond the control of man."[16]

The patriarchy encoded in the Matthean text and the androcentrism manifest in the ideological perspectives and linguistic usage are also key analytic categories that I used in the first book-length study of the Gospel of Matthew from a feminist perspective, *Towards a Feminist Critical Reading of the Gospel According to Matthew*, published in 1991.[17] The focus of this study was the way female characters function within texts. I demonstrated the pervasiveness of patriarchal structures and androcentric perspectives in those texts and in their literary and sociocultural contexts. I concluded that such a critical study "must be extended until all the patriarchal constructs and androcentric perspectives evident in the text are uncovered."[18] But, like Anderson, I also discovered that "tension, ambiguity, and anomaly mark the Matthean Gospel at the points where women function as significant characters in the narrative."[19] Patriarchy/kyriarchy and androcentrism do not prevail

Western feminists. See K. Pui Lan, *Discovering the Bible in the Non-biblical World*, BALS (Maryknoll: Orbis, 1995).

[14] J. C. Anderson, "Mary's Difference: Gender and Patriarchy in the Birth Narratives," *JR* 67.2 (1987): 183–202.

[15] Anderson, "Mary's Difference," 185–86.

[16] Anderson, "Mary's Difference," 190. For a more extensive study of the infancy narratives in Matthew and Luke from a feminist perspective, see J. Schaberg, *The Illegitimacy of Jesus: A Feminist Theological Interpretation of the Infancy Narratives* (San Francisco: Harper & Row, 1987).

[17] See Wainwright, *Towards a Feminist Critical Reading*, 28–29, for a brief theoretical discussion of this terminology. For an abbreviated version of this work, see "The Gospel of Matthew," in *Searching the Scriptures Volume Two: A Feminist Commentary*, ed. E. Schüssler Fiorenza (New York: Crossroad, 1994), 635–67.

[18] Wainwright, *Towards a Feminist Critical Reading*, 354.

[19] Wainwright, *Towards a Feminist Critical Reading*, 353.

absolutely in the Matthean narrative and this could be because gender is never a fixed construction but one that is constantly negotiated. Feminist historiographical studies of the late Hellenistic and early Roman era, the context of emerging Christianity and its texts, have demonstrated that this was a period of significant gender negotiation.[20]

The uncovering of androcentrism and patriarchy within the Matthean text and context has only just begun. These two key categories of critical analysis must continue to function in any feminist reading of Matthean texts so that they do not subtly but profoundly shape Christian perspectives and interpretations or naturalize what has been constructed as a result of their pervasive influence. They will, however, be continually nuanced as feminist studies develop. As early as 1995, Rosemary Pringle drew attention to this nuancing of the term *patriarchy* within feminist studies in a way that may have signaled its demise. She, however, advocated the ongoing need to "identify and destabilize patriarchal residues in the world of the symbolic, in texts and in psyches."[21] Given the profound impact of the "patriarchal symbolic" in ecclesial/theological as well as sociocultural contexts, and given the centrality of "texts" to New Testament studies, this task continues to be urgent and needs to be pervasive, focusing on every aspect of the Matthean text, on reconstructions of its context, and on interpretations through history. The context for analyzing these systemic categories early in the twenty-first century is, however, globalization and the violence and domination present in both economic and cultural as well as physical and rhetorical systems within the globalized reality that impacts each localized feminist interpretive project.

Prior to the 1990s, feminist New Testament studies generally and feminist Matthean studies in particular paid little attention to the way patriarchy and androcentrism intersected with, were shaped by, and in turn shaped race, class, colonial imperialism, and other social and cultural

---

[20] See by way of example R. S. Kraemer, *Her Share of the Blessings: Women's Religions among Pagans, Jews, and Christians in the Greco-Roman World* (New York: Oxford University Press, 1992), and C. Osiek, M. Y. Macdonald, with J. H. Tulloch, *A Woman's Place: House Churches in Earliest Christianity* (Minneapolis: Fortress, 2006), noting their nuancing of this claim on 1–2. Source materials demonstrating the situation of women in the Greco-Roman world are listed in n. 38.

[21] R. Pringle, "Destabilising Patriarchy," in *Transitions: New Australian Feminisms*, ed. B. Caine and R. Pringle (St. Leonards: Allen & Unwin, 1995), 199.

categories.[22] Musa Dube and Leticia Guardiola-Sáenz were responsible
for extending the feminist reading paradigm in relation to Matthean
studies to foster more explicit and focused attention to these factors. In
1996, Dube contributed an article to a volume of *Semeia* entitled *"Reading With": An Exploration of the Interface between Critical and Ordinary
Readings of the Bible.*[23] In this, we see the initial stages of her postcolonial
feminist reading. The postcolonial lens she brings to the text leads her
to ask the question, "What has been the role of the Bible in justifying
imperialism and why?" Her feminist biblical perspective leaves her not
content simply with readings that fight gender oppression and affirm
the agency of women, but she proposes to link such readings to a consideration of the role of the Bible in "the subjugation and exploitation
of one's nation and continent."[24] Her reading with women from the
African Independent Churches in Botswana leads her to conclude that
these women readers offer us strategies of interpretation that are born
out of a struggle with issues of imperialism and sexism.

Dube develops her postcolonial feminist approach to biblical interpretation in her book-length study, *Postcolonial Feminist Interpretation of the
Bible*, with Matthew 15:21–28 being one of the focal texts.[25] Initially she
brings what she calls "the postcolonial condition" into dialogue with the
Bible and with feminist biblical interpretation. She suggests that "imperialism" rather than "patriarchy" or "kyriarchy" should be the critical
category used in feminist interpretation: "[W]e therefore need a mode of
reading that takes seriously the presence of both imperialism and patriarchy, and seeks for liberating interdependence between genders, races,
nations, economies, cultures, political structures and so on."[26] Within
such a paradigm the biblical texts need to be placed alongside not only

[22] M. W. Dube, "Rahab is Hanging out a Red Ribbon: One African Woman's Perspective
on the Future of Feminist New Testament Scholarship," in Wicker, Miller, and Dube,
Feminist New Testament Studies, 181–86, makes this critique. The essays within this
volume generally provide insights into the effect of globalization and colonization
on feminist New Testament studies from African-American, Latin American, Asian,
African, Caribbean, European, and Northern American perspectives.

[23] See M. W. Dube, "Readings of *Semoya*: Botswana Women's Interpretations of Matt.
15:21–28," in *"Reading With": An Exploration of the Interface between Critical and Ordinary Readings of the Bible*, ed. G. West and M. W. Dube, *Semeia* 73 (Atlanta: Society of
Biblical Literature, 1996), 111–29.

[24] Dube, "Readings of *Semoya*," 122.

[25] M. W. Dube, *Postcolonial Feminist Interpretation of the Bible* (St. Louis: Chalice, 2000).

[26] Dube, *Postcolonial Feminist Interpretation*, 39.

Jewish texts but sacred texts from the two-thirds world and interpreters from this world need to be heard.

Dube turns her decolonizing lens to a reading of Matthew 15:21–28 and demonstrates how Empire functions in this text. One of her conclusions is that "[t]he form and ideology of Matthew 15:21–28 reflects that of the land possession type-scene, thus embracing imperialistic values and strategies as well as employing gender images that reinforce the oppression of women."[27] She turns then from text to reader using the same decolonizing lens. The readers she engages with from her critical postcolonial and feminist perspective are divided into White Western Male Readers and White Western Feminist Readers of Matthew 15:21–28. (The latter include Janice Capel Anderson, Amy-Jill Levine, Elisabeth Schüssler Fiorenza, and myself.) One of the major critiques Dube makes of the second group is what she sees as a failure to critique imperialism and/or power relationships. This critique underscores the necessity to nuance patriarchy quite significantly and to situate it within all relationships of power. She rightly concludes with a call to "depatriarchalize as well as to decolonize texts before any attempt is made to reclaim them."[28] Postcolonial theories and reading strategies can inform such decolonized readings. Patriarchy and androcentrism are not replaced, but function within the context of an analysis of both global and local contexts with imperialism, violence, and domination as key analytic categories.[29]

Using Gender (or Woman) as Key Analytic Category

It is already evident in the preceding discussion that gender is a significant analytic category within a feminist reading of texts. It is a defining element in Anderson's initial study, "Gender and Reading," and her citing of feminist literary critics highlights again the importance of dialogue with

---

[27] Dube, *Postcolonial Feminist Interpretation*, 155.

[28] Dube, *Postcolonial Feminist Interpretation*, 184.

[29] In relation to this, see E. Schüssler Fiorenza, *The Power of the Word: Scripture and the Rhetoric of Empire* (Minneapolis: Fortress, 2007). In this work, Schüssler Fiorenza engages with what she calls "Empire Studies" as a new field in biblical interpretation, and she discusses the ways in which feminist and postcolonial studies can converge when biblical interpreters "adopt a critical analytic for interpreting the inscriptions of kyriarchal power in biblical texts and their possible internalizations by biblical readers" (p. 129).

feminist theorists in the development of a distinctive feminist approach to biblical interpretation.[30] She does not define *gender* but speaks of its "symbolic significance" in the text.[31] It is also the key analytic category she uses in her second article, "Mary's Difference," already discussed briefly earlier. Here, she demonstrates the way in which the gendering of characters functions symbolically to shape readings of texts that can be patriarchal/androcentric or critical.[32]

Schüssler Fiorenza gives explicit attention to the sex–gender system in her 1994 study, *Jesus: Miriam's Child, Sophia's Prophet*. She critiques the naturalizing of the sex–gender binary difference that has been so constructed over millennia, noting four levels of such construction:

1. the *sociopolitical*, which recognizes the constructed nature of both sex and gender and their intersection with other such constructions as race;
2. the *philosophical*, which recognizes a long history of constructions in both Western and human thought and behavior;
3. the *natural* or *factual*, which understands the sex–gender dualism as simply the way the world is; and
4. the *theological*, which has taken the system into the heart of religious and theological articulations that have circulated for millennia as truth.[33]

What her work makes clear is that feminist analyses cannot be limited to a focus on women or female characters in texts. Rather, the entire sex–gender system and its impact on texts and on our reconstruction of history need serious scholarly attention.

---

[30] Anderson, "Gender and Reading."

[31] Anderson, "Gender and Reading," 4–6.

[32] I note here that in *Towards a Feminist Critical Reading*, 28, I define gender in terms of a social construction of "cultural roles which are considered appropriate to either men or women in a given society," noting that it "may not necessarily mirror the historical situation to which it refers or out of which it arose." R. Braidotti offers this definition of gender: "a notion that offers a set of frameworks within which feminist theory has explained the social and discursive construction and representation of differences between the sexes." See "What's Wrong with Gender?" in *Reflections on Theology and Gender*, ed. F. van Dijk-Hemmes and A. Brenner (Kampen: Kok Pharos, 1994), 52. Braidotti goes on to point out that within this system, the masculine is taken as the norm or "the human" and the feminine is rendered "other."

[33] Schüssler Fiorenza, *Jesus*, 34–43.

Emily Cheney, in her book *She Can Read: Feminist Reading Strategies for Biblical Narrative*, uses "gender" as a key analytic category in her development of the feminist reading strategies that she brings to bear on chosen Matthean texts.[34] She does not limit her focal texts to those in which women function as characters but turns her gender reading lens on Matthew 1:18–25, 10:5–15, 23:1–12, 26:20–29, and 28:16–20. One of the reading strategies that she develops in dialogue with feminist literary critics is that of "gender reversal."[35] She recognizes that "[a] knowledge of ancient literary and cultural conventions about gender roles is therefore necessary in order to sense that a protagonist of the reversed gender would be unusual for the action of a story or scene." After reversing the roles in the Matthean text, she then compares "the dominant action of these scenes to the portrayals of women and men in a selection of ancient writings to assess the conventional role behavior attached to that dominant action."[36] To my knowledge, her proposal of gender reversal as a feminist approach to reading biblical texts has not been taken up by other feminist interpreters of Matthew's Gospel, perhaps because of the very "unnatural" aspect of such a reading task (the very point she is making). What she has highlighted, however, is the importance of a knowledge of gender construction in ancient texts, which enables feminist critics to identify and critically evaluate the gender construction within the Matthean text and to determine whether it is representative of the naturalizing perspectives of the dominant culture or whether it is constructing/reconstructing gender in a different way.[37]

---

[34] E. Cheney, *She Can Read: Feminist Reading Strategies for Biblical Narrative* (Valley Forge: Trinity Press International, 1994).

[35] Her other two categories are analogy and women as exchange objects. For her explanation of these categories, see *She Can Read*, 36–42.

[36] Cheney, *She Can Read*, 46.

[37] There is now a wide range of sources on which feminist New Testament critics can draw for their analysis of gender constructions in antiquity. Here I can simply name a representative selection: B. J. Brooten, *Women Leaders in the Ancient Synagogue*, BJS 36 (Chico: Scholars, 1982); M. R. Lefkowitz and M. B. Fant, eds, *Women's Life in Greece and Rome: A Source Book in Translation*, 3rd ed. (Baltimore: Johns Hopkins University Press, 2005); R. S. Kraemer, ed., *Maenads, Martyrs, Matrons, Monastics: A Sourcebook on Woman's Religions in the Greco-Roman World* (Philadelphia: Fortress, 1988); and U. E. Eisen, ed., *Women Officeholders in Early Christianity: Epigraphical and Literary Studies*, trans. L. M. Maloney (Collegeville: Liturgical, 2000). I draw significantly on such sources in my reconstruction of the role and function of women in the Matthean community in *Towards a Feminist Critical Reading*, 339–352.

Gender and difference, as two related categories of analysis in feminist-critical theory in the late 1990s,[38] shaped my own construction of a feminist paradigm for rereading the Matthean Jesus in *Shall We Look for Another? A Feminist Rereading of the Matthean Jesus*. The use of the term *engender* to characterize a new reading, an engendered reading, enabled me to combine the critical aspect that had come to be associated with gender as demonstrated previously with the creative aspect of a new reading, which the term *engender* evokes. This engendered reading took account of text, reader, and context, giving particular attention to difference as it functioned across these three parameters. In particular, the recognition of different households or communities of reading in the Matthean context allowed me to hear the different meanings that may have been given to the text from within these different contexts.[39] Gender and gendering function in both the critical and constructive phases of a feminist reading and will continually intersect with other reading categories such as difference.

As with patriarchy and androcentrism, however, it has been recognized within feminist studies that gender as an analytic category intersects not only with imperialism (as noted earlier) but also with race, class, sexuality, and age. These and a range of other aspects may be structured into every rhetorical and social context (e.g., exile and diasporic living, as feminist interpreters find themselves living across national boundaries; and multifaith dimensions of life, as women engage the religious traditions of their ancestors or of current contexts).[40] Positionality is recognized as multiple within today's feminisms and as such will shape readings of Matthew's Gospel into the future as feminist interpreters raise up their multiple voices from the wide range of positionalities that represent today's interpreters.

This recognition turns attention to two nuanced aspects of a reading of gender that have characterized Matthean feminist criticism but which need critical analysis. First, the use of gender as an analytic category for reading may not necessarily indicate that the work is a feminist

---

[38] See, for instance, R. Braidotti, *Nomadic Subjects: Embodiment and Sexual Difference in Contemporary Feminist Theory*, GC (New York: Columbia University Press, 1994).

[39] Wainwright, *Shall We Look for Another?*, 19–32, for the development of the reading paradigm, and 35–49, for differences between the reading communities.

[40] These latter are two of the categories that Wicker highlights. See "Introduction," in Wicker, Miller, and Dube, *Feminist New Testament Studies*, 6–8.

interpretation; and second, focus on women may not constitute either a gendered or a feminist approach. If such studies are not integrated into an explicitly feminist paradigm, then "woman"[41] or "gender"[42] can function simply as an analytic lens for reading the text. There is little or no exploration of the way either of these categories functioned within the text or within the historico-literary context of the first century toward the construction of patriarchy or the maintenance of androcentrism and imperialism, nor of the ways that these latter had already shaped the text and continue to inform its interpretation. On the other hand, it has been demonstrated that both "woman" and "gender" are significant categories in Matthean feminist interpretations. It is important not to confuse these different types of readings but also to recognize how a range of readings can contribute in different ways to the goals of feminist interpretation, namely, a critique of all processes and systems that oppress wo/men[43] and the subsequent transformation of perspective and praxis in relation to wo/men and society.[44]

"Gender" as analytic category emerging from within feminist studies has generated two related fields of study, namely, gender studies and

[41] J. Kopas, "Jesus and Women in Matthew," *Theology Today* 47 (1990): 13–21, and M. J. Selvidge, "Violence, Woman and the Future of the Matthean Community: A Redactional Critical Essay," *Union Seminary Quarterly Review* 39 (1984): 213–23, are two examples of an early focus on women as characters in the early stages of feminist studies of the Matthean text. Levine's commentary, "Matthew," in *Women's Bible Commentary: Expanded Edition with Apocrypha*, ed. C. A. Newsom and S. H. Ringe (Louisville: Westminster John Knox, 1998), 339–49, shares in the focus of the entire collection, namely, a reading of not only portions of the Bible that deal explicitly with female characters and symbols but also sections that bear on the condition of women more generally. There is little development of a feminist reading paradigm. Similarly with G. Jackson, *"Have Mercy on Me": The Story of the Canaanite Woman in Matthew 15.21–28*, JSNTSS 228 (New York: Sheffield Academic Press, 2002).

[42] S. L. Love has provided some excellent perspectives on the gendering of Matthew in "The Household: A Major Social Component for Gender Analysis in the Gospel of Matthew," *BTB* 23 (1993): 21–23. But Love recognizes that he has not addressed "the hermeneutical question for Christians and churches in an advanced industrial society" (p. 29), feminism being a significant element of this question. See also S. L. Love, "The Place of Women in Public Settings in Matthew's Gospel: A Sociological Inquiry," *BTB* 24.2 (1994): 52–65.

[43] See n. 6 and Schüssler Fiorenza's "thinking twice" so that wo/men includes men as well as women.

[44] S. M. Schneiders defines feminism as "a comprehensive ideology which is rooted in women's experience of sexual oppression, engages in a critique of patriarchy as an essentially dysfunctional system, embraces an alternative vision for humanity and the earth, and actively seeks to bring this vision to realization." See *Beyond Patching: Faith and Feminism in the Catholic Church* (New York: Paulist, 1991), 15.

men's or masculinity studies.[45] Feminist interpretation of Matthew will need to engage critically with such studies and to extend its gender focus to include male gendering. This needs to be done with caution, however, as the power of the normativity of masculinity in both texts and the consciousness of interpreters remains strong.

In this section, it has been demonstrated that "wo/man" and "gender" can function as key analytic categories within feminist interpretation. Both, however, have to function critically within a well-constructed feminist framework, the topic that will be taken up in the next section, where they will be seen to intersect with a range of analytic categories rising from the contemporary positionalities of feminist interpreters such as nationality, diaspora, hybridity, and sexuality.

Constructing a Feminist Interpretive Framework

Feminism as a critical ideology has been characterized by two major moments: the first is *deconstructive*, consisting of a critique of all that oppresses wo/men; and the second *reconstructive*, seeking transformation of society so that justice prevails for all, but especially for women.[46] This twofold approach underlies and informs Schüssler Fiorenza's construction of what she calls a feminist model of biblical interpretation in her 1984 publication, *Bread Not Stone*.

She extends the twofold movement to a fourfold one.[47] Within the deconstructive moment she includes a *hermeneutics of suspicion* that she characterizes as starting from "the assumption that biblical texts and their interpretations are androcentric and serve patriarchal functions." This critical perspective must be directed to the text, its context of origin, the history of its interpretation, and its rhetorical impact in contemporary contexts in order to determine how these functioned for women within and at all these layers of interpretation. She makes this more explicit at the contemporary layer as a *hermeneutics of proclamation* that "assesses

---

45 See S. D. Moore and J. C. Anderson, eds, *New Testament Masculinities, Semeia* 45 (Atlanta: Society of Biblical Literature, 2003), especially the two articles that focus on Matthew: J. H. Neyrey, "Jesus, Gender, and the Gospel of Matthew," 43–66, and J. C. Anderson and S. D. Moore, "Matthew and Masculinity," 67–91.

46 See S. Benhabib and D. Cornell, "Introduction: Beyond the Politics of Gender," in *Feminism as Critique*, ed. S. Benhabib and D. Cornell (Minneapolis: University of Minnesota Press, 1987), 1.

47 Schüssler Fiorenza, *Bread Not Stone*, 15–20.

the Bible's theological significance and power for the contemporary community of faith."

Her lens then turns to the reconstructive or what she calls *a critical hermeneutics of remembrance.* Here she proposed using "a historical-critical reconstruction of biblical history from a feminist perspective" to recover "*all* biblical traditions." This entails a reclaiming not only of women's agency within both biblical traditions and history but also of "their sufferings and struggles" as a "dangerous" or "subversive" memory. To this, she adds *a hermeneutics of creative actualization* that uses "historical imagination, artistic recreation, and liturgical ritualization" to "allow women to enter the biblical story" anew and for this story to function to shape a new imagination for those engaged in the struggle against patriarchal oppression. This is one example of a feminist-critical paradigm, and Schüssler Fiorenza's approach, as it has developed across the last twenty-five years, has provided a foundation or at least dialogue partner for the development of the particular paradigms scholars have used in their studies of Matthew's Gospel.[48]

It was such a dialogue with Schüssler Fiorenza's fourfold model that shaped my own construction of a feminist framework for reading Matthew's Gospel in *Towards a Feminist Critical Reading of the Gospel According to Matthew.* My approach was both critical and reconstructive, and I nuanced the analytic category of "liberation" with that of "inclusion." Using a narrative-critical approach, I examined, in Stage One, *the inclusion of women in the text.* Then, using redaction criticism, I examined, in Stage Two, the *inclusion of women in the formation of the text* – the way in which women's traditioning may have shaped that process. The insights from these two stages of analysis were brought into dialogue with the ever-increasing body of resources relating to women's participation in the Greco-Roman world to inform Stage Three: *the inclusion of women within history* – the role women may have played in the emerging Matthean community that produced the text of the Gospel according to Matthew.[49] A feminist paradigm informed a range of

[48] Schüssler Fiorenza has developed her feminist-critical hermeneutics for biblical interpretation further in *Wisdom Ways: Introducing Feminist Biblical Interpretation* (Maryknoll: Orbis, 2001). It is now multidimensional rather than fourfold and seeks to incorporate the development of her thinking over the two decades since the publication of *In Memory of Her* in 1983.

[49] Wainwright, *Towards a Feminist Critical Reading*, 25–55.

biblical methodologies to achieve the particular goal of the project being undertaken.

It should be noted here that Dube critiques my use of the categories of "liberation" and "inclusion," pointing to my failure to take account of their function within an imperialist perspective, stating that "liberative inclusion will need to be qualified in order to differentiate it from imperialist inclusions which usually entail subjugation of difference and inequality of subjects."[50] Feminist categories as we have used them in developing a feminist paradigm for reading Gospel texts need to be nuanced in light of our current awareness of the complex web woven by imperial modes of oppression and domination. What can appear as liberating perspectives can be subtly shaped by the dominant global rhetoric and structures. As a Western feminist, I need to be attentive to the "Western imperialist rhetoric" that can permeate my interpretation of texts that I have intended to be liberative.

Schüssler Fiorenza continued to develop her feminist-critical framework for biblical interpretation in *But She Said*, in which her turn to the rhetorical began. She called her developing approach "a critical feminist rhetorical model"[51] and shifted her critical gaze to the ways in which texts functioned to shape meaning in historical contexts and continue to create meaning and shape consciousness in contemporary sociopolitical and theologico-religious contexts.

Developments in sociorhetorical methodology within biblical studies generally and Schüssler Fiorenza's incorporation of a rhetorical perspective into a feminist-critical framework influenced the development of my feminist paradigm for rereading Jesus in the Gospel of Matthew. An "engendered reading" sought to capture the critical or deconstructive aspect of reading from a gender perspective and to evoke the reconstructive or creative rereading that attention to difference and gender makes possible within the context of a feminist-critical approach. I developed a three-tiered framework that would enable such an approach to inform reading.[52] A *Poetics* of Engendered Reading focused on the *text*: how genre, characterization of Jesus, and metaphors used for Jesus functioned in the first-century interpretation of the text, and how they might

---

[50] Dube, *Postcolonial Feminist Interpretation*, 178–79.
[51] Schüssler Fiorenza, *But She Said*, 40–48.
[52] Wainwright, *Shall We Look for Another?*, 21–32.

continue to function today.[53] The *Rhetorics* of Engendered Reading turned attention to the *reader(s)*: those persons within different types of first-century households constituting the Matthean community (some scribal, some more egalitarian, some identified along class and status lines) who would have influenced the meaning given to Jesus as the Gospel was heard in their communities. Finally, the third stage of this reading gave attention to the *Politics* of Engendered Reading whose focus was *context* – the contexts of both the first and the late twentieth centuries. The goal of this reading paradigm was, therefore,

to bring to light new perspectives that highlight and creatively weave together aspects of the text and its subtext that have been neglected, silenced, or forgotten during centuries of patriarchal Christianity. Such a reading will, therefore, create a new symbolic universe that can shape the reader and according to which a new view of the world can be created.[54]

This feminist "map for reading" provided the guidance necessary to undertake selected soundings across the Matthean text. What emerged were indeed different voices, multiple voices that I claim would have been present in the Matthean first-century community of households reading the text, just as a variety of interpretive voices are present in today's different households of faith that constitute the church. Feminist-critical categories of gender and difference combined with a sociorhetorical approach or methodology informed by feminism enabled such a reading. Such a feminist paradigm must, however, come into dialogue with the imperial, the ecological, and other critical lenses.[55]

It has been Levine who has brought a necessary and critical Jewish perspective to feminist readings of Matthew's Gospel. In a 1996 article, she critiqued the way in which Christian feminist interpretations have focused unnecessarily on purity codes and have interpreted

---

[53] C. Deutsch explores the metaphor of wisdom in relation to the characterization of Jesus. See "Jesus as Wisdom: A Feminist Reading of Matthew's Wisdom Christology," in Levine, *Feminist Companion*, 88–113; *Lady Wisdom, Jesus, and the Sages: Metaphor and Social Context in Matthew's Gospel* (Valley Forge: Trinity Press International, 1996).

[54] Wainwright, *Shall We Look for Another?*, 32.

[55] I develop what I called a multidimensional hermeneutics that integrates feminist, ecological, and postcolonial perspectives in E. M. Wainwright, *Women Healing/Healing Women: The Genderization of Healing in Early Christianity* (London: Equinox, 2006), 7–32. This work includes a chapter on women and healing in the Gospel of Matthew.

them ahistorically. She claims that this leads to a supersessionist rather than reformist interpretation of the Jesus story.[56] Almost a decade later in a roundtable discussion in the *Journal of Feminist Studies of Religion* entitled "Anti-Judaism and Postcolonial Biblical Interpretation," Levine extended her Jewish critique to include the emerging international readings of the Gospels from some of the different positionalities already discussed earlier.[57] Given the intensity of the discussion that emerged in response to Levine's critique,[58] it is clear that there is internal controversy within the field of feminist studies of Matthew and feminist New Testament studies. It is also evident how profoundly anti-Judaism like imperialism has shaped the Christian consciousness of all its adherents. Attention to this is, therefore, an essential element in any contemporary and future feminist interpretation of the Matthean Gospel.

This tracking of feminist-critical readings of the Gospel of Matthew has demonstrated that the feminist paradigm or hermeneutic is becoming multidimensional. We have seen how postcolonial studies, especially as articulated in relation to Matthean studies by Dube, have brought the category of empire/imperialism to the center of the feminist paradigm. Likewise, Guardiola-Sáenz introduced the important category of "border" as it relates to the positionality of exile and diaspora.[59] Violence and domination permeate all aspects of contemporary social and rhetorical systems and hence must nuance feminist readings,[60] with one particular manifestation of this being ecological. In the future, we will need to be ever attentive to those dimensions of which we are not yet aware that must constitute a feminist reading paradigm as our recognition of layers of injustice and domination becomes more acute.

[56] A.-J. Levine, "Discharging Responsibility: Matthean Jesus, Biblical Law and Hemorrhaging Woman," in *Treasures New and Old: Recent Contributions to Matthean Studies,* ed. D. R. Bauer and M. A. Powell (Atlanta: Scholars Press, 1996), 379–97; reprinted in Levine, *Feminist Companion,* 70–87.

[57] A.-J. Levine, "Anti-Judaism and Postcolonial Biblical Interpretation," *JFSR* 20.1 (2004), 91–99.

[58] K. Pui-lan, M. Kanyoro, A. Reinhartz, H. Kinukawa, and E. M. Wainwright, "Anti-Judaism and Postcolonial Biblical Interpretation," *JFSR* 20.1 (2004): 99–125.

[59] L. Guardiola-Sáenz, "Borderless Women and Borderless Texts: A Cultural Reading of Matthew 15:21–28," in *Reading the Bible as Women: Perspectives from Africa, Asia, and Latin America,* ed. P. Bird, K. D. Sakenfeld, and S. H. Ringe, *Semeia* 78 (Atlanta: Society of Biblical Literature, 1997), 69–81.

[60] Wicker, "Introduction," 4–5.

What has emerged in this section is that there is no single feminist
framework for reading biblical or Matthean texts.[61] Rather each project
will differ as the interpreter undertakes her own unique inquiry, for as
Sandra Schneiders suggests, "[t]he interpretive project begins with the
proper formulation of the questions one wishes to ask of the text."[62]
It is the questions particular to each unique project that will constitute the particular categories that will enable each new reading project
to be undertaken and completed. There are, however, shared feminist
principles, which are always developing and being nuanced anew, and
demonstrated ways in which these can shape biblical methodologies in
order to provide each particular interpreter with her feminist framework.

FEMINIST CRITICISM: INTERPRETATION OF MATTHEW
27:57–28:15

In what follows, a feminist hermeneutic will be combined with a socio-
rhetorical approach. This will focus on four of the textures outlined in
the work of Vernon Robbins: the inner texture, the intertexture, social
and culture texture, and ideological texture.[63] When exploring the *inner
texture* my focus will be on the narrative and rhetorical features in the
text, drawing on the methodologies of narrative and rhetorical criticism.
Intertexture recognizes that each text exists within a network of other
texts. Attention to the *sociocultural texture* of the text focuses on the
sociocultural world that the text creates and that can be explored by way
of sociological and cultural anthropological analyses that will be drawn
into my reading as appropriate. The *ideological texture* of a text permeates
the previous three textures and many of the feminist categories explored
previously will inform this layer of analysis, which cannot be separated
from the first three.

The Gospel of Matthew, like all the literature of the New Testament,
emerges from the context of Empire. Whether its origin was in Syrian

---

[61] This is likewise demonstrated in the collection by Levine cited earlier, *A Feminist
Companion to Matthew*. See in particular her insightful introduction, pp. 13–23, which
provides an overview of the varied approaches taken in the articles included in the
collection.

[62] S. M. Schneiders, *The Revelatory Text: Interpreting the New Testament as Scripture* (San
Francisco: Harper, 1991), 152.

[63] V. K. Robbins, *Exploring the Texture of Texts: A Guide to Socio-Rhetorical Interpretation*
(Valley Forge, PA: Trinity Press International, 1996).

Antioch, Sepphoris, or the arc of cities joining Antioch to upper Galilee, colonization by Rome characterized the region.[64] Rome is likewise foregrounded in the text under consideration (Matt. 27:57–28:15) as it immediately follows from the death of Jesus by crucifixion, an instrument of Roman oppression (27:1–50). Also, twice in this text, the chief priests and Pharisees or chief priests and elders interact with Pilate, the Roman governor of the region, in relation to the body of Jesus (27:62–66; 28:11–15). Power, domination, subservience, and violence characterize context and text. It is in such a context that gender and kyriarchy need to be analyzed.

Examining the Confines of the Narrative/Text

One of the first considerations of a biblical interpreter is an examination of the parameters of a text, where the unit begins and ends and how it is situated within its literary context.[65] A rhetorical approach determines the rhetorical units, and narrative criticism seeks to situate a text in its narrative context. A feminist analysis will bring a complex gendered lens to these undertakings, questioning how the chosen beginning and end points function in relation to male and female characterization, power relationships, and imperialist and anti-Jewish perspectives.

The section of Matthew's Gospel proposed to me as contributor to this volume (27:57–28:15) contains the following rhetorical units:

27:57–60   A disciple (Joseph of Arimathea) entombs Jesus.
27:61   Two women disciples remain at the tomb.
27:62–64   Counteraction of opponents of Jesus and his disciples.
28:1–10   Women disciples at the tomb discover Jesus has been raised.
28:11–15   Opponents of Jesus and his disciples continue counteraction.

I will not go into detail here as to the determinants of these units, but even brief attention to the beginning and ending of each scene provides a clear indicator.

---

[64] See the work of W. Carter, *Matthew and the Margins: A Sociopolitical and Religious Reading* (Maryknoll: Orbis, 2000), and *Matthew and the Empire: Initial Explorations* (Harrisburg: Trinity Press International, 2001).

[65] Robbins, *Exploring the Texture of Texts*, 19–21, discusses "opening-middle-closing texture and pattern."

Attention to the narrative structure of this section of the Matthean Gospel informed by a feminist lens would suggest that the section for analysis should be extended on either side in order to better interpret 27:57–28:15. Frank Matera's narrative construction of the Matthean text on the basis of the theory of "kernels" and "satellites" supports the separation of the final verses of the Gospel (28:16–20) from the preceding narrative,[66] a division that is also affirmed by Donald Senior.[67] But my own narrative construction demonstrates that the entire passion/resurrection narrative (i.e., Matt. 26–28) is framed thus:

1. Jesus's instructions to his disciples (Matt. 26:1–2; 28:16–20);
2. the assembling or gathering of the chief priests and elders (26:3–5 and 28:11–15);[68] and
3. the actions of women, one who pours perfumed ointment over the head of Jesus (26:6–13) and others who witness the empty tomb and are commissioned to proclaim that Jesus has been raised (28:1–10).[69]

This suggests that 28:16–20 is intimately interwoven with the other two elements of the frame, a claim that is further substantiated by the instruction given to the women at the tomb to go to tell the eleven male disciples that they must go to Galilee to encounter the risen one as the women have done outside the empty tomb. A gendered reading will, therefore, link these final accounts in Matthew 28, recognizing that there are significant interconnections between the female disciples at the tomb and the male disciples on the mountain in Galilee. Although I will not be able to examine it in detail here, if 28:16–20 is allowed to stand alone, it is easily informed by the androcentric perspective that reads the commissioning

---

[66] F. J. Matera, "The Plot of Matthew's Gospel," *CBQ* 49.2 (1987): 233–53. The choice of kernels and satellites will always be shaped by each interpreter's perspective and a feminist critique of Matera's division could offer an alternative but I will not be able to explore this further here.

[67] D. Senior, *What Are They Saying about Matthew?*, rev. ed. (New York: Paulist, 1996), 36–37. Elsewhere, Senior argues that Matt. 27:55–56 is the terminal point of the passion narrative; hence, beginning a new narrative section at 27:57 fits with his structuring. See *The Passion Narrative According to Matthew: A Redactional Study* (Leuven: University of Leuven Press, 1982), 328.

[68] The verb *synagō* is used in both 26:3 and 28:12 to designate their gathering; *symbouleuō* (26:4) and the noun *symboulion* (28:12) also point to the opponents consulting together.

[69] See Wainwright, *Toward a Feminist Critical Reading*, 122–23.

of eleven male disciples as the ultimate postresurrection commissioning. Ideally, a feminist gendered reading would extend the text under consideration to include 28:16–20.

Similarly when one turns to the opening verses of the chosen section, a gendered postcolonial reading raises questions as to why two human responses to the death of Jesus prior to that of Joseph of Arimathea are omitted from the chosen text. Matthew 27:50 records the death of Jesus followed by the extraordinary phenomena of the tearing of the curtain of the temple and the splitting open of the tombs (27:51–53) – the earth responds to the crucifixion of Jesus.[70] A series of human responses ensues: the centurion acclaims Jesus (27:54); women are present at the site of the crucifixion (27:55–56); Joseph of Arimathea buries the body of Jesus (27:57–60); two of the women continue their watch at the tomb (27:61); and the chief priests and Pharisees seek to extend the guard/watching at the cross of Jesus to the tomb (27:62–66). The Matthean strategy of intertwining the imperial and the gendered response in 27:54 and 27:55–56 with what follows will, therefore, be given consideration later.

Reading the Textures of the Text: Responses to the Death of Jesus

The first related human response to Jesus's yielding up of his spirit in 27:50 is that of a centurion and others with him who are keeping watch. Their response is not, however, to the dehumanizing execution by crucifixion of a Galilean whom they had colonized but rather it is to the earth's trembling and to the rocks' splitting.[71] Their exclamation, "Truly this one was a son of God," together with their recognition of divine phenomena surrounding this death, encodes in the text intertextually the type of portents that accompanied the death of a Roman hero.[72] This initial response is an imperial one and it is couched in the language of the Gospel's portrayal of Jesus as being G*d's son (see Matt. 4:3, 6; 8:29; 14:33; 16:16; 26:63; 27:40, 43). Dube notes the way in which imperial responses

---

[70] A multidimensional feminist hermeneutic that includes an ecological perspective would need to give significant attention to this response.

[71] The Matthean text reads, "[When they] saw the earthquake and what took place."

[72] F. W. Danker, "God with Us: Hellenistic Christological Perspectives in Matthew," *Currents in Theology and Mission* 19 (1992): 433–39. He cites pseudo-Callisthenes' reporting of the sun darkening at the death of Alexander as one among many examples.

are portrayed positively and set over against those of the Jewish leaders who are characterized in opposition to the Matthean community that is authoring this story of Jesus.[73] In this way the Empire is exonerated and "sanctified" especially when the words of the centurion and those keeping watch are called a "confession."[74] This interpretation of John Paul Heil demonstrates such a reading:

The soldiers' climactic confession illustrates God's vindication of the trust Jesus has placed in him as his Son by remaining on the cross. By proclaiming, "Truly this (*houtos*) was the Son of God," these Gentile soldiers not only contradict the bystanders' misunderstanding but also transform their own mockery of the crucified Jesus in the previous scene into a profession of faith in the crucified Jesus' profound identity.[75]

A feminist postcolonial *hermeneutics of suspicion* must be brought to the response of the centurion and its affirmation in the predominantly male-stream history of interpretation of the text in contrast to other responses. Only then might it be possible for the response of the centurion to be reclaimed, within a *hermeneutics of reclamation,* as an outsider recognizing what is of G*d in the death of the Galilean preacher of the *basileia* (kingdom) of the heavens. (Matthew 4:17 is programmatic of the mission of Jesus in the Gospel of Matthew.)

The exclamation of the centurion and his companions reflects one of the central metaphors or titles used to characterize Jesus in the Gospel of Matthew, namely "Son of God." The imagery is androcentric; it evokes the patriarchal and kyriarchal household of the first century (the relationship between son and father, with father being one of the dominant images used for the divine in the Matthean Gospel) and as such participates in

---

[73] Dube, *Postcolonial Feminist Interpretation,* 133–35. A recognition of Christian anti-Judaism warns against interpreting a possible conflict internal to the Jewish community of the Matthean context or between two Jewish communities, and reflected in the Matthean text, as theological superiority leading to supersessionist theology.

[74] In *Shall We Look for Another?,* 110, I noted the way in which "confession" is privileged among a number of male scholars over against the faithful discipleship of women and other nonelites in this section of the narrative. This gendered critique can now be integrated with the critique of imperialism as discussed earlier.

[75] J. P. Heil, *The Death and Resurrection of Jesus: A Narrative-Critical Reading of Matthew 26–28* (Minneapolis: Fortress, 1991), 87. Carter, *Matthew and Margins,* 537, claims that "the soldiers act as disciples," thereby privileging the imperial. He does, however, go on to indicate that the words of the centurion proclaim "Rome's certain defeat."

the imperial theology.[76] A feminist reading will read against the grain of this response to the death of Jesus, recognizing the crucified one as the prophet or child of Sophia G*d whose death was the result of the threat that his proclamation of a new vision, a new *basileia*, posed to the Empire.[77]

The second response to the death of Jesus, namely that of the "many women," has received significant attention in feminist interpretation. Rhetorically, the Matthean narrative places a number of women, three of whom are explicitly named and identified, at the scene of the death of Jesus (27:55–56). The opening phrase of 27:55 (*ēsan de ekei*) parallels v. 61 (*ēn de ekei*) except for the plural and singular of the verb. What follows is a reference in 27:55 to the many women and in 27:61 to the two designated women, Mary Magdalene and "the other Mary," who have already been named in v. 56. These latter two will also be the women who go to the tomb on the first day of the week (28:1). A study here of 27:55–56 with 27:61 will inform the interpretation of 28:1–10.

There is a certain ambivalence created around the women of 27:55. They are said to be "there" (*ekei*), an adverb that locates them in relation to the previous verse in which a group of men keep watch presumably in close proximity to the cross on which Jesus has been crucified. Verse 36 seems to indicate that the watchers sat down where they had crucified him. The women, however, are also said to be looking on, witnessing the death of Jesus "from a distance" (*apo makrothen*). For the attentive reader, this phrase will recall Peter's following Jesus from a distance into the courtyard of the high priest (26:58) after presumably having been among "all the disciples" who forsook Jesus and fled (26:56).

---

[76] See Schüssler Fiorenza, *Power of the Word*, 199–213, for a more extensive examination of such theologizing, together with Sheffield, "The Father in the Gospel of Matthew," 52–69, and my reading of the metaphor of "son of God" as heteroglossal in *Shall We Look for Another?*, 107, where I suggest that for some households it would have functioned to sustain patriarchy but for others it may have evoked "intimacy, love and fidelity."

[77] See Schüssler Fiorenza, *Jesus*, 97–128, for her critique of those theologies of the death of Jesus that are founded on cosmic and divine violence and victimization and that are silent about the sociopolitical causes of Jesus's death and her proposals for a rereading and retheologizing of the death of Jesus. In *Shall We Look for Another?*, 111–12, I also propose ways in which the Matthean account of the death of Jesus could be interpreted, "as the suffering just one who remained faithful to God even in the face of unjust persecution and torment at the hands of enemies." I did not, however, in that earlier work, recognize the imperial nature of the centurion's response to the death of Jesus.

Gender, gender stereotyping, and the construction of gender seem to be at play within these verses. These will be examined together with attention to other categories with which they may be linked. In contrast to the male centurion and his fellow watchers who are associated with the Empire, the women are described in relation to Jesus, the crucified Galilean. They have followed Jesus from Galilee (*ēkolouthēsan*) and have been ministering to him (*diakonousai autō*). It is well established among scholars that the verb "follow" designates discipleship in Matthew's Gospel.[78] I have also shown that *diakoneō* associates followers with the ministry or work of Jesus.[79] These Galilean women can, therefore, be read rhetorically as faithful disciples of Jesus in contrast to Peter whose earlier looking on from a distance did not culminate in his presence at the foot of the cross with the women. They are also contrasted with the disciples who fled.[80]

Gender intersects with socioeconomic constructs in relation to the women characters in these verses. The verb *diakoneō* can be read not only as symbolic of discipleship but also as indicative of the women's status in relation to resources used for the itinerant Jesus movement.[81] Such a recognition may stand to blunt the gender-reversal process that seems to be in play in these verses, for it could suggest to readers that it is women with access to material resources who function as faithful disciples. How women without such access will find a reading position in relation to this text is a question.

Kathleen Corley has explored both the literary and sociocultural intertextuality as well as the sociocultural texture of the narratives of

---

[78] See J. D. Kingsbury, "The Verb *Akolouthein* ('To Follow') as an Index of Matthew's View of His Community," *JBL* 97 (1978): 56–73.

[79] Wainwright, *Towards a Feminist Critical Reading*, 85–86.

[80] R. E. Brown, *The Death of the Messiah: From Gethsemane to the Grave: A Commentary on the Passion Narratives in the Four Gospels*, 2 vols. (New York: Doubleday, 1994), represents what seems to be androcentric reactions to the work of feminist scholars whom he says lack evidence to support their attempt to contrast the women at the cross with the male disciples whose fleeing was mentioned some sixty verses before (referring to the passion story in Mark, though the same point could supposedly be made with regard to Matthew). Unfortunately Brown does not explicitly cite any of the feminist scholars he is seeking to refute. It is also common practice for biblical scholars to cite intratextual connections across much more than sixty verses of text, 2:1157.

[81] M. Sawicki explores possible characteristics of the Galilean women in the entourage of Jesus, especially through the lens of Luke 8:1–3. See "Magdalenes and Tiberiennes: City Women in the Entourage of Jesus," in *Transformative Encounters: Jesus and Women Re-viewed*, ed. I. R. Kitzberger (Leiden: Brill, 2000), 181–202.

the women at the cross and tomb.[82] The focus of her investigation is the historical plausibility of the presence of the women at the crucifixion. My focus is rhetorical and seeks to understand the way the text functions for its Matthean readers attentive as they would have been to the sociocultural texture of the text.[83]

Turning first to Mary Magdalene, Mary the mother of James and Joseph, and the mother of the sons of Zebedee who stand witness to the death of Jesus and examining their faithful presence from Galilee to the foot of the cross through a gender lens reveals that a gender reversal may be functioning. Women were certainly involved in funerary rituals, mourning, visiting the graves of loved ones, and keeping watch on their tombs.[84] Literary intertextuality suggests, however, that women's mourning was characterized by loud wailing and they were often dismissed from the scene prior to death. The male family members or disciples of a dying hero would remain to the end, mourning silently.[85] There is a gender reversal in Matthew 27:55–56, as the women remain faithful to the end, mourning silently, suggesting that gender is being constructed by this text, possibly representing the rhetoric of the Matthean household(s) that I have characterized as "more egalitarian."[86] The Matthean Gospel functions at this late point in the narrative to characterize discipleship as both female and male, suggesting significant gender construction functioning in the Matthean households (or at least in some).

There is, however, a tension in this text that may encode some of the struggles entailed in communities when cultural mores such as gender were being negotiated. The three women at the cross represent faithful discipleship generally characterized as male, namely staying with the dying loved one until death occurs and mourning silently. That they are, however, depicted in a way that is characteristic of male mourners rather

[82] K. E. Corley, *Women and the Historical Jesus: Feminist Myths of Christian Origins* (Santa Rosa: Polebridge, 2002), 107–39.

[83] R. Strelan notes how gestures and postures take on meaning in shared cultural worlds in "To Sit Is to Mourn: The Women at the Tomb (Matthew 27:61)," *Colloquium,* 31/1 (1999): 31.

[84] See Corley, *Women and the Historical Jesus,* 107–18.

[85] Corley, *Women and the Historical Jesus,* 118–23. While Strelan ("To Sit Is to Mourn") argues that the women at the tomb are portrayed culturally as mourning, he does not take account of the gender distinctions that typify such mourning in the first century as does Corley.

[86] Wainwright, *Shall We Look for Another?,* 45–49.

than female mourners who express much more emotion could function rhetorically to denigrate women's traditional mourning rituals – they can function as disciples but only within male norms.

Also, two of the women are identified in terms of their traditional sexual roles: they are mothers of significant sons and both have appeared already in the narrative in relation to those sons (27:56; cf. 13:55, in which Mary – the mother of Jesus – is linked narratively to the brothers of Jesus, the first two of whom are named as "James and Joseph"; and 20:20–28, in which the mother of the sons of Zebedee asks Jesus for a place for them in his *basileia*). This depiction of the two faithful women disciples in terms of sexual function can affirm rhetorically cultural stereotypes and can blunt the portrayal of the women's fidelity and discipleship. On the other hand, the presence of these mothers of the "brothers" of Jesus and of two of his inner circle of male disciples (James and John; cf. 4:21–22, 10:2, 17:1) draws attention to familial and fictive kinship connections to Jesus among the women who stand by his cross. Corley notes "the potential for national protest through the vehicle of family mourning (especially that of women) following a state (presumably Roman) execution."[87] The presence of the women may signify elements of the anti-imperial potential of the narrative as it was developing in the Matthean households with the maternal relationship pointing to this.

The ambivalence of the placement of the women "there" at the foot of the cross and yet "looking on from a distance" further enhances the tension around this text. It places these female characters in a borderland space evoking a reading space that can be taken up by contemporary women whose context(s) place them in such a space on account of ethnicity, age, sexual preference and function, or other factors. Reading from such spaces could constitute a feminist *hermeneutics of reclamation,* opening the possibility of new and more inclusive theologies from the position of women of different and wide-ranging positionalities.

The response of the women who are characterized as faithful disciples, members of the Jesus movement, is set alongside that of the centurion. Theirs has been long-term fidelity as designated by their having followed Jesus from Galilee and their ongoing ministering to him into

---

[87] Corley, *Women and the Historical Jesus,* 117.

the present.[88] A feminist reading will take care not to privilege confession that is generally associated with male characters (cf. Matt. 16:13–20) over other forms of fidelity.[89] This caution can inform a turn now to the third response to the death of Jesus, namely that of Joseph of Arimathea.

From a gender perspective, 27:57–60 foreground masculinity as did 27:54, and in these verses masculinity is once more portrayed as intersecting with wealth and privilege. Joseph of Arimathea is explicitly named as rich and as having ready access to Pilate, the symbol of imperial power, and so, on the sliding scale of mapped masculinity in Matthew as discussed by Anderson and Moore, he is among the "supreme exemplars of hegemonic masculinity" since he has both power and resources.[90] He is characterized as having been discipled.[91] As with the response of the centurion, the characterization of Joseph of Arimathea needs to be read through the lens of a hermeneutics of suspicion that critiques the patriarchal perspectives of "ideal" masculinity prior to an exploration of his representation of ideal discipleship.

The *kai autos* that precedes the aorist passive indicative of the verb "to disciple" (*mathēteuō*) in 27:57 carries the sense that "he too" had been discipled. This links him, therefore, with the women of 27:55–56 who were characterized as having been disciples in/from Galilee. Joseph, however, like the other male disciples, does not carry out the mourning task expected of male disciples, namely, to remain with the friend or loved one until his death. He is, however, associated with a second aspect of male mourning and male rituals surrounding death, namely, the burial of the body.[92]

Cultural anthropology provides tools that can assist in our understanding of the sociocultural texture of this text, in particular, the model of honor/shame and the processes of labeling and making prominent.[93]

---

[88] Such a reading contrasts with the claim of Heil, *The Death and Resurrection of Jesus*, 92, who contrasts the activity of Joseph of Arimathea with "the passivity of the 'many women.'"

[89] See Wainwright, *Shall We Look for Another?*, 110.

[90] Anderson and Moore, "Matthew and Masculinity," 68–69.

[91] He stands in contrast to the young man of many possessions of Matthew 19:16–22, who went away grieving because he could not respond to the call to discipleship.

[92] Corley, *Women and the Historical Jesus*, 117–18.

[93] B. J. Malina and J. H. Neyrey employ these tools in their reading of Matthew 26–27. See *Calling Jesus Names: The Social Value of Labels in Matthew* (Sonoma: Polebridge, 1988), 69–131.

As Byron R. McCane says so succinctly, "the historical Jesus was buried in shame."[94] If he was convicted by a Jewish court that had access to Roman authority, then his death was that of a condemned criminal – a death willed by the society. He would have been forbidden public ritual mourning including an honorable burial,[95] preventing family and community from undertaking the customs of mourning whose function it was to heal the wound that death brought to family and society.[96] Jewish custom, however, demanded that bodies even of condemned criminals be buried promptly (Deut. 21:22–23), and since their condemnation was intended to sever family ties, communal burial places were reserved for this purpose.

These cultural codes constitute something of the social and cultural texture of Matthew 27:57–60 and its story of Joseph of Arimathea. They function in the narrative to create meaning. That this story is part of the fabric of the narrative being woven within early Christian traditions making Jesus prominent or restoring honor to him in the face of his dishonorable death and the negative labeling accompanying that death is evident in the designation given to Joseph in the Matthean narrative in comparison with the earlier Markan story. There Joseph is called a "respected member of the council" (Mark 15:43) and as such he undertakes a task that would have been that of the council, to ensure the burial of a condemned criminal before sundown. The Markan narrative is, however, also beginning the process of reversal in its telling of Jesus's death. Rather than simply being associated with the opponents of Jesus, Joseph is also named as "looking for the kingdom of God" (15:43). Thus, the burial is not simply what would be expected of the council in the case of a condemned Jewish criminal but an element of a story that seeks to reverse the dishonor.

---

[94] B. R. F. McCane, "'Where No One Had Yet Been Laid': The Shame of Jesus' Burial," in *SBL Seminar Papers 32*, ed. E. H. Lovering (Atlanta: Society of Biblical Literature, 1993), 473.

[95] This may be a further explanation of the women at the cross and the tomb. They do not perform the traditional mourning rituals associated with women's grief but rather are presented as standing at the cross looking on from a distance, seated at the tomb, and going to see the tomb again on the first day of the week. This may have represented the beginning stages of reversing the shame of the death of Jesus as a criminal. Women are, therefore, at the heart of the stories that seek to reverse the cultural labeling of Jesus from that of dishonored criminal to the honorable one unjustly condemned.

[96] McCane, "Where No One Had Yet Been Laid," 477–80.

The Matthean narrative furthers that process by naming Joseph as "being discipled." As a member of the Jesus movement, he undertakes one of the roles of the faithful family, friends, and community in the face of the death of a loved one. He buries the one who has died, and according to the Matthean narrative, this burial is in his "own new tomb," seeking further to characterize his action as that appropriate to a new fictive kinship group that honorably buried a beloved one.[97] This enables, through the storytelling, the healing of the wounds of both death and shame. Rhetorically, both male and female disciples are represented as honoring the dishonored one. A critique of status must, however, continue to accompany the reading of Joseph of Arimathea as it did the women with resources.

Each of the four responses explored earlier – the centurion and other watchers, the woman at the cross, Joseph of Arimathea, and the two women who sit opposite the tomb – contributes to the reversal of the shame of Jesus's death and his probable burial in a criminal grave. They honor Jesus by their faithful presence, their proclamation of his fidelity to G*d in the face of death and G*d's reciprocal fidelity, and their burial of Jesus in a new tomb, not of his family but of a member of the new fictive kinship group that his ministry has established. Attention has been paid to the gendering of these responses as well as to other factors such as imperial connections and access to resources and to power that subtly shape characterization and hence reading. My feminist hermeneutics was informed by attentiveness to gender as it intersects with these multiple elements of positionality. I brought a hermeneutics of suspicion to these elements of the text and the ways in which they underpin androcentrism, kyriarchy, imperialism, and other categories of domination. This critique, as it informed a sociorhetorical reading of texts, has enabled new meanings to emerge.

Reading the Textures of the Text: Counteraction of the Opponents of Jesus and His Disciples

As we saw in the previous section in relation to the women at the cross and the tomb, so too in the remainder of the narrative, stories involving

---

[97] McCane, "Where No One Had Yet Been Laid," 482, for a more extensive discussion of this aspect of the retelling, the reclaiming of the body of Jesus.

similar character groups constitute the narrative web. Mary Magdalene and "the other Mary" weave their way through 27:55–56, 61 and into 28:1–10. Similarly, the chief priests with either the Pharisees or the elders thread together 27:62–65 and 28:11–15. These two stories can, therefore, be examined together in this section.[98]

The two feminist-critical categories of *imperial power* and *anti-Judaism* will inform the reading of these accounts of the opponents of Jesus plotting against him even beyond his death. Levine, in discussing Matthew 28:11–15, points out that it makes no sense from an historical perspective but functions to vilify "the Jews."[99] A similar argument could be mounted in relation to Matthew 27:62–65. Both stories are unique to the Matthean Gospel and seem, at this point in the narrative, to function rhetorically to keep before readers the strong association between designated Jewish leaders and Roman authority in relation to the death of Jesus. These must, therefore, be read in the context of Matthean intra-Jewish polemic and not universalized into Christian anti-Judaism.

Power over the body of Jesus, a power that has moved between the Jewish and Roman elite, has characterized the narrative of Jesus's death from its beginning when the "chief priests and elders took counsel together" (*synebouleusanto*) to arrest and kill Jesus (26:4). His teachings had brought him into conflict with the scribes and the Pharisees, and Jesus had brought this conflict to Jerusalem (where the "chief priests and elders" had authority),[100] at the time of the Passover. Such Jewish leaders in Roman-occupied Jerusalem/Palestine functioned as retainers in the imperial power structure, often representing Rome's colonizing power among their own people. For them to retain that power, it was necessary that they both recognize the power of Rome as their source of power and that they exercise similar power in relation to their own people. Imperial narratives or imperial perspectives even in narratives

---

[98] Brown (*Death of the Messiah*, 1287) also notes the interrelationship of these two stories in what he designates the final section of Matthew's narrative, 27:57–28:15.

[99] A.-J. Levine, *The Misunderstood Jew: The Church and the Scandal of the Jewish Jesus* (New York: HarperSanFrancisco, 2006), 113–14. This is the only time that the phrase "the Jews" is used in the Gospel apart from within the title "King of the Jews" (see 2:2; 27:11, 29, 37) and it carries an extremely negative connotation. Levine highlights this aspect of their characterization: they knew the truth and deliberately attempted to suppress it.

[100] See Matt. 26:3, 47; 27:1, 3, 12, 20, 41; 28:12.

of resistance like the Gospel can exonerate the imperial power, as Dube has shown in relation to the account of the death of Jesus in Matthew: Pilate points the finger at Jesus's own leaders who bring many charges against him (the colonizer who turns the colonized against one another – Matt. 27:13); he is portrayed as offering the Jewish people a choice between Jesus and a notorious Jewish criminal (27:16); and his wife is the recipient of a divine revelation that "confirms Pilate's conviction that Jesus is an innocent man."[101] The colonizer is presented favorably using the belief systems and processes of the colonized who are condemned.

In these final narratives of the passion/resurrection segment, as at the beginning, the Jewish leaders are presented as gathering and conspiring with imperial power to prevent a manifestation of G*d's power (27:62, 65–66) and when this is unsuccessful, manufacturing a story to counteract the Matthean community's account of that manifestation (28:12). A feminist reading for liberation will read against the grain of the rhetoric that renders Jesus's fellow religionists more guilty than Rome's top-level representatives and hence against the anti-Jewish rhetoric of the Matthean text. What can be reclaimed, however, is the critique of power (of imperial rulers and their colonized retainers wherever and however this is manifest) that seeks to control the power of G*d, who has promised the vindication of the righteous proclaimer of the *basileia*.

Reading the Textures of the Text: The Women at the Tomb Who Encounter the Risen Jesus

The story of Jesus and of discipleship to Jesus reaches its climax in 28:1–10.[102] It opens with Mary Magdalene and the "other Mary" going to see (*theōrēsai*) the tomb, just as they were previously looking on (*theōrousai*) at the cross of Jesus (27:55). The location at the tomb likewise reminds readers of the vigil of these same two named women at the tomb in

---

[101] Dube, *Postcolonial Feminist Interpretation.*

[102] In *Shall We Look for Another?*, 14–18, I argue that it is essential to a feminist reading of the Gospel and of Jesus that we avoid what I call an "isolated focus on Jesus." Rather, attention must be given to the narrative where a wide range of characters, as we have already seen in the closing sections of the Gospel explored earlier, function within and in the shaping of the story of Jesus.

27:61.[103] The climactic story of 28:1–10 is, therefore, woven into the fabric of the Matthean narrative as it moves to a conclusion, seeking to honor the one who was crucified as a Roman criminal.[104]

Earlier, attention was given to the maternal status of the two women who stood with Mary Magdalene at the cross and questions were raised about the possible socioeconomic status of all these ministering women. It is Mary Magdalene, however, who stands at the head of each group of women and who is also common to the named groups of women at the cross and/or tomb in the other canonical Gospels.[105] The Matthean Gospel gives us no indicators of other characteristics of Mary Magdalene that intersect with her gender except the geographic location Magdala, which suggests she is Galilean. She will appear in a more developed way in ongoing Christian tradition, but that does not concern us here.

The first thing the women encounter is not a sealed tomb as they had previously seen on their vigil, but a great earthquake and the rolling back of the stone that had been sealed and guarded at the request of the chief priests and Pharisees (27:62–66). Earth responded to the death of the faithful one of G*d, manifesting G*d's recognition of Jesus's fidelity to his *basileia* mission (27:51–53). Earth here gives witness to the power of G*d over death. And it is to the women, Mary Magdalene and "the other Mary," that the message is given: Jesus who was crucified is not here, for he has been raised as he said (28:5–6). In the Gospel of Matthew, it is the faithful women disciples who are entrusted with the kerygmatic proclamation that the crucified one has been raised and they are the ones who are given the commission to begin the proclamation process: go quickly and tell his disciples that he has been raised from the dead (28:7).[106] The women's witness to the empty tomb points forward to

---

[103] Many aspects of these two named women have been explored previously and will not be repeated here.

[104] Both T. R. W. Longstaff, "What Are Those Women Doing at the Tomb of Jesus? Perspectives on Matthew 28.1," in Levine, *Feminist Companion*, 196–204, and C. Osiek, "The Women at the Tomb: What Are They Doing There?" in Levine, *Feminist Companion*, 205–20, explore the sociocultural and religious codes that inform meaning-making in relation to the presence of the women at the tomb.

[105] Mark 15:40–41, 47; 16:1–8; Luke 23:49, 55; Luke 24:1–11; John 19:25–27; 20:1–18.

[106] Here my focus is the rhetorical function of the Matthean text. Osiek ("Women at the Tomb," 103) notes, however, that such "cycles of stories may have originated in women's storytelling circles." See Wainwright, *Towards a Feminist Critical Reading*, 300–14, for a more detailed analysis of the development of this tradition within the Matthean community.

include the disciples. They are commissioned to reconcile these disciples and to incorporate them back into relationship with Jesus, whom the disciples have betrayed. The final commissioning of these male disciples from the mountain of authority (28:16–20) cannot, therefore, stand alone but circles back rhetorically to the women at the empty tomb.[107] Gender functions here, when read from a feminist *hermeneutics of reclamation*, to affirm male and female discipleship, male and female commissioning, with the message that the crucified one has been raised, that the power of G*d and the mission to proclaim G*d's vision or dream that was named *basileia* can overcome Empire.[108] Such a reading will critique any meaning-making that affirms kyriarchal and imperial power as contrary to the liberating message of G*d's *basileia* vision.

Turning a feminist reading lens onto Jesus in this narrative reveals that androcentric and kyriarchal metaphors and images such as Son of God, Son of Man, and *Kyrios*/Lord have disappeared. The raised one is Jesus who was crucified. It is not Jesus's masculinity that is foregrounded but rather his fidelity to G*d through his proclamation of the *basileia* that brought him to the cross. Rhetorically, the text also affirms the power of the G*d of Jesus.[109] This recognition provides a challenge to Christian theologizing even as it has been undertaken in the earlier sections of the Matthean storytelling with its focus on male-centered titles and metaphors.

It is also the crucified and raised one whom the women encounter as they go away from the tomb on their commission to reconcile the male disciples. The women's greeting is not accompanied by titles but they do worship Jesus, recognizing the power of G*d that has raised Jesus as the angel told them. They are commissioned by the risen Jesus but with a similar commission as that given by the angel. The key difference is that Jesus refers to the disciples as "brothers," a pointer toward the

---

[107] For a much more extensive exploration of this, see Wainwright, *Shall We Look for Another?*, 112–18.

[108] A more extensive study of Matt. 28:16–20 would have to take account of the postcolonial critique of the universal commission and the way it has accompanied colonial imperialism.

[109] Schüssler Fiorenza, *Jesus*, notes that crucifixion does not have the last word. The dream that was named *basileia* can overcome Empire. Such a reading will critique any meaning-making that affirms kyriarchal and imperial power as contrary to the liberating message of G*d's *basileia* vision.

reconciliation that is necessary because of their betrayal. Jesus commissions the women to go and to tell, as he will commission the male disciples. As I have argued elsewhere, "the male and female commissions may have been read cyclically as authorizing both women and men, thus crossing gender boundaries according to the way these have been constructed transgressively in this section of the text."[110]

The Matthean story links women not only with the empty tomb tradition but also with a resurrection appearance. Carolyn Osiek notes that 28:9–10 seem to add nothing to the angel's message at the empty tomb.[111] It is significant, however, that the first appearance of the risen Jesus is to women disciples. John Dominic Crossan analyzes the function of appearance stories noting that their focus does not seem to be "trance, ecstasy, apparition, or revelation, but – authority, power, leadership, and priority."[112] It is not unthinkable, in light of women's heading of households, house churches, and synagogue,[113] and their participation in labors in the public arena during the first century of the Common Era,[114] that this text could be an authorizing of women as leaders of households in the Matthean community. The appearance of Jesus to Mary Magdalene and "the other Mary" could have been an authorizing text for such leadership just as 28:16–20 functioned to authorize male leadership.

CONCLUSION

What has emerged from this study has been a comprehensive account of feminist studies of the Matthean Gospel that can take its place among the many undertakings that have explored feminist New Testament studies more generally. It is not, however, simply a history or a theoretical exposition of feminist biblical interpretation. It brings the key categories that have developed and are continuing to develop within feminist Matthean and New Testament studies to a reading of a selected Matthean text. This segment is, however, not comprehensive, but simply highlights some of the potentialities for a feminist-critical reading of this text of

[110] Wainwright, *Shall We Look for Another?*, 116.
[111] Osiek, "Women at the Tomb," 99.
[112] J. D. Crossan, *A Revolutionary Biography* (San Francisco: Harper, 1994), 166.
[113] Brooten, *Women Leaders*; and Osiek and Macdonald with Tulloch, *A Woman's Place*.
[114] Lefkowitz and Fant, *Women's Life in Greece and Rome*.

Matthew 27:57–28:15. I have been able to bring out "the new and the old" in characteristic Matthean fashion, but much remains to be done from the variety of different reading positions that will characterize potential readers. It is to be hoped, however, that as this reading concludes, others will begin until the justice and righteousness characteristic of the Matthean *basileia* vision comes to fruition.

4

↓

Historical Jesus Studies and the Gospel of Matthew

CRAIG A. EVANS

S CHOLARLY, POPULAR, AND RELIGIOUS INTEREST IN THE HIS-
torical Jesus has never been greater. Not a year goes by without at
least one new major book and at least one new documentary, almost
always claiming to have discovered something novel. Indeed, in recent
years the public has been told that Jesus was married and had children,
that he wrote letters to Jewish leaders denying his divinity, that he faked
his death and fled Israel, or that he really did die but was not resur-
rected and that his tomb and DNA have been found. Genuine scholars
do not take any of this seriously, but this has not discouraged the production of a seemingly unending stream of outlandish books and television
documentaries.

Notwithstanding the nonsense, most scholars and most clergy agree
that the historical Jesus is important and that careful, rigorous study is
necessary. Competent scholarly books, as well as popular books, that
engage this significant subject are welcome and on the whole advance
the discussion in useful ways. But the task is not easy.

THE GOALS AND METHODS THAT GUIDE HISTORICAL
JESUS STUDIES

The goals and methods, or operating principles, that guide scholars
engaged in research into the historical Jesus vary. Most agree that the
primary goal of this research is to reconstruct a portrait of Jesus that
has good claim to historicity (in contrast, e.g., to pious imagination
or centuries of untested tradition). Disagreements arise with respect to
methods, or operating principles, and the various sources that we have at

our disposal. That there are such disagreements is not surprising, given the difficulty and complexity of the task.

Serious, competent study of the historical Jesus is very complicated. This is the case for several reasons. First of all, study of the historical Jesus entails a measure of competence in several disciplines, such as foreign languages (Greek, Hebrew, and Aramaic, among others), foreign culture and customs, geography and topography, history, and archaeology. There is also a vast amount of literature (secondary and primary) to be mastered.

Historical Jesus studies are difficult also because of the personal biases and preferences of researchers, reflected at times in diverse, competing scholarly conclusions. Scholars have to make educated choices and sometimes guesses, and one's bias will unavoidably come into play. Theoretical possibilities are legion, probabilities are much fewer, and certainties are rare.

The biggest problem of all is that we are in possession of only some of the facts, and not all agree on what really are the facts. It is not unlike having some of the pieces of a puzzle and then trying to put it together. Distortions and false conclusions are hard to avoid. Yet, careful work will yield positive results.

There are three basic questions that must be addressed in the study of the historical Jesus. First, where do we find information about Jesus (i.e., in what ancient sources will we find the most reliable information about him)? Second, where should we place Jesus (i.e., in what historical and social context should he be seen, and how was he perceived by his contemporaries)? Third, how do we assess the material that ostensibly provides us with information about Jesus (i.e., what methods and criteria should we employ in our study)? Let us address these questions in the order they have been raised.

Question 1: Where to Find Information about Jesus?

For more than nineteen centuries historians interested in the historical Jesus turned to the four Gospels of the New Testament: Matthew, Mark, Luke, and John. Gospels and Gospel-like sources that appeared in the second, third, and later centuries were not taken seriously. All this has changed in the last three decades or so.

One of the most controversial aspects of Jesus research revolves around the question of what sources are best. Although almost all scholars believe that the four New Testament Gospels, which date from the first century, remain our best sources for the historical Jesus, some scholars insist that a few of the extracanonical Gospels may be just as valuable, and in some cases may actually contain older material that more accurately reflects what Jesus said and how he understood himself.

In the scholarly and popular press of today the most frequently mentioned writings outside of the New Testament are the *Gospel of Thomas*, the *Gospel of Peter*, Egerton Papyrus 2 (or *Egerton Gospel*), and the *Secret Gospel of Mark*.[1] Many people had probably not heard of these writings until recently, and even now they may hear of them only in connection with a book or television documentary making sensational claims. Until recently, extracanonical Gospels such as these were not taken seriously as potential sources for Jesus research. Three quarters of a century ago Rudolf Bultmann, who was not a traditionalist in any sense, regarded these Gospels and related writings as nothing more than legendary adaptations and expansions of the canonical Gospel tradition.[2] Almost no one in his generation disagreed. Today, the picture has changed.

Some scholars recently argued that *early editions* of the *Gospel of Thomas* and the *Gospel of Peter* reach back to the middle of the first century, that the *Egerton Gospel* predates Mark and John – and indeed may have been on the writing table of the evangelist Mark himself – and that the *Secret Gospel of Mark* may represent an earlier form of the canonical Gospel of Mark. It is no wonder then – if these early dates and hypothetical early forms of these writings are held to be valid – that some scholars make use of these extracanonical sources in their reconstructions of the historical Jesus. Accordingly, the Jesus Seminar's assessment of the authentic words of Jesus came out under the title *The Five Gospels*, the fifth gospel being the *Gospel of Thomas*.[3] What are we to make of all this?

---

[1] Other Gospels are frequently mentioned, such as the *Gospel of Mary* (Magdalene). But serious historians do not appeal to these sources in historical Jesus research.

[2] R. Bultmann, *The History of the Synoptic Tradition* (Oxford: Blackwell, 1972), 374.

[3] For the results of the Jesus Seminar, see R. W. Funk, R. W. Hoover, and the Jesus Seminar, *The Five Gospels: The Search for the Authentic Words of Jesus* (Sonoma: Polebridge, 1993). The Jesus Seminar became notorious for color coding the Jesus tradition. Words thought to derive, accurately, from Jesus are printed in red; words approximating Jesus's statements are printed in pink; doubtful words are printed in gray; words felt not to

Is there really solid evidence that these writings outside the New Testament truly date to the first century and contain sayings from Jesus and/or
stories about him that are early, independent, and perhaps even superior
to what is found in Matthew, Mark, Luke, and John?

THE *GOSPEL OF THOMAS*. Thirteen leather-bound books (or codices),
written in the Coptic language, dating to about C.E. 350–380, were found
in Egypt sometime near the end of 1945 (near a place called Nag Ham-
madi). One of these books contains a writing that begins with the words
"These are the secret words that the living Jesus spoke and Judas, even
Thomas, wrote," and ends with the words "the Gospel according to
Thomas." Third- and fourth-century church fathers had mentioned a
Gospel that went by the name of the apostle Thomas.[4] It seemed, then,
that the *Gospel of Thomas* mentioned by Christian theologians seventeen
centuries earlier had turned up in the dry sands of Egypt.

When the new discovery was read and translated (and was found to
contain a prologue and 114 sayings, or logia, mostly attributed to Jesus),
scholars realized that parts of the *Gospel of Thomas* had in fact been found
a half-century earlier, in the 1890s, in a different part of Egypt, in a place
called Oxyrhynchus. Three Greek papyrus fragments published at the
turn of the century contain about 20 percent of the *Gospel of Thomas*, at
least as compared with the Coptic version. The Greek fragments range
in date from C.E. 200 to 300.

The *Gospel of Thomas* is an esoteric writing, purporting to record
the secret (or hidden) teachings of Jesus, teachings reserved for those
qualified to hear these teachings. Almost all scholars allow that *Thomas*
was composed at least as early as the middle of the second century. How
much earlier (or later) is hotly debated.

There is compelling evidence that leads to the conclusion that *Thomas*
is a late writing, not an early one. First, the *Gospel of Thomas* evinces

derive from Jesus are printed in black. Only 18 percent of the words attributed to Jesus
in the New Testament Gospels are given red or pink ratings. See also R. W. Funk, ed.,
The Acts of Jesus: What Did Jesus Really Do? The Search for the Authentic Deeds of Jesus
(San Francisco: HarperCollins, 1998). The Jesus Seminar's results here are similar to
their earlier results.

[4] For reference to the *Gospel of Thomas* in early church fathers, see Hippolytus, *Haer.*
5.7.20; Origen, *In Luc. Hom.* 1.5.13–14; Jerome, *Comm. in Matth.* Prologue; and Ambrose,
Expositio evangelii Lucae 1.2.10.

at least half of the New Testament writings. This strongly tells against a first-century publication. Second, *Thomas* contains parallels to Gospel material that scholars regard as late, such as material special to Matthew and Luke, as well as elements from the Gospel of John. Third, *Thomas* evinces familiarity with later editing in the Gospels (e.g., Matthean and Lukan redaction). Fourth, *Thomas* shows familiarity with traditions distinctive to eastern, Syrian Christianity, traditions that did not emerge earlier than the middle of the second century. These traditions include readings distinctive to the Syriac form of the Gospels, as well as readings distinctive to Tatian's harmony of the Gospels (the *Diatessaron*), a work composed in Syria in the Syriac language. Evidence such as this strongly cautions against the use of the *Gospel of Thomas* as a source on par with the first-century Gospels, Matthew, Mark, Luke, and John.

A few scholars still argue that the *Gospel of Thomas* contains primitive, pre-Synoptic tradition.[5] This is possible theoretically, but there are numerous difficulties that attend efforts to cull from this collection of logia, or sayings, material that can, with confidence, be judged primitive, independent of the New Testament Gospels, and even authentic.

EGERTON PAPYRUS 2. The work that is officially identified as Egerton Papyrus 2 was found somewhere in Egypt and fell into the hands of scholars in 1934. It consists of four fragments. The fourth fragment yields nothing more than one illegible letter. The third fragment yields little more than a few scattered words. The first and second fragments, however, offer four (or perhaps five) stories that parallel stories found in John and in the Synoptic Gospels (such as Jesus's healing the leper and Jesus being threatened with stoning). Papyrus Köln 255, discovered sometime later, constitutes a related fragment of the text.[6]

---

[5] Scholars who believe that the *Gospel of Thomas* contains primitive, pre-Synoptic tradition include G. Quispel, "The Gospel of Thomas and the New Testament," *VC* 11 (1957): 189–207; H. Koester, "Q and Its Relatives," *Gospel Origins & Christian Beginnings*, ed. J. E. Goehring et al. (Sonoma: Polebridge, 1990), 49–63, here 61–63; R. D. Cameron, "The Gospel of Thomas: A Forschungsbericht and Analysis," *ANRW* II.25.6 (1988): 4195–251; S. L. Davies, "Thomas: The Fourth Synoptic Gospel," *BA* 46 (1983): 6–9, 12–14. Davies makes the astonishing claim that "the *Gospel of Thomas* may be our best source for Jesus's teachings" (p. 9). See also, S. L. Davies, *The Gospel of Thomas and Christian Wisdom* (New York: Seabury, 1983).

[6] For the Greek text of the London fragments of Egerton Papyrus 2, see H. I. Bell and T. C. Skeat, *Fragments of an Unknown Gospel and Other Early Christian Papyri*

John Dominic Crossan's analysis of these fragments led him to conclude that Papyrus Egerton 2 represents a tradition that predates the New Testament Gospels. Crossan thinks that "Mark is dependent on it directly" and that it gives evidence of "a stage before the distinction of Johannine and Synoptic traditions was operative." Helmut Koester agrees with Crossan's second point, saying that in Papyrus Egerton 2 we find "pre-Johannine and pre-synoptic characteristics of language [which] still existed side by side." He thinks it is unlikely, against other scholars, that "the author of this papyrus could have been acquainted with the canonical Gospels and would have deliberately composed [it] by selecting sentences" from them.[7]

Theoretically, Crossan and Koester could be correct in this assessment. If they are correct, then Papyrus Egerton 2 could potentially make an important contribution to the study of the historical Jesus. There are, however, some serious questions that must be raised. First, there are several instances in which various editorial improvements that Matthew and Luke made in their source material appear in Egerton. Thus, we have the same problem observed in the case of the *Gospel of Thomas*. We would not expect sources that predate the Synoptic Gospels to contain editorial touches evident in the latest stage of the Synoptic tradition.

A second question arises in response to Koester's statement about the improbability that the author of the Egerton Papyrus "would have deliberately composed [it] by selecting sentences" from the canonical Gospels. Is this not the very thing that Justin Martyr and his disciple

---

(London: British Museum, 1935), 8–15, 26; H. I. Bell and T. C. Skeat, *The New Gospel Fragments* (London: British Museum, 1951), 29–33. A critical edition has been prepared by G. Mayeda, *Das Leben-Jesu-Fragment Papyrus Egerton 2 und seine Stellung in der urchristlichen Literaturgeschichte* (Bern: Haupt, 1946), 7–11. See also K. Aland, ed., *Synopsis Quattuor Evangeliorum*, rev. ed. (Stuttgart: Deutsche Bibelgesellschaft, 1985), 60, 323, 332, 340, 422. The text of the more recently discovered Köln fragment has been made available in M. Gronewald, "Unbekanntes Evangelium oder Evangelienharmonie (Fragment aus dem Evangelium Egerton)," in *Kölner Papyri*, Sonderreihe Papyrologica Coloniensia 7 (Cologne: Bibliothèque Bodmer, 1987), 136–45; and in D. Lührmann, "Das neue Fragment des PEgerton 2 (PKöln 255)," in *The Four Gospels 1992*, 3 vols., ed. F. Van Segbroeck, C. M. Tuckett, G. Van Belle, and J. Verheyden, BETL 100 (Leuven: Peeters, 1992), 3.2239–55.

7 On the claims that Egerton Papyrus 2 is early and independent of the New Testament Gospels, see J. D. Crossan, *Four Other Gospels: Shadows on the Contours of Canon* (New York: Harper & Row, 1985), 183; H. Koester, *Ancient Christian Gospels: Their History and Development* (London: SCM, 1990), 207. Crossan (*Four Other Gospels*, 86) argues that Mark is actually "directly dependent" on the (Egerton) papyrus text.

Tatian did? Sometime in the 150s, Justin Martyr composed a *Harmony* of the Synoptic Gospels and twenty years later Tatian composed a harmony (i.e., the *Diatessaron*) of all four New Testament Gospels. If Justin Martyr and Tatian, writing in the second century, could compose their respective harmonies through the selection of sentences and phrases from this and that Gospel, why could not the author of the Egerton Papyrus have done the same thing? Indeed, it is probable that this is the very thing that he did do.

A third question arises out of Koester's suggestion that the mixture of Johannine-like and Synoptic elements is primitive, while their separation into the existing canonical forms is secondary. If Koester's suggestion were correct, then the *Egerton Gospel* would indeed derive from the middle of the first century, as Crossan argues. It would have to be this early, if it were used by the Synoptic evangelists (as well as by the author of John's Gospel). But if this were the case, we would have to wonder why it is that we have no other fragment, nor any other evidence, of the existence of this extraordinarily primitive Gospel. How is it that we do not have other papyri, extracanonical Gospels, or patristic quotations attesting this primitive pre-Synoptic, pre-Johannine unified tradition?

Admittedly, while the hypothesis of Crossan, Koester, and others remains a theoretical possibility, the evidence available at this time suggests that, in all probability, Papyrus Egerton 2 (or *Egerton Gospel*) represents a second-century combination of elements from the Synoptic Gospels and the Gospel of John, rather than primitive first-century material on which the New Testament Gospels depended.

THE *GOSPEL OF PETER*. Church historian Eusebius of Caesarea (C.E. 260–340) states that the first letter of Peter (i.e., 1 Pet.) is accepted and has been used by the ancient Christian elders, but other writings attributed to the apostle Peter have been rejected (*Hist. Eccles.* 3.3.1–4). The rejected writings that are attributed to Peter include the second letter (presumably 2 Pet.), the Apocalypse (i.e., the *Apocalypse of Peter*), the Gospel (i.e., the *Gospel of Peter*), and the preaching or sermons (i.e., the *Kerygmata Petrou*). Later in his history Eusebius refers to "writings that are put forward by heretics under the name of the apostles containing Gospels such as those of Peter, and Thomas, and Matthias, and some others besides" (*Hist. Eccles.* 3.25.6). Still later Eusebius once again mentions that "the Gospel attributed to Peter," this time in reference to Serapion, bishop of Antioch (in office 199–211). Eusebius quotes a portion of the bishop's letter, in which he says that the *Gospel of Peter* was produced by Docetists (*Hist. Eccles.* 6.12.3–6). Unfortunately, neither Serapion nor Eusebius provides any actual quotations from the *Gospel of Peter* itself.

In the winter of 1886–87, during excavations at Akhmîm in Egypt, a codex was found in the coffin of a Christian monk. The manuscript comprises a fragment of a Gospel, fragments of Greek *Enoch*, the *Apocalypse of Peter*, and written on the inside of the back cover of the codex, an account of the martyrdom of the legendary St. Julian. The Gospel fragment bears no name or hint of a title, for neither the beginning nor the conclusion of the work has survived. Nevertheless, it has been widely assumed that the fragment belongs to the *Gospel of Peter* mentioned by Eusebius. This conjecture is based on the following observations: the apostle Peter appears in the text, narrating in the first person ("But I, Simon Peter"); the work is said to have a Docetic orientation (i.e., one in which the physical reality of Jesus is discounted); and the work was found in the company of the *Apocalypse of Peter*.[8]

This Akhmîm Gospel fragment (possibly to be identified as a fragment of the otherwise lost *Gospel of Peter*) contains some unusual material. It begins with Pontius Pilate washing his hands and giving Jesus up to be crucified. Jesus is pushed, shoved, mocked, crucified, and buried. A large contingent of soldiers, including Jewish elders, keep watch at the tomb. On Easter morning, two tall men (angels) enter the tomb and escort Jesus from it, with his cross following. The heads of the two men reach the clouds; the head of Jesus reaches above the clouds. A voice from heaven

---

[8] The ninth-century Akhmimic Greek Gospel fragment was published five years after its discovery, in U. Bouriant, "Fragments du texte grec du livre d Enoch et de quelques écrits attribués à Saint Pierre," in *Mémoires publiés par les membres de la Mission archéologique française au Caire* 9.1 (Paris: Librairie de la Société asiatique, 1892), 137–42. Edited and corrected editions of the text can also be found in J. A. Robinson and M. R. James, *The Gospel According to Peter, and the Revelation of Peter* (London: C. J. Clay, 1892); H. von Schubert, *Das Petrusevangelium* (Berlin: Reuther & Reichard, 1893); H. von Schubert, *The Gospel of St. Peter* (Edinburgh: T&T Clark, 1893); and more recently in M. G. Mara, *Évangile de Pierre*, Sources chrétiennes 201 (Paris: Éditions du Cerf, 1973). The Greek text of the *Gospel of Peter* is also found in K. Aland, ed., *Synopsis Quattuor Evangeliorum* (Stuttgart: Deutsche Bibelgesellschaft, 1985), 479–80, 484, 489, 493–94, 498, 500, 507.

asks if Jesus has preached to the dead (lit. "to those who sleep") and the cross answers "Yes."

Critical assessments of this Gospel fragment diverged widely, with some scholars, such as Percival Gardner-Smith, claiming that the fragment was independent of the New Testament Gospels, and others, such as Henry Barclay Swete, claiming that the fragment is dependent on the New Testament Gospels.[9] Throughout this debate no one seriously asked if the Akhmîm fragment really was part of the late second-century *Gospel of Peter*. It was simply assumed that it was.

In recent years, Koester and a circle of colleagues and students have given new life to Gardner-Smith's position. According to Koester, the *Gospel of Peter*'s "basis must be an older text under the authority of Peter which was independent of the canonical Gospels." Koester's student Ron D. Cameron agrees to this, concluding that this Gospel is independent of the canonical Gospels, may even predate them, and "may have served as a source for their respective authors."[10] This position has been worked out in detail by Crossan who accepts the identification of the Akhmîm fragment with Serapion's *Gospel of Peter*. In a lengthy study that appeared in 1985, Crossan argued that the *Gospel of Peter*, though admittedly in its final stages influenced by the New Testament Gospel tradition, preserves

---

[9] The scholarly assessments of the relationship between the alleged *Gospel of Peter* and the Synoptic Gospels diverge greatly. Those who argue that the newly discovered Gospel fragment depends on the Synoptic Gospels include T. Zahn, *Das Evangelium des Petrus* (Erlangen: Deichert, 1893); H. B. Swete, *EUAGGELION KATA PETRON: The Akhmîm Fragment of the Apocryphal Gospel of St. Peter* (London: Macmillan, 1893), xiii–xx. Robinson and James (*Gospel According to Peter*, 32–33) speak of "the unmistakable acquaintance of the author with our Four Evangelists ... He uses and misuses each in turn." Those who argue that the fragment is independent of the Synoptic Gospels include A. Harnack, *Bruchstücke des Evangeliums und der Apokalypse des Petrus*, TU 9 (Leipzig: Hinrichs, 1893); A. Harnack and H. V. Schubert, "Das Petrus-evangelium," *TLZ* 19 (1894): 9–18; P. Gardner-Smith, "The Gospel of Peter," *JTS* 27 (1925–26): 255–71; "The Date of the Gospel of Peter," *JTS* 27 (1925–26): 401–407.

[10] On recent scholarly support of the antiquity of the *Gospel of Peter*, see H. Koester, *Introduction to the New Testament. Volume 2: History and Literature of Early Christianity* (Berlin: de Gruyter, 1982) 163; cf. H. Koester, "Überlieferung und Geschichte der frühchristlichen Evangelienliteratur," *ANRW* II.25.2 (1984): 1463–1542, esp. 1487–88, 1525–27; R. D. Cameron, *The Other Gospels: Non-Canonical Gospel Texts* (Philadelphia: Westminster, 1982), 78. Another Koester student, B. A. Johnson (*The Empty Tomb Tradition in the Gospel of Peter* [dissertation; Cambridge: Harvard University, 1966]), has argued that Peter's empty tomb tradition is not based on the canonical Gospels, but on an older tradition.

a very old tradition, on which the Passion accounts of all four of the canonical Gospels are based.[11] This old tradition is identified as the *Cross Gospel.*

As intriguing as the possibility of the antiquity and independence of the Akhmîm Gospel fragment is, several troubling questions arise. First, there are many details in this fragment that look late and secondary and sometimes reflect ignorance of first-century Palestinian realities. According to 8.31 and 10.38 the Jewish elders and scribes camp out in the cemetery, as part of the guard keeping watch over the tomb of Jesus. Given Jewish views of corpse impurity, not to mention fear of cemeteries at night, the author of our fragment is astonishingly ignorant. Who could write such a story only twenty years after the death of Jesus? And if someone did write such a work at such an early time, can we really believe that the evangelist Matthew, who was surely Jewish and was knowledgeable of Jewish customs, would make use of such a poorly informed writing? One can scarcely credit this scenario.

Second, can it be seriously maintained that the Akhmîm fragment's resurrection account, *complete with a talking cross and angels whose heads reach heaven*, constitutes the most primitive account of Jesus's passion and resurrection? Is this the account that the New Testament Gospel writers had before them? Or, is it not more prudent to conclude that such features are exemplary of the secondary, fanciful nature of this apocryphal writing?[12]

Thus, the evidence suggests that the Akhmîm Gospel fragment is little more than a blend of details from the four New Testament Gospels, especially from Matthew, that has been embellished with pious imagination,

---

[11] J. D. Crossan, *The Cross That Spoke: The Origins of the Passion Narrative* (San Francisco: Harper & Row, 1988).

[12] The fantastic elements in the Akhmîm Gospel fragment strongly tell against its antiquity. On the great height of Jesus, see *Shepherd of Hermas* 83.1 ("a man so tall that he rose above the tower"). The *Shepherd of Hermas* was composed sometime between C.E. 110 and 140. The mid-second-century addition to 4 Ezra (i.e., 2 Esd. 1–2) likewise describes the "Son of God" as possessing "great stature, taller than any of the others" (2:43–47). The Akhmîm Gospel fragment's description of the Cross that exits the tomb with the Risen Jesus parallels late Ethiopic tradition, attested in two works, whose compositions probably dated no earlier than the middle of the second century. For citations, see J. K. Elliott, *The Apocryphal New Testament: A Collection of Apocryphal Christian Literature in an English Translation Based on M. R. James* (Oxford: Clarendon, 1993), 566, 600.

apologetic concerns, and a touch of anti-Semitism. It should be regarded as a late work, not an early work, even if we attempt to find an earlier substratum (gratuitously) shorn of imagined late additions.

Even more pressing, however, is the question of whether the existing ninth-century Akhmîm Gospel fragment *really is* a fragment of the late second-century *Gospel of Peter* condemned by Bishop Serapion in the early third century. The extant Akhmîm fragment does not identify itself, nor do we have any quotations from the lost *Gospel of Peter* with which we could make comparison and possibly settle the question. Nor is the Akhmîm Gospel fragment obviously Docetic, as many asserted shortly after its publication. If the fragment is not Docetic, then the proposed identification of the fragment with the *Gospel of Peter* is weakened still further. After all, the one thing that Serapion emphasized was that the *Gospel of Peter* was used by Docetists to advance their doctrines.[13] And finally, as Paul Foster has shown, the connection between the Akhmîm Gospel fragment and the small papyrus fragments that may date as early as 200–250 is quite tenuous.[14] Thus, we have no solid evidence that allows us to link the extant Akhmîm Gospel fragment with any confidence to a second-century text, be that the *Gospel of Peter* mentioned by Bishop Serapion or any other writing. Given its fantastic features and coherence with late traditions, it is not advisable to make use of this Gospel fragment for Jesus research.

SECRET GOSPEL OF MARK. At the annual Society of Biblical Literature meeting in New York in 1960, Morton Smith announced that during his sabbatical leave in 1958, at the Mar Saba Monastery in the Judean wilderness, he found the first part of a letter of Clement of Alexandria (c. 150–215) penned in Greek, in what was argued to be an eighteenth-century

[13] The evidence of Docetic Gnosticism in the Akhmîm Gospel fragment is slim and probably nonexistent. In 4:10 it says that Jesus "himself was silent, as having no pain," but this does *not* say that Jesus felt no pain; it implies only that he was silent, even though the experience was indeed painful. Also, the cry from the Cross, "My power, [my] power, you have abandoned me!" (5.19), is taken by some to indicate Docetism. But what we have here is probably no more than influence from a variant form of Psalm 22:1, where one of the Greek recensions reads "strength" (or "power"), instead of "God": "My strength, my strength, why have you abandoned me?" For further discussion on this issue, see J. W. McCant, "The Gospel of Peter: Docetism Reconsidered," *NTS* 30 (1984): 258–73.
[14] See P. Foster, "Are There Any Early Fragments of the So-Called *Gospel of Peter*?" *NTS* 52 (2006): 1–28.

hand, inscribed in the back of a seventeenth-century edition of the letters of Ignatius. In 1973 Smith published two editions of his find, one learned and one popular. From the start, scholars suspected that the text was a forgery and that Smith was himself the forger. Still, many scholars – including several members of the Jesus Seminar – defended Smith and the authenticity of the Clementine letter.

What made the alleged find so controversial were two quotations in the letter of a mystical or secret version of the Gospel of Mark. These quotations cited passages not found in the public Gospel of Mark. In these passages, Jesus raises a dead man and then later, in the nude, instructs the young man in the mysteries of the kingdom of God. The homoerotic orientation of the story is hard to miss. This mystical version of Mark that Smith claims Clement was quoting would become known as the *Secret Gospel of Mark*.

No one besides Smith would ever study the actual physical document on which this letter was allegedly written, nor would the paper and ink ever be subjected to the kinds of tests normally undertaken to determine authenticity of ancient writings. Nevertheless, many scholars accepted the Clementine letter as genuine and so accepted its testimony that there really was in circulation, in the second century, a secret version of the Gospel of Mark. Indeed, some scholars have suggested that *Secret Mark* may help us better understand how the Gospels of Matthew, Mark, and Luke related to one another, and of course, some scholars have suggested that *Secret Mark* is older and more original than public Mark, the version of the Gospel in the New Testament. Learned studies continue to appear, including two recent monographs.[15]

The sad thing is that all this labor has been misspent; the Clementine letter and the quotations of *Secret Mark* embedded within it constitute a

---

[15] For a sampling of scholarship concerned with the *Secret Gospel of Mark*, see M. Smith, *Clement of Alexandria and a Secret Gospel of Mark* (Cambridge: Harvard University Press, 1973); M. Smith, *The Secret Gospel: The Discovery and Interpretation of the Secret Gospel According to Mark* (New York: Harper & Row, 1973); F. F. Bruce, *The Secret Gospel of Mark* (London: Athlone, 1974); M. W. Meyer, *Secret Gospels: Essays on Thomas and the Secret Gospel of Mark* (Harrisburg, PA: Trinity Press International, 2003). For two recent monographs, see E. Rau, *Das geheime Markusevangelium: Ein Schriftfund voller Rätsel* (Neukirchen: Neukirchener Verlag, 2003); and S. G. Brown, *Mark's Other Gospel: Rethinking Morton Smith's Controversial Discovery* (Waterloo, Ontario: Canadian Corporation for the Studies in Religion, 2005). An early and outstanding critical review of Smith's books was written by Q. Quesnell, "The Mar Saba Clementine: A Question of Evidence," CBQ 37 (1975): 48–67.

modern hoax and Smith almost certainly is the hoaxer. Several scholars
have for years suspected this to be the case, but the recently published,
clear, color photographs of the document[16] have given experts in the
science of the detection of forgeries the opportunity to analyze the handwriting of the document and compare it with samples of the handwriting
of the late Professor Smith. The evidence is compelling and conclusive:
Smith wrote the text himself.[17]

In addition to these four extracanonical works, other sources have been
brought into the discussion. These include various Gospels or Gospel-
like writings that survive as fragments, either as fragments of papyrus or
as quotations in early Christian writings. Jesus is also mentioned briefly
in various Jewish sources, such as Josephus and rabbinic literature. He is
also mentioned in passing by various Greek and Roman writers. Some
of this material has been slightly helpful, but none of it sheds any new
light on the person and world of Jesus. As interesting as some of the
extracanonical Gospels and Gospel-like sources are, they are not as old
and are not as well connected to the first generation of Jesus's movement
as are the New Testament Gospels of Matthew, Mark, Luke, and John.
Critical study of the historical Jesus has no other choice but to focus on
the New Testament Gospels and other early Christian sources (such as
the letters of Paul and James).

Question 2: Where to Place Jesus: Why Historical Context Is Crucial?

Just exactly who Jesus was and how he fit into his society are ongoing
questions. They are important questions too. Was Jesus a Cynic philosopher? Was he a rabbi? Was he a prophet? Did he hold political aspirations?

---

[16] For good-quality color photographs of the Clementine letter, see C. W. Hedrick, "Secret
Mark: New Photographs, New Witnesses," *The Fourth R* 13/5 (2000): 3–16. Hedrick
thought that his photographs supplied evidence supporting the authenticity of the
Clementine letter. As it turns out, they had the opposite effect.

[17] For convincing evidence that the Clementine letter (supposedly containing quotations
and discussion of *Secret Mark*) is a hoax, see S. C. Carlson, *The Gospel Hoax: Morton
Smith's Invention of Secret Mark* (Waco, TX: Baylor University Press, 2005); P. Jeffrey, *The
Secret Gospel of Mark Unveiled: Imagined Rituals of Sex, Death, and Madness in a Biblical
Forgery* (New Haven, CT: Yale University Press, 2006). A number of anachronisms have
also been detected, including the fact that a peculiar interpretation of Mark 4:11 ("the
mystery of the kingdom of God") that occurs in the letter of Clement "discovered"
by Smith at Mar Saba just happens to be an interpretation that Smith himself had
proposed some time before "discovering" that letter.

Did he proclaim the end of the world? Over the last century or so Jesus has been presented as a Pharisee (of one stripe or another), an Essene, a prophet, and an ethicist. In more recent times, Jesus has been interpreted as a philosopher, a rabbi, a sage, a charismatic holy man, and a magician. Indeed, some of these portraits combine two or more of these categories.[18] The teachings of Jesus have also been compared to those credited to the Buddha.[19]

In sorting through all these different ideas, we must ask what archaeology can tell us about the world of Jesus. What do we know about Nazareth, the village in which Jesus grew up? What do we know about the larger region of Galilee, in which Nazareth is located and in which larger cities at one time existed, including Sepphoris, only four miles from Jesus's hometown? Investigation into these and related questions will help us better contextualize Jesus and gain a clearer understanding of who he was and what his hopes and intentions were.

Jesus grew up and was publicly active in Galilee in the first three decades of the first-century c.e. His environment was thoroughly Jewish. His home village was Nazareth. Although the village was small (somewhere between two hundred and four hundred inhabitants), there was a synagogue. There were no pagan temples or schools. In all likelihood not a single non-Jew lived in Nazareth at that time.

Recent excavations in and around Nazareth suggest that the village in the time of Jesus may not have been a sleepy, isolated place (as many have

[18] On the diverse portraits of Jesus in modern scholarship, see C. G. Montefiore, *Some Elements of the Religious Teaching of Jesus* (London: Macmillan, 1910); J. Klausner, *Jesus of Nazareth: His Life, Times, and Teaching* (London: Macmillan, 1925; 3rd ed., 1952); A. Finkel, *The Pharisees and the Teacher of Nazareth* (Leiden: Brill, 1964; repr., with corrections, 1974); G. Vermes, *Jesus the Jew: A Historian's Reading of the Gospels* (London: Collins, 1973); G. Vermes, *Jesus in His Jewish Context* (London: SCM, 2003); M. Smith, *Jesus the Magician* (San Francisco: Harper & Row, 1978); H. Maccoby, *Jesus the Pharisee* (London: SCM, 2003).

[19] On comparing Jesus with Buddha, see the remark in J. D. Crossan, *In Parables: The Challenge of the Historical Jesus* (San Francisco: Harper & Row, 1985), 77: "But it must be emphasized that Jesus' use of proverbs and parables is far closer to that of Zen Buddhism than it is to conventional Hebrew wisdom." This is very misleading. Jesus's use of proverbs and parables is far closer to that of the early rabbis, who in turn derived much of their material and style from Hebrew Scripture itself. For parallels between Jesus and the proverbs and parables of the rabbis, see C. A. Evans, *Jesus and His Contemporaries: Comparative Studies* (Leiden: Brill, 1995), 251–97. For a convenient presentation of the parallels between Jesus and Buddha, see M. Borg, *Jesus and Buddha: The Parallel Sayings* (Berkeley, CA: Ulysses, 1997).

imagined it). There is evidence of vineyards and grape presses, of terrace farming, of olive presses and the manufacture of olive oil, and even of stone masonry. The old, quaint notion that the inhabitants of Nazareth had to look for work in nearby villages and cities is now quite obsolete. The economy of Nazareth was more than sufficiently active to keep her inhabitants fully occupied.

Of course, Nazareth was not isolated from the rest of Galilee. Nazareth is only a few miles from Sepphoris, a major city; and Nazareth is near a major highway that connects Caesarea Maritima (on the Mediterranean) to the southwest to Tiberias (on the Sea of Galilee) to the northwest. Sepphoris, Caesarea Maritima, and Tiberias were the three largest and most influential cities in Galilee; Jesus grew up near one of them and near the highway that linked the other two.

THE CYNIC HYPOTHESIS. In his popular book on the historical Jesus, Crossan argued that Jesus was a "peasant Jewish Cynic" and that Jesus and his followers were "hippies in a world of Augustan yuppies."[20] Who were the Cynics of late antiquity, what did they believe, and how did they live? Cynicism was founded by Diogenes (c. 412–321 B.C.E.). The nickname "Cynic" comes from the Greek word *kynarion*, meaning doggish or doglike. Cynics earned this dubious sobriquet because of their ragged, unkempt appearance. Attractive apparel and grooming meant nothing to them. And, like dogs, Cynics would urinate and defecate in public. In a certain sense, then, they were a bit like twentieth-century "hippies."

The Cynic typically carried a cloak, a beggar's purse, a staff, and usually went barefoot. In a letter to his father, Diogenes says, "Do not be upset, Father, that I am called a dog and put on a double, coarse cloak, carry a purse over my shoulders, and have a staff in my hand."[21] It was this dress code of sorts that has encouraged a few scholars to see significant parallels between Jesus and Cynics. After all, so goes the argument, Jesus gave his disciples similar instructions:

---

[20] On Jesus as Jewish Cynic, see J. D. Crossan, *The Historical Jesus: The Life of a Mediterranean Jewish Peasant* (San Francisco: HarperCollins, 1991), 421–22. The quotation is from p. 421.

[21] A. J. Malherbe, *The Cynic Epistles* (Missoula, MT: Scholars, 1977), 99.

- "He charged them to take nothing for their journey except a staff; nor bread, no bag, no money in their belts; but to wear sandals and not put on two tunics" (Mark 6:8–9).
- "Take no gold, nor silver, nor copper in your belts, no bag for your journey, nor two tunics, nor sandals, nor a staff; for the laborer deserves his food" (Matt. 10:9–10).
- "Take nothing for your journey, no staff, nor bag, nor bread, nor money; and do not have two tunics" (Luke 9:3).
- "Carry no purse, no bag, no sandals; and salute no one on the road" (Luke 10:4).

These instructions in fact do not agree with Cynic dress and conduct; they contradict them. The very things Jesus tells his disciples *not* to take with them (no bag, no tunic, and no staff either, if we follow the version in Matthew and Luke) are the characteristic markers of the true Cynic. As one observer from late antiquity put it: "What makes a Cynic is his purse and his staff and his big mouth."[22]

The only parallel between Jesus and a Cynic leader here is that both are reported as having given instructions concerning what to wear and what to take on one's journey. The only *specific* agreement is taking the staff (if we follow Mark; if we do not, then there is no agreement at all). The staff, however, is hardly distinctive to Cynics. On the contrary, in the Jewish context the staff has a long and distinguished association with the patriarchs, such as Jacob and Judah (Gen. 32:10, 38:18), and the great lawgiver Moses and his brother Aaron (Exod. 4:4, 7:9). Moreover, the staff is also a symbol of royal authority, figuring in texts that in later interpretation take on messianic and eschatological significance (e.g., Gen. 49:10; Isa. 11:4; Ezek. 19:14).

Besides the question of dress, some scholars suggest that Jesus's worldview is Cynic. Instead of being caught up with materialism and vanity, the Cynic lives a life of simplicity and integrity before God. According to one ancient writer, the "end and aim of the Cynic philosophy . . . is happiness, but happiness that consists in living according to nature."[23]

---

[22] On the dress and behavior of Cynics, see the comments in ancient writers, such as Epictetus 3.22.50; cf. Lucian, *Peregrinus* 15; Diogenes Laertius, *Lives of Eminent Philosophers* 6.13; Ps.-Diogenes 30.3. The quotation is from Epictetus.

[23] On the Cynic living according to nature, see Julian, *Orations* 6.193D.

Living according to nature also means treating fellow human beings as equals. A few scholars apparently think that is more or less what Jesus taught. Was it? Here are teachings that are sometimes cited to make this point:

- "And why are you anxious about clothing? Consider the lilies of the field, how they grow; they neither toil nor spin; yet I tell you, even Solomon in all his glory was not arrayed like one of these. But if God so clothes the grass of the field, which today is alive and tomorrow is thrown into the oven, will he not much more clothe you, O men of little faith? Therefore do not be anxious, saying, 'What shall we eat?' or 'What shall we drink?' or 'What shall we wear?' For the Gentiles seek all these things; and your heavenly Father knows that you need them all. But seek first his kingdom and his righteousness, and all these things shall be yours as well" (Matt. 6:28–33).
- "You shall love your neighbor as yourself" (Mark 12:31; cf. Lev. 19:18).
- "For if you forgive people their trespasses, your heavenly Father also will forgive you; but if you do not forgive people their trespasses, neither will your Father forgive your trespasses" (Matt. 6:14–15).

Superficially, Jesus's teaching is at points comparable to Cynic teaching. But Jesus's teaching is very different at other significant points. For one, Jesus did not teach his disciples to pursue happiness and to live according to nature. What he taught was that nature reveals important things about God, namely, that God is loving, good, and generous. Jesus urges his disciples to have faith and live in light of God's goodness and care. But in the end, the disciple is to seek God's kingdom (or rule) and righteousness. Then all the rest will fall into place. When the core values are understood, the profound differences between Jesus and the Cynics cannot be missed.

And, as mentioned already, Cynics were known for flouting social custom and etiquette, such as urinating, defecating, and engaging in sexual intercourse in public.[24] Cynics could be very coarse and very rude. In fact, one was remembered to have retorted: "What difference does it make to me, from which end the noise comes?"[25] There simply is no

---

[24] On Cynic crudeness, see Cicero, *De officiis* 1.128; Diogenes Laertius, *Lives of Eminent Philosophers* 6.69; Epictetus, *Discourses* 2.20.10: Cynics "eat and drink and copulate and defecate and snore."

[25] For the quotation, see Seneca, *Moral Epistles* 91.19.

parallel to this kind of thinking or behavior in the teaching and lifestyle of Jesus and his disciples.

Jesus did indeed criticize some of his contemporaries for their religiosity, hypocrisy, and mean-spiritedness toward the poor and marginalized:

- "Thus, when you give alms, sound no trumpet before you, as the hypocrites do in the synagogues and in the streets, that they may be praised by people" (Matt. 6:2).
- "And when you pray, you must not be like the hypocrites; for they love to stand and pray in the synagogues and at the street corners, that they may be seen by people" (Matt. 6:5).
- "And when you fast, do not look dismal, like the hypocrites, for they disfigure their faces that their fasting may be seen by people" (Matt. 6:16).
- "Woe to you, scribes and Pharisees, hypocrites! For you tithe mint and dill and cummin, and have neglected the weightier matters of the law, justice and mercy and faith; these you ought to have done, without neglecting the others" (Matt. 23:23).
- "Woe to you, scribes and Pharisees, hypocrites! For you build the tombs of the prophets and adorn the monuments of the righteous, saying, 'If we had lived in the days of our fathers, we would not have taken part with them in shedding the blood of the prophets'" (Matt. 23:29– 30).
- "You leave the commandment of God, and hold fast the tradition of people" (Mark 7:8).

Admittedly, all this criticism could well have been uttered by a Cynic. But this represents only one aspect of Jesus's teaching. Jesus criticized some of his critics, but he was not crude, nor did he suggest that religious faith was pointless. Herein lies a telling difference between the worldview of Jesus and the world view of Cynics. Whereas the latter railed against religion because the gods, they thought, were indifferent, Jesus urged his followers to believe in God because he does take notice and cares deeply. Indeed, some of the preceding utterances go on to assure that "your Father who sees in secret will reward you" (Matt. 6:6, 18). Accordingly, Jesus urges his disciples to pray, "for your Father knows what you need before you ask him" (Matt. 6:8). This is not the teaching of the Cynics.

Furthermore, Jesus proclaimed God's rule and urged his disciples to look to God for deliverance. Jesus longed for the redemption of his people and believed deeply that the God of Israel would fulfill the prophecies and promises of old. These hopes and beliefs are not consistent with Cynic ideology. Accordingly, most scholars concerned with the historical Jesus find the Cynic thesis unlikely.[26]

Archaeology does not support the Cynic hypothesis either. Excavations at Sepphoris, a major city just a few miles north of Nazareth, have provided evidence that has called into question the assumption of the presence of Cynics in Galilee. How Jewish or Greek was Sepphoris, the city near the village of Nazareth, in the time of Jesus? This is a very important question. Much of the archaeological work in the 1970s and 1980s revealed the extent of building. Besides paved, colonnaded streets and large buildings, a public theater was also excavated. Although it is disputed, it is likely that the first phase of the theater was built in the 20s and later expansion and renovation took place later in the century. Such discoveries suggested to some that this city may have had extensive Greek influence, but further archaeological work in the 1990s, which included discovery of the city dump, led to the conclusion that Sepphoris was a thoroughly Jewish city in the days of Jesus after all. The dump was a great find, because garbage reveals a lot about the people who lived at a particular time. In the dump at Sepphoris, prior to C.E. 70, archaeologists have found virtually no pig bones, which is hard to explain if we are to imagine the presence of a significant non-Jewish population. In stark contrast to this finding, after C.E. 70 (i.e., after the destruction of Jerusalem by the Roman army) when there was a sizable growth in the non-Jewish population, pig bones come to represent 30 percent of the animal remains. What this suggests is that prior to the Jewish revolt, the population of Sepphoris was Jewish and observed Jewish laws and customs. It was only after the revolt that support for Jewish law began to erode. This means that in the time of Jesus (a generation or more before the revolt), there was little and possibly no non-Jewish presence in Sepphoris. And that means, no Cynics.

[26] For studies by scholars who find the Cynic hypothesis unconvincing, see D. E. Aune, "Jesus and Cynics in First-Century Palestine: Some Critical Considerations," in *Hillel and Jesus: Comparisons of Two Major Religious Leaders*, ed. J. H. Charlesworth and L. L. Johns (Minneapolis: Fortress, 1997), 176–92; H. D. Betz, "Jesus and the Cynics: Survey and Analysis of a Hypothesis," *JR* 74 (1994): 453–75; C. M. Tuckett, "A Cynic Q?" *Bib* 70 (1989): 349–76; Tuckett, *Q and the History of Early Christianity: Studies on Q* (Edinburgh: T&T Clark, 1996), 368–91; B. Witherington, III, *Jesus the Sage: The Pilgrimage of Wisdom* (Minneapolis: Fortress, 1994), 123–43.

There is still more evidence that supports this conclusion. More than one hundred fragments of stone vessels have been unearthed thus far, dating from before C.E. 70, again pointing to a Jewish population at Sepphoris concerned with ritual purity (i.e., because stone vessels – unlike ceramic vessels – cannot easily be made unclean; cf. John 2:6). Also consistent with concern over personal purity is the presence in Sepphoris of many *miqva'ot*, or ritual bathing pools. Furthermore, a Hebrew pottery fragment and several lamp fragments bearing the image of the menorah (the seven-branched candelabra) have also been found, dating from the early period.

Coins minted at Sepphoris during the pre–C.E. 70 period do not depict the image of the Roman emperor or pagan deities (as was common in the coinage of this time). And, the excavations have not uncovered any structures typically present in a Greco-Roman city (such as pagan temples, gymnasium, odeum, nymphaeum, or shrines and statues, all which were offensive to Jewish sensibilities). It is only in the post–C.E. 70 period that pagan art and architecture begin to make their appearance. All this evidence leads to the conclusion that Sepphoris in Jesus's day was a thoroughly Jewish city. There is little reason to think that there may have been Cynics wandering the streets of Sepphoris, who could have influenced Jewish youths from nearby villages.

Commitment to the Jewish laws and customs is in fact seen throughout Galilee; it is not limited to Sepphoris. Throughout Galilee the distribution of Jewish and non-Jewish pottery is very suggestive of this conclusion. Whereas non-Jews purchased Jewish pottery, the Jews of Galilee did not purchase and make use of pottery manufactured by non-Jews. The point here is that because non-Jews had no purity issues in the use of ceramic and pottery, they were happy to buy ceramic from any source – Jewish or non-Jewish; but not so in the case of Jews. Because, in their view, ceramic was susceptible to impurity, Jews purchased pottery only from Jews, never from non-Jews. Accordingly, Jewish pottery that dates prior to C.E. 70 is found in Jewish and non-Jewish sectors in and around Galilee, while non-Jewish pottery is found only in the non-Jewish sectors. These patterns of distribution strongly suggest that the Jewish people of Galilee were scrupulous in their observance of Jewish purity laws.[27] Jesus grew

---

[27] On the Jewish character of Galilee and Sepphoris in the time of Jesus, see J. F. Strange, "First Century Galilee from Archaeology and from the Texts," in *Archaeology and*

up and conducted his public ministry in a world characterized by such observances. It is very unlikely that he understood himself as a Cynic or that his followers viewed him this way.

Question 3: How to Study Jesus: Why Methods and Criteria Are So Important?

Once the investigator has identified the most promising sources (in this case, the New Testament Gospels) and has recognized the most probable cultural and social context (Galilee, dominated by Jews loyal to Israel's faith and traditions), he or she must come to think through assumptions about history and the criteria needed to distinguish history from legend. These criteria are variously termed the "criteria of authenticity" or the "authenticity criteria." This may sound terribly technical and complicated, but actually it is only an attempt to apply common sense to determine if ancient documents are trustworthy sources for learning what happened and discerning who said what.

No matter what perspective one brings to the New Testament Gospels (and extracanonical Gospels, for that matter), one needs to have criteria. The word *criterion* (plural *criteria*) is a Greek word that means "judgment" or "basis for passing judgment." We all have criteria for passing judgment with respect to many things in life. When someone says, "I think this story is true," and you respond, "Why do you think so?" you are asking the person to explain his or her criteria, or basis for making the judgment.

Some traditional Christians will, of course, respond simply by saying, "Whatever the New Testament Gospels say Jesus said or did I accept as historical." That may work for those who do not doubt the historicity and authority of the Bible. But what about those who would like to have sound, compelling reasons for accepting the Gospel narratives as reliable? Asserting that the Bible is inspired and therefore true, without providing any criteria that historians would recognize, will not satisfy everyone.

the Galilee: Texts and Contexts in the Graeco-Roman and Byzantine Periods, ed. D. R. Edwards and C. T. McCollough (Atlanta: Scholars, 1997), 39–48; M. A. Chancey, The Myth of a Gentile Galilee, SNTSMS 118 (Cambridge: Cambridge University Press, 2002); M. A. Chancey, Greco-Roman Culture and the Galilee of Jesus, SNTSMS 134 (Cambridge: Cambridge University Press, 2005).

So, historians apply criteria for assessing the historical worth of documents. They ask questions, such as "When was this document written?" "Who wrote this document?" "Do the details in this document cohere with other known and trusted sources?" "Was the author of this document in a position to know what really happened and what really was said?" "Are claims in this document supported by archaeological evidence and geographical realities?"

Over the years, biblical scholars have developed historical and literary criteria for assessing biblical literature. Discussions of criteria for the study of the Gospels have been especially intense, with a great number of criteria proposed. Some "hairsplitting" studies have been published that list as many as twenty-five criteria. Some of these criteria seem unnecessarily complex. Some criteria are very questionable. But a few of the criteria are consistently invoked.[28] We may review what most scholars regard as the best criteria. One will also be discussed that is often misused and misapplied.

HISTORICAL COHERENCE. When the Gospels tell us things that cohere with what we know of Jesus – historical circumstances and principal features of his life and ministry – it is reasonable to believe that we are on solid ground. Jesus drew a following, attracted the attention of the authorities, was executed, and yet was proclaimed Israel's Messiah and God's Son. Deeds and sayings attributed to him in the Gospels that cohere with these major elements and, indeed, help us understand these major elements should be judged authentic.

This criterion provides a basis for accepting the narrative of Jesus in the temple precincts, quarreling with and criticizing the ruling priests (as we see in Mark 11–12 and parallels). This criterion also encourages us to accept as authentic Jesus's affirmation that he is indeed Israel's Messiah and God's Son (Mark 14:61–63), for this makes sense of his crucifixion on the grounds of his claim that he is "king of the Jews" (Mark 15:26). It is less likely that Jesus would have been executed in this fashion if he were little more than an annoying teacher.

---

[28] For assessments of the criteria of authenticity, see Evans, *Jesus and His Contemporaries*, 13–26; J. P. Meier, *A Marginal Jew: Rethinking the Historical Jesus. Volume One: The Roots of the Problem and the Person* (New York: Doubleday, 1991), 167–95.

MULTIPLE ATTESTATION. This criterion refers to sayings and actions attributed to Jesus that appear in two or more independent sources (such as Mark and the sayings source used by Matthew and Luke). When sayings and actions of Jesus appear in two or more independent sources, we have reason to believe that reports of those sayings and actions were circulated widely and early and that they were not invented by a single writer. The fact that there is a goodly amount of material that enjoys multiple attestation is itself a witness to the antiquity and richness of our sources.

Here are a few examples: Jesus's saying on the lamp appears in Mark (at 4:21) and in the sayings source (at Matt. 5:15 and Luke 11:33). This saying is followed by the saying on what is revealed, which appears in Mark (at 4:22) and in the sayings source (at Matt. 10:26 and Luke 12:2). Jesus's saying on the evil generation that seeks a sign is found in Mark (at 8:12) and in the sayings source (at Matt. 12:39 and Luke 11:29). Jesus's conversation with the centurion, whose servant (or son) was ill, is another example of a story that is multiply attested (in Q at Matt. 8:5–13, Luke 7:1–10, and in the fourth Gospel at John 4:46–55). This story is examined in the second part of this chapter.

EMBARRASSMENT. This criterion begs to be misunderstood. All it means is that material that potentially created awkwardness or embarrassment for the early church is not likely to be material that a Christian invented sometime after Easter. Potentially "embarrassing" sayings and actions are therefore ones that are sure to reach back to the ministry of Jesus and, therefore, like it or not, they cannot be deleted from the Jesus data bank.

Perhaps the classic example of an embarrassing tradition is the baptism of Jesus (Mark 1:9–11 and parallels). What makes Jesus's baptism embarrassing? John's baptism called for repentance of sins and yet, according to Christian teaching, Jesus was sinless (Heb. 4:15). So why would sinless Jesus go to John for baptism? No Christian would invent such a story. Its preservation in the Gospels argues strongly that it is authentic material. The fact that it is preserved in the Gospels and not deleted also shows that the writers of the Gospels made every effort to tell the truth, even when what they were reporting might seem to conflict with developing Christian doctrine.

Another important example of "embarrassment" is seen in the narrative in which the imprisoned John sends messengers to Jesus, asking: "Are you he who is to come, or shall we look for another?" (Matt. 11:2–6 = Luke 7:18–23). Jesus answers John's question in an indirect, almost veiled way, "Go and tell John what you hear and see." Who would make up a story in which John – an ally of Jesus – expresses doubts about Jesus's identity and mission? And, why would an invented reply by Jesus fail to make explicit his messianic identity and mission? Why not have Jesus affirm loudly and clearly: "Go and tell John that I *am* he who is to come"? The story as preserved in Matthew and Luke strikes historians as an accurate report of an exchange between John and Jesus rather than as a later Christian fiction.

DISSIMILARITY. No criterion has been more discussed than the criterion of dissimilarity. Used properly, it can lend support to the conclusion that a given saying or deed is authentic. Applied improperly, it unnecessarily and unreasonably rules out of bounds a host of sayings and deeds. Improperly applied it requires sayings and deeds that are deemed authentic to be dissimilar to (or inconsistent with) the theology of the early church with the tendencies and emphases within the Judaism of Jesus's day. At this point the logic of the criterion is a bit strained. The intention is to rule out sayings and deeds that may have originated in Jewish circles, on the one hand, or in early Christian circles, on the other. So, if a saying is not dissimilar to both these contexts, there is no guarantee that the saying (or deed) originated with Jesus. The problem with the criterion applied in this way is that it rules out almost *everything* attributed to Jesus. After all, Jesus was Jewish and much of what he taught reflected themes and concepts current among religious teachers of his day (not to mention Israel's scripture). We would rather expect Jewish tendencies and emphases to be present in authentic teachings of Jesus. And, of course, the early church clung to Jesus's teaching as precious and formed its thinking and practices in conformity with that teaching. So, again, we should expect lines of continuity between Jesus and the movement that he founded.

Nevertheless, the criterion of dissimilarity does prove useful when it is applied in a positive fashion. There *is* some material in the New Testament Gospels that is not particularly consistent with the theology and practice of the early church, and there is also some material that does not present Jesus as typical with respect to Jewish tendencies. Jesus's free and easy association with sinners was not the sort of thing that religious teachers in his day did (and even Christians in the early church could be reserved in that matter). So, Jesus's practice of associating freely with sinners may represent an instance in which his reported actions are at variance with those of both his Jewish contemporaries and his Christian followers. The reports of such a practice would be deemed authentic through positive application of the criterion of authenticity.

SEMITISMS AND PALESTINIAN BACKGROUND. This criterion, which is sometimes subdivided into two or more criteria, suggests that sayings and deeds that reflect the Hebrew or Aramaic language (Semitisms), or that reflect first-century Palestine (geography, topography, customs, commerce), exhibit features we would expect of authentic material. Of course, material that enjoys the support of this criterion may derive from early Jewish Christians and not necessarily from Jesus. But this criterion, nevertheless, is important. After all, the Gospels were written in Greek and yet they purport to preserve the sayings of Jesus who spoke Aramaic and the deeds of Jesus who ministered in first-century Palestine. If these Greek Gospels faithfully preserve the sayings and deeds of Jesus, then these Greek Gospels should show evidence of Semitism and Palestinian background; and this they do.

COHERENCE (OR CONSISTENCY). Finally, the criterion of coherence (or consistency) is also useful and functions in some ways as a catchall. According to this criterion, material that is consistent with material judged authentic on the basis of the other criteria may also be regarded as authentic.

All these criteria have their place and have made useful contributions to the scholarly study of the historical Jesus. They enable historians to give good reasons for judging this saying or that deed attributed to Jesus as authentic. The problem is in assuming that everything that is attributed to Jesus that does not enjoy support from one or more of the criteria should be regarded as *inauthentic*. Lack of support from the authenticity criteria does not necessarily mean that the saying or deed in question *cannot* derive from Jesus.

HISTORICAL JESUS STUDIES: INTERPRETATION
OF MATTHEW 8:5–13

In this part of the chapter the principles and methods discussed previously are applied to a specific passage. This passage is Matthew 8:5–13 (with parallels in Luke and John), a passage that tells the story of a desperate man who appeals to Jesus for help.

Here is a literal translation of Matthew 8:5–13:

[5]When he entered Capernaum a centurion came to him, beseeching him, [6]and saying, "Sir, my servant lies at home paralyzed, terribly tormented." [7]And he says to him, "Coming I will heal him." [8]And the centurion, answering, said, "Sir, I am not worthy that you should come under my roof; but only say the word and my servant shall be healed. [9]For I also am a man under authority, having soldiers under me, and I say to this one, 'Come,' and he comes, and to my servant, 'Do this,' and he does it."[10] When Jesus heard this he marveled and said to his followers, "Truly, I say to you, from no one have I found such faith in Israel. [11]But I say to you that many will come from east and west and they shall recline with Abraham and Isaac and Jacob in the kingdom of heaven, [12]but the sons of the kingdom shall be cast into the outer darkness, where there shall be weeping and gnashing of teeth." [13]And Jesus said to the centurion, "Go, let it be to you as you have believed." And the servant was healed at that very moment.

Let us examine this interesting story in light of the three questions raised in the first part of this chapter.

Question 1: Assessing the Sources

There is no parallel in Mark, but we do find the same story in Luke 7:1–10 and apparently also in John 4:46–54. The absence of the story in Mark and its presence in Matthew and Luke encourage us to think that the evangelists Matthew and Luke found the story in that body of material that scholars call Q. Moreover, it is probable that in Q the story directly followed the Sermon on the Mount. In the Gospel of Luke, the story immediately follows Luke's version of that sermon (Luke 6:20–49), and in Matthew's Gospel it follows a transitional passage that links the sermon (Matt. 5–7) with a series of healings, several of which are drawn from Mark.

In both the Matthean and Lukan contexts the centurion thus typifies the type of person Jesus called for in his sermon. He is a person of faith who "does" what someone "says" (cf. Matt. 8:9, "I say . . . to my slave, 'Do this!' and he does it," with Matthew 7:21 "Not every one who says . . . but he who does the will of my Father"). However, Matthew inserts his version of the healing of the leper, which he derived from Mark 1:40–45, between the ending of the sermon and the story of the centurion's servant. In Luke there is no interruption; Jesus finishes the Sermon on the Plain (as Luke's version is usually called), enters Capernaum in 7:1, and then encounters the worried centurion in 7:2–10.

The appearance of a very similar story in the Gospel of John encourages us to view the healing story as very early and well known. It survived and circulated among first-generation Christians, even if the Q and Johannine versions of the story differed at points. These differences suggest that we have in our possession two distinct streams of tradition. Even the Q version preserved in Matthew and Luke was remembered in somewhat different ways. Thus we can say that we have three versions in all. Each deserves careful attention.

We begin with Matthew's version of the story.[29] The story takes place in Capernaum, which is situated on the northwest shore of Kinneret Lake, better known as the Sea of Galilee. Jesus is approached by a centurion (8:5). This officer is not necessarily a Roman soldier, for Galilee was not a Roman province until C.E. 44. He could have been a captain in Herod's provincial militia or a member of a Roman auxiliary. However, historians tell us that some Romans were stationed in Galilee at this time and that this centurion very likely was a Roman. (That he was a Gentile is implied by Luke 7:5.) The word "centurion" comes from the Latin *centurio*, that

---

[29] In addition to the major commentaries on Matthew one should consult D. C. Allison, "Who Will Come from East and West? Observations on Matt. 8.11 12/Luke 13.28 29," *IBS* 11 (1989): 158–70; R. A. J. Gagnon, "The Shape of Matthew's Q Text of the Centurion at Capernaum: Did It Mention Delegations?" *NTS* 40 (1994): 133–42; W. Grimm, "Zum Hintergrund von Mt 8.11f./Lk 13.28f.," *BZ* 16 (1972): 255–56; S. H. Hooke, "Jesus and the Centurion: Matthew viii.5 13," *ExpTim* 69 (1957): 79–80; T. W. Jennings, "Mistaken Identities but Model Faith: Rereading the Centurion," *JBL* 123 (2004): 467–94; S. Loffreda and V. Tzaferis, "Capernaum," in *The New Encyclopedia of Archaeological Excavations in the Holy Land*, 4 vols, ed. E. Stern (Jerusalem: The Israel Exploration Society, 1993), 1:291–96; D. B. Saddington, "The Centurion in Matthew 8:5–13," *JBL* 125 (2006): 140–42; G. Zuntz, "The 'Centurion' of Capernaum and His Authority (Matt. VIII.5 13)," *JTS* 46 (1945): 183–90.

is, a commander of a *centuria*, a "hundred (troops)." The evangelist Matthew uses the Greek equivalent *hekatonarchos*, that is, "ruler of one hundred."

Parts of first-century Capernaum have been excavated. A third- or fourth-century limestone synagogue has been partially restored. It rests on a much older basalt foundation that archaeologists believe dates back to the time of Jesus. Accordingly, we may actually have recovered the floor plan and foundation of the synagogue in which Jesus sometimes taught (cf. Mark 1:21). Archaeologists have also uncovered the foundations and lower wall portions of several homes, including one that some think may have been the home of Simon Peter, the very home in which Jesus resided while at Capernaum (cf. Mark 1:29–31; 2:1; 9:33). And even more recently, archaeologists think they have identified the remains of what had been the headquarters and home of the centurion, who would have commanded the small garrison at Capernaum.

The centurion tells Jesus that his servant lies at home paralyzed and in terrible distress (8:6). Assuming that the man wishes Jesus to return with him to his home, Jesus offers to go with him and heal the servant (8:7). The centurion, however, responds in a way not seen before, saying, "Lord, I am not worthy to have you come under my roof; but only say the word, and my servant will be healed" (8:8). He goes on to explain: "For I am a man under authority, with soldiers under me; and I say to one, 'Go,' and he goes, and to another, 'Come,' and he comes, and to my slave, 'Do this,' and he does it" (8:9).

When the centurion says "only say the word, and my servant will be healed," he may have alluded to Psalm 107:20 ("He sent His word and healed them"). Is this plausible? According to the parallel story in Luke, the centurion built Capernaum's synagogue (cf. Luke 7:5). In all probability he regularly attended this synagogue (as a "God-fearer"; cf. Acts 10:22, 13:43) and heard the scriptures read and interpreted. Therefore, it should occasion no surprise that he used a biblical phrase when addressing a Jewish teacher and prophet.

Jesus is quite astonished at the centurion's declaration. He admits, "Truly, I say to you, not even in Israel have I found such faith" (8:10). In Luke's version of the story, Jesus says no more. All that Luke's readers are told is that when those who approached Jesus returned home, they found the servant healed. But in Matthew's version Jesus goes on to exclaim: "I tell you, many will come from east and west and sit at table with Abraham, Isaac, and Jacob in the kingdom of heaven, while the sons of the kingdom will be thrown into the outer darkness; there men will weep and gnash their teeth" (8:11). Although this saying does not appear in Luke's story of the centurion, it does appear in Luke 13:28–30. Most interpreters see this saying as belonging to Q, which Matthew has placed in the context of the exchange with the centurion. Why did the evangelist do this? First, it gives the evangelist the opportunity to elaborate on Jesus's remark that the centurion's faith exceeds the faith found in Israel. Matthew can now hint at the mission to the Gentiles that will later be developed more directly (cf. Matt. 10:16–23, 28:19–20). Second, the Matthean evangelist may well have caught the allusion to Psalm 107, both in the centurion's statement and in Jesus's saying. For the saying about coming "from east and west" echoes Psalm 107:1–3 ("Oh give thanks to the Lord . . . He has redeemed . . . and gathered from the lands, from the east and from the west, from the north and from the south").

Psalm 107 originally referred to the return of Jewish captives, who had been exiled from the land of Israel. Later Jewish writers understood this passage and others the same way: "Look toward the east, O Jerusalem, and see the joy that is coming to you from God! Behold, your sons are coming, whom you sent away; they are coming, gathered from east and west, at the word of the Holy One, rejoicing in the glory of God" (Bar. 4:36–37); and "Gather together our scattered people, set free those who are slaves among the Gentiles . . . Plant your people in your holy place, as Moses said" (2 Macc. 1:27–29). According to the Aramaic paraphrase of scripture (i.e., the Targum), Israel's exiles will be gathered by the Messiah (e.g., Tg. Isa. 28:1–6, 53:8, the Messiah "will bring our exiles near"; Tg. Hosea 14:8, "they shall be gathered from among their exile, they shall dwell in the shade of their Messiah"; Tg. Mic. 5:1–3, "from you shall come forth before Me the Messiah . . . and they shall be gathered in from among their exiles").

Jesus's saying, as embedded in Q and as found in its context in Luke (cf. Luke 13:22–30), probably assumed the same meaning. The Jews of Jerusalem, perhaps presuming on a privileged status, were warned that they may be pushed aside, to make room for Jews from Galilee and even from outside the land itself. But the context of the saying in Matthew 8 takes on a new nuance. Those from "east and west" will include Gentiles,

Gentiles like the centurion, who have faith greater even than the faith of God's privileged, covenant people.

Those who come from east and west will "sit at table with Abraham, Isaac, and Jacob in the kingdom of heaven" (Matt. 8:11). Luke 13:29 reads more simply that "they will recline at the table in the kingdom of God." The patriarchs – Abraham, Isaac, and Jacob – are mentioned in Luke 13:28, but Matthew's relocating them to the banqueting table itself heightens the expected bitterness of the scene. Those far away, who have "come from east and west," will sit at the table, but those close by (in Jerusalem and Judea) will miss out. The imagery of the banquet is part of eschatology and messianism, which envisioned many blessings for Israel. The imagery of banquets and eating and drinking in the kingdom of God is seen elsewhere in Matthew (cf. Matt. 5:6, "those who hunger and thirst . . . they shall be satisfied") and in Israel's ancient scriptures (cf. Ps. 107:1–9; Isa. 25:6–8; Ezek. 39:17–20; 1 Enoch 62:14; 2 Bar. 29:4).

Not only will those far away, Gentiles as well as Israelites, enjoy the anticipated banquet of God, "the sons of the kingdom will be thrown into the outer darkness" (Matt. 8:12). The "sons of the kingdom" are the Jewish people who live in Israel, to whom, it was supposed, belonged the kingdom of God. Because they live in the land (perhaps in the vicinity of Jerusalem itself), which was thought in itself to be a blessing, surely they would be the very first to benefit in the restoration of Israel. But no, Jesus says, those far away are more likely to benefit than those right in the land itself. This is consistent with Jesus's teaching elsewhere that the first will be last and the last first (cf. Matt. 19:30, 20:16; and especially Luke 13:30).

This interpretation helps us understand better some of the material that is unique to the Gospel of Matthew, such as the parable of the wise and foolish maids (Matt. 25:1–13), the parable of the wheat and weeds (Matt. 13:24–30, 36–43), and the parable of the drag net (Matt. 13:47–50). In Matthew, the kingdom of God (or heaven) is identified with Israel – to whom belongs the kingdom (as in 1QSb 5.21, "He shall . . . establish the kingdom of His people"; cf. 4Q252 5.4, "the kingdom of His people") – but not all Israel will in fact enter the kingdom (or, in Pauline terms, "they are not all Israel who are descended from Israel [i.e., from the patriarch Jacob]"; cf. Rom. 9:6). Repentance and faith, in response to Jesus's message, are the determining factors. Those who respond in faith will be included; those who do not will not be included. The irony, Jesus says, is that those far away – those one thinks enjoy no advantages – will be included in the kingdom in greater numbers than those who have the privilege of living in the holy land itself.

The sons of the kingdom will be thrown "into the outer darkness; in that place there shall be weeping and gnashing of teeth" (8:12). This is the first of three passages in the Gospel of Matthew, in which we hear of outer darkness, weeping, and gnashing of teeth (cf. Matt. 22:13, 25:30). These graphic depictions of hell are found only in Matthew. That the allusion is to hell is confirmed by the parallel with 1 Enoch 10:4a, "And He said to Raphael, 'Go, Raphael, and bind Azael hand and foot, and cast him into the darkness'." In the context of 1 Enoch, it is clear that the archangel Raphael has been ordered to bind the evil angel Azael and to cast him into hell. Similar language is found in the Dead Sea Scrolls, where we are told that the wicked face "everlasting damnation in the wrath of God's furious vengeance, never-ending terror and reproach for all eternity, with a shameful extinction in *the fire of Hell's outer darkness*" (1QS 4.12–13, emphasis added).

Matthew's version of the story concludes with Jesus telling the centurion: "Go; be it done for you as you have believed" (Matt. 8:13). This word of assurance is not found in Luke's version of the story (cf. Luke 7:10). It may well have been added by Matthew to underscore the importance of faith, a theme that is very important to the evangelist (cf. Matt. 8:26, 9:28–29, 14:31, 15:28, 23:23). Of course, in speaking the word, Jesus lives up to the centurion's earlier assertion that all Jesus need do is say the word. Jesus has spoken the word and, indeed, "the servant was healed at that very moment" (Matt. 8:13).

LUKE'S VERSION OF THE STORY. Luke's version (Luke 7:1–10) differs from Matthew's at several points.[30] First, we are told that the centurion's slave "was dear to him" and "at the point of death" (Luke 7:2). When

---

[30] In addition to the major commentaries on Luke one should consult T. R. S. Broughton, "The Roman Army," in *The Beginnings of Christianity*, 5 vols, ed. F. J. Foakes Jackson and K. Lake (London: Macmillan, 1920–33), 5:427–45; J. D. M. Derrett, "Law in the New Testament: The Syro-Phoenician Woman and the Centurion of Capernaum," *NovT* 15 (1973): 161–86; M. Gourges, "Du centurion de Capharnaum au centurion de Césarée. Luc 7,1 10 et sa fonction proleptique par rapport à Actes 10,1–11,18," in *Forschungen zum Neuen Testament und seiner Umwelt*, ed. C. Niemand (Frankfurt: Peter Lang, 2002), 259–70; J. A. G. Haslam, "The Centurion at Capernaum: Luke 7:1 10," *ExpTim* 96 (1984–85): 109–10; R. P. Martin, "The Pericope of the Healing of the 'Centurion's' Servant/Son

the centurion learns that Jesus has arrived in Capernaum, "he sent to him elders of the Jews, asking him to come and heal his slave" (7:3): the sending of Jewish elders to the Jewish Jesus shows the centurion's respect for Jewish customs and sensitivities and at the same time gives the centurion people who can vouch for his piety and integrity. The Jewish elders provide an excellent reference for the centurion, telling Jesus: "He is worthy for You to grant this to him" (7:4). The centurion is worthy because "he loves our nation, and it was he who built us our synagogue" (7:5). The synagogue to which reference is made is probably the very one that once stood on the basalt stone foundations uncovered by archaeological excavation. As one enters the building, the assembly room for worship is on the left, while to the right is what may have been a social hall.

On his way to the centurion's house Jesus is intercepted. The centurion has sent friends to tell Jesus that he is not worthy to have Jesus in his house and that he therefore did not presume himself to come to Jesus (7:6–7). Here the details of coming and going and of who meets whom are somewhat confused. Matthew's version seems to imply that the centurion met Jesus in person (cf. Matt. 8:5–6), but Luke implies that Jesus and the centurion in fact did not meet face to face. Matthew says nothing about delegates.

Luke's version of the story ends on a slightly different note. Whereas Matthew concludes with the notation that "the servant was healed at that very moment" (Matt. 8:13), Luke says, "And when those who had been sent returned to the house, they found the slave well" (Luke 7:10).

JOHN'S VERSION OF THE STORY. John's version of the story (John 4:46–54) differs at several points.[31] First, whereas Matthew and Luke tell us that the man was a centurion (Matt. 8:5; Luke 7:2), John says it was a "royal"

(Matt. 8:5 13 par. Luke 7:1–10): Some Exegetical Notes," in *Unity and Diversity in New Testament Theology*, ed. R. A. Guelich (Grand Rapids: Eerdmans, 1978): 14–22.

[31] In addition to the major commentaries on John one should consult M.-E. Boismard, "Saint Luc et la redaction du quatrième évangile (Jn. iv, 46–54)," *RB* 69 (1962): 185–211; A. Feuillet, *Johannine Studies* (Staten Island, NY: Alba House, 1965), 39–51; F. Neirynck, "John 4,46–54: Signs Source and/or Synoptic Gospels," *ETL* 60 (1984): 367–75; R. Schnackenburg, "Zur Traditionsgeschichte von Joh 4, 46–54," *BZ* 8 (1964): 58–88; E. Schweizer, "Die Heilung des Königlichen, Joh 4, 46–54," *EvT* 11 (1951): 64–71; E. F. Siegman, "St. John s Use of the Synoptic Material," *CBQ* 30 (1968): 182–98; G. Van Belle, "Jn 4,48 et la foi du centurion," *ETL* 61 (1985): 167–69.

official (John 4:46). Second, whereas Matthew and Luke tell us that the sick person was a servant (Matt. 8:6; Luke 7:2), John says he was a son (John 4:46). Third, in John's version there is nothing remarkable about the worried man's faith, no word of commendation, no comparison with Israel or Israel's lack of faith (as in Matt. 8:10, 13; Luke 7:9). Fourth, at the conclusion of the story, when we are told that the boy was on the mend (John 4:51), the Johannine evangelist goes into much greater detail, complete with checking the time ("Yesterday at the seventh hour the fever left him") and discovering "that it was at that hour in which Jesus said to him, 'Your son lives'" (John 4:52–53).

These differences notwithstanding, there are several important agreements that suggest we probably do have three versions of one healing episode. First, all three Gospels agree that the setting is Capernaum (Matt. 8:5; Luke 7:1; John 4:46). Second, all three stories involve an official, identified as a *centurion* in Matthew and Luke, but in John as a *royal* official, which in itself does not exclude the possibility that the official was a centurion. Third, there is urgency on the part of the petitioner. And fourth, all three stories remark on the immediacy of the healing of the sick son/servant (Matt. 8:13; Luke 7:10; John 4:52–53).

Two other considerations should be taken into account. First, the difference between son and servant is not necessarily a major difference. Matthew's word for "servant" (*pais*) can also refer to a son. This ambiguous word could account for what may be a bifurcation of this detail in the transmission of the story: the *pais* ("son"/"servant") of Matthew, which is perhaps how the text originally read in Q, becomes a "servant"/"slave" (*doulos*) in Luke, but a "son" (*huios*) in John. Second, Matthew and Luke are different from one another in major details (e.g., almost nothing of Luke 7:2–6 has an equivalent in Matthew), which argues against the simplistic conclusion that John's differences necessarily point to a wholly different episode.

In light of such research, it is reasonable to conclude that we have in Matthew 8:5–13 one version of a very old story, one that reaches back to the ministry of Jesus and has also been preserved in other, variant accounts. Essential details are remembered, as outlined previously, but other details, in the telling and retelling of the story, were dropped out or added, perhaps due to the influence of other stories and reminiscences of events that took place in the ministry of Jesus. The appearance of this story in three forms and in what are probably two very distinct literary traditions (Synoptic and Johannine), as well as the many discrepancies of minor details, tells against late wholesale fabrication of the story.

Question 2: Assessing the Role of Jesus in His World

We should now ask how this remarkable story in the life and ministry of Jesus of Nazareth would have been understood. Jesus is remembered as a teacher and wonder-worker, at least according to first-century Jewish historian and apologist Josephus Flavius (*Ant.* 18.63–64). Modern historians have compared Jesus to early rabbis and Jewish holy men. One story in particular has caught the attention of scholars. It is related to the Babylonian Talmud:

Once the son of Rabbi Gamaliel fell ill. He sent two scholars to Rabbi Hanina ben Dosa to ask him to pray for him. When he saw them he went up to an upper chamber and prayed for him. When he came down he said to them: "Go, the fever has left him." They said to him, "Are you a prophet?" He replied, "I am neither a prophet nor the son of a prophet, but I have learned this from experience. If my prayer is fluent in my mouth, I know that he [the sick person] is accepted; but if not, I know that he is rejected." They sat down and made a note of the exact moment. When they came to Rabbi Gamaliel, he said to them, "By the temple service! You have not been a moment too soon or too late, but so it happened at that very moment the fever left him and he asked for water to drink" (b. Ber. 34b).

There are many stories told of Hanina ben Dosa. He was renowned for his piety and mysticism, for his answered prayers, for healings, and even for successful encounters with evil spirits. Not surprisingly, some scholars think that Jesus and Hanina should be compared.[32] In the story of Hanina's fluent prayer for the son of Gamaliel, the parallel with John 4:52–53 is striking. And, as in Luke's version of the story, a delegation is sent to the holy man.

Without claiming that Jesus would have been viewed by his contemporaries as nothing more than another holy man, the parallels with the

---

[32] See Vermes, *Jesus the Jew*, 58–83. For further work on Jesus as rabbi, see B. D. Chilton, *A Galilean Rabbi and His Bible: Jesus' Use of the Interpreted Scripture of His Time* (Wilmington Del.: Glazier, 1984); B. D. Chilton, *Rabbi Jesus: An Intimate Biography. The Jewish Life and Teaching that Inspired Christianity* (New York: Doubleday, 2000).

story told of Hanina ben Dosa do suggest that Jesus's activities and the stories told about him would have been viewed by first-century Jews in Palestine as right at home in Israel and in Jewish piety. The specific story of Jesus's encounter with the centurion agrees with the general observations learned through history and archaeology (viz., that there really were Roman soldiers and officials in Galilee and that there probably were a centurion and garrison in Capernaum itself) and is consistent with what is known in other sources of Jewish charismatic piety.

Question 3: What Do We Learn from Our Study?

Critical investigation of the story of the healing of the centurion's servant (or son) provides reasonably solid evidence for the historicity of the event. The story is found in three Gospels that date to the first century. The Q source shared by Matthew and Luke may even date as early as the 1940s and 1950s. Even within this single source the diversity of details suggests that the story of the centurion circulated in more than one form, in turn suggesting early and widespread circulation. The appearance of a literarily independent version of the story in the fourth Gospel lends additional support to this supposition. Finally, the coherence of the story with what is known of Jewish history and culture in pre–c.e. 70 Galilee, complete with what appears to be coherence with archaeological excavations of Capernaum, where the event is said to have taken place, strongly encourages us to view the story as reflecting a genuine event from the life and ministry of Jesus.

Our critical study has also helped us understand better the significance of the story, both for those who originally witnessed it and for those who heard and retold it in the years that followed. In Luke's Gospel the respect that the centurion showed Jesus, as well as his piety, foreshadows the receptivity of Roman officials to the Christian message, as we see in the book of Acts, which narrates the expansion of the young church (cf. Acts 10:1–48, 13:4–12). The details of the delegation (Luke 7:3–5) provide the opportunity for the evangelist to bear witness to this man's faith in God and how, as such, he becomes a very promising candidate who will respond positively to Jesus. In Matthew's Gospel details appear in the story that warn of judgment befalling the "sons of the kingdom" and the Christian mission to those "from east and west." The latter part anticipates the Great Commission that the risen Jesus will give to his apostles (Matt. 28:18–20), with which the Gospel of Matthew draws to a close.

In John's Gospel the story of the healed son is part of schema of miracles as "signs" that attest to Jesus's heavenly origin and mission. In fact, the evangelist links the miracle of Capernaum very closely to the miracle of Cana, where Jesus changed the water into wine (John 2:1–12, 4:45–46). For the fourth evangelist the healing of the official's son is to produce faith in the hearers – that they might come to believe that Jesus is Israel's true Messiah and Son of God (John 20:30–31).

The story of the centurion provides us with an instructive example of the preservation and interpretation of an authentic event in the life and ministry of Jesus of Nazareth. But this event was not simply preserved as a static, unaltered recounting of something that took place; it was preserved in three creative, interpretive presentations, suggesting new meaning and significance for the emerging Church.

↓

5

Social-Scientific Approaches and the Gospel of Matthew

BRUCE J. MALINA

*M*ANY SCHOLARS WHO USE SOCIAL-SCIENTIFIC APPROACHES to the New Testament employ perspectives derived from the academic study of the social sciences, for example, from the infamous Sociology 101. Since the goals and principles of social-scientific (not "sociological") approaches elude most interpreters, it seems useful to present a simple overview of the definitions and organizing principles supporting social-science perspectives. These definitions should help.

Sociology is the study of human beings in groups in one's own society. The study of human beings in groups in foreign societies is called *anthropology*. Human beings in groups interact in terms of the *social system* into which they have been socialized. These social systems consist of social institutions, values, and ways of "being person" – all directed toward a meaningful, human, social existence for all group members.

- *Social institutions* are fixed forms of phases of social life. Generally four major fixed forms are used for analysis: kinship (naturing/nurturing); politics (taking effective collective action); economics (provisioning society); and religion (relating people to the general order of existence, from which they derive ultimate meaning, belonging, and comfort). Specialized fixed forms of social life in Western societies include education and medicine (both deriving from kinship and/or religion), and the legal system and the military (both deriving from politics and/or religion). Social institutions are ways or means to the general end/goal of a meaningful, human, social existence for all group members. The specific qualities constituting a meaningful, human, social existence derive from group values.

- *Values* are qualities and quality sets shaping and directing agents and their behaviors via cues of perception, action, reaction, and the like. Core values are embedded in value objects (self, others, nature, time, space, God[s]) as well as in interactions between/among value objects. For example, in the United States, the core value in interaction is efficiency or instrumental mastery. U.S. citizens pride themselves personally on efficiency and expect it from other value objects as well. Values contribute to and largely constitute culture. *Culture* can be characterized as the set of persons, things, and events endowed with meaningfulness (valued meaning, or meaning + feeling) within some specific social system.

- *Ways of "being person":* There are two major ways of "being person" in specific social systems, perhaps falling along a spectrum. These are individualism (focus on self-reliance) and collectivism (focus on family/group integrity). Most of the world's societies are collectivistic.

Sociological theory deals with attempts to explain why human beings in groups interact as they do. There are three major and irreconcilable approaches to this "why?" question.

First, there are *structural-functional theories.* All human interaction follows repeated pathways governed by norms of behavior, perception, reaction, and so on. These are social structures consisting of statuses, roles, and norms. These structures exist for determined ends or goals, the attainment of which is their function. Every human being acts with a purpose (to fulfill needs), within the social boundaries provided by a social system. People in groups seek to have things work properly; that is, they seek equilibrium and homeostasis (often called "law and order"). Disruptions are abnormal and social system devices are in place to minimize disruptions and restore equilibrium. In this perspective, human beings interact to fulfill needs in a harmonious way (latent or obvious).

Second, there are *conflict theories.* All societies consist of interrelated social structures comprising statuses, roles, and norms, and these structures exist for determined ends or goals that favor the social elite over against the nonelite. The social elite wish to avoid change at all costs. The nonelite hope for a change in their situation. The result is constant, "normal" grievance on the part of the nonelite. The change sought by the

aggrieved to alleviate their grievance results in conflict. When the conflict is resolved, it necessarily leads to new grievance since social agents
differ from each other in statuses, roles, and other characteristics (gender, age, and abilities). In this perspective human beings interact to allay
grievances in a conflictual way (latent or obvious).

Finally, there are *symbolic theories*. Every human being acts with the
primary purpose of making sense of human existence to and with other
human beings. Human experience is socially interpreted experience. All
human interaction follows socially agreed upon pathways of behavior
judged to be meaningful in terms of socially contrived norms of behavior, perception, reaction, and so on. These are socially interpreted and
evaluated structures with their statuses, roles, and norms. These structures exist for determined ends or goals, namely, to allow the individual
and the group to make sense of their existence. Every human being acts
so as to have meaning for others and, secondarily, to have meaning for
himself or herself. The basic need of all humans is to have meaning, or
simply "to mean." According to symbolic sociological theories, human
beings interact to make sense, to *mean* to others.

As initially noted, sociology and anthropology are related. Sociology is
the study of human beings in groups in one's own society. Anthropology
(cultural/social) is the comparative study of human beings in alien groups
compared with one's own society. When the focus is on comparative
social institutions (a field developed and favored by the British), it is
called *social anthropology*; when the focus is on comparative values, value
objects, and value sets (a field developed and favored by Americans),
it is called *cultural anthropology*. In either case, however, the work is
comparative. Anthropology compares; this is its hallmark.

Culture looks to values and value orientations. The core value in the
ancient Mediterranean world was family (group) integrity. Society was
kinship focused, with value objects (self, others, nature, time, space,
God) assessed in terms of kinship concern regarding gender. Male/female
identity in specific families and locations formed the primary self-
determinant and offered a way to see the world.

Every society has social-psychological sanctions for deviance, as well
as rewards for compliance. These run the gamut from anxiety (and tran-
quility), or shame (and honor), to guilt (and innocence). Mediterranean
societies favored shame and honor, notably in a collectivistic mode.

Person types as integral parts of the social system are the concern of social psychology. Characteristics of individualists and collectivists are radically different. If the self be considered in terms of the private self (what the individual thinks of self), the public self (what society at large thinks of the individual), and the group self (what the in-group thinks of the individual), then:

- in *collectivistic society* private self and group self must coincide.
- in *individualistic society* private self and public self must coincide.

Hypocrisy in a collectivistic society is a group characteristic; in an individualistic society it is an individual characteristic. A lie in collectivistic society is nonconformity between what one thinks and what one says to the in-group. In individualistic society, a lie is nonconformity between what one thinks and what one says to any member of the public (including one's own group).

SOCIAL-SCIENTIFIC APPROACHES TO NEW TESTAMENT INTERPRETATION

Social-scientific approaches to New Testament interpretation are rooted in the insight that the people who wrote the documents in the Bible as well as the people described in those documents are all foreigners to the modern Western world. The scholarly attempt to understand foreigners on their own terms emerged with the academic disciplines of social (British) or cultural (American) anthropology, largely in the second half of the twentieth century. The application of Mediterranean anthropology to biblical documents in the last quarter of the twentieth century resulted in what might best be called *historical anthropology* (Craffert 2007).[1] The historical dimension is intended to filter out the anachronistic features that modern readers bring to their reading, while the anthropological component attempts a comparative understanding of those ancient foreigners to overcome a reader's ethnocentrism.

---

[1] *Editor's note:* This chapter of the book employs a method of citing sources widely used in social-scientific literature. Superscripted numerals are not used. Instead, an author's surname is provided in parentheses (followed sometimes by a date and/or a page number). This parenthetical reference points the reader to a source that is included in "Works Cited" given at the end of the chapter.

A first step to understanding social-scientific interpretation is to realize that all the features that have emerged in Mediterranean societies over the past two millennia did not exist for people described in the New Testament. It is well known that the majority of Bible readers today read the Gospels through the lens of the fourth-century Nicene Creed, though original readers would not have read them in this way. But there are other lenses as well: science and scientism, technology and technologism, the industrial revolution, Romanticism and individualism, the Enlightenment and rationalism, a sense of history, the separation of church and state and of bank and state, universities, Talmudic Jewishness formed in the fifth century and in the Khazar (Ashkenazi) conversion of the ninth century, Christendom and political Christianity – all these perspectives intrude on any proper understanding of the New Testament and inevitably affect assumptions about first-century biblical peoples.

Where do we begin? We may start with the observation that the social systems, cultural values and behaviors, and person types of Mediterraneans are all alien to modern Western readers. The way to access those social systems begins with a comparative understanding of *contemporary* Mediterranean people and their traditional values. Thus, we may access some of the social systems of biblical peoples through comparative analysis of villagers in Italy, Greece, Lebanon, Palestine, and Egypt (but not Israelis, since Israelis are a non-Semitic, central European people of Turkic origin). While social structures apart from kinship have often undergone "modernization," the values and behaviors of people traditional to this region have remained fairly stable.

Historical Overview of What Led to the Use of Social-Scientific Approaches

Social-scientific approaches to New Testament interpretation involve first selecting a suitable model accepted in the social-scientific community and then using that model to form adequate scenarios for directing the reading of a New Testament document. Forming adequate scenarios involves retrojecting an appropriate model to the first-century Mediterranean culture by a process of abduction while making it applicable through the use of filters that keep out anachronism and ethnocentrism.

In other words, social-scientific interpretations of the New Testament are literary and historical interpretations of biblical documents coupled with a set of explicit perspectives deriving from the social sciences. Social-scientific approaches employ a collection of appropriate generalizations and models from the social sciences in the task of the historical interpretation of biblical documents.

What makes a social-scientific generalization or model appropriate depends on social-scientific and historical judgment.

The *social-scientific judgment of appropriateness* relates to whether the behaviors in question conform to the social system of the Eastern Mediterranean cultural region, with its traditional values (e.g., gender roles and concern for honor) and social structures (e.g., kinship focus and endogamous marriage). There are some who deny that the Mediterranean forms a cultural region, but a reading of Horden and Purcell's history of the area indicates otherwise (Horden and Purcell 2000). To study comparative culture areas, the Human Relations Area File (begun by George P. Murdock, now on CD) serves very well. In that file, every society on the planet is described in terms of its institutions, values, and notable behavioral features. The fruit of such a collection has been to understand other people on their own terms through comparative generalizations. The outcome has been the awareness of culture areas, areas in which various people hold similar cultural values and modes of perception and assessment of life experiences. Murdock and his team, for example, produced a small book (Murdock 1980) in which he took 186 societies and compared them in terms of similarities and differences relative to sickening (see later). Thanks to his categorizations, he surfaced the main theories of sickness common to various groupings of these various societies. One of Murdock's unexpected conclusions was to discover a theory of illness characteristic of and distinctive to the circum-Mediterranean region, regardless of the particular histories of the distinctive ethnic or national groups:

Trial and error showed, however, that if North Africa were detached from sub-Saharan Africa and the Near East from Asia, and if both were grouped with Europe to form a composite Circum-Mediterranean region, this would yield three regions reasonably comparable not only to one another but also to each American continent and the Insular Pacific. The experimental tabulation of the incidence of the major theories of illness in these ad hoc regions led to a serendipitous discovery: the theories actually showed some tendency toward segregation by region (Murdock 1980:42).

Illness theories are replications of the interpretive themes of a culture, and common illness theories would point to common interpretive themes. Thus, Murdock shows that the Mediterranean cultural area is distinctive with regard to illness perception.

The *historical judgment of appropriateness* relates to whether generalizations and models can be shown to trace back to the *first-century* eastern Mediterranean area. To make such a historical judgment, the historian must remove the previously noted filters rooted in phases of the historical development of modern Western society. Each of these historical episodes introduced social features that, unless removed, would obfuscate an understanding of the first-century eastern Mediterranean area. With regard to illness theory, it is the judgment of Murdock that the Mediterranean's distinctive features can be traced to antiquity.

The requisite historic awareness of social features that have emerged over the past two millennia indicates that social-scientific approaches are always a form of historical study. Unlike most historians, however, scholars who use social-scientific approaches explicitly state which generalizations and models they use and why. They explicitly define the terms used in their generalizations and models, and then describe the models that undergird the generalizations. In other words, those using social-scientific approaches study the available sources with specific historical questions in mind, with a view to locating the information generated by those questions within some historically and culturally appropriate theoretical framework of concepts and hypotheses to produce intelligibility and interpretations. Most historically oriented biblical scholars proceed in the same way,

but in practice there are two main differences. The first is that the historian's conceptualization tends to be implicit, arbitrary, and unsystematic, whereas the social scientist's is explicit and systematic. The second is the historian's tendency, because his sources usually provide him with some sort of loose narrative pattern to which the facts can be related, to evade so far as possible the theoretical issues, and also to deal for preference less with the underlying structure than with events and personalities, which are usually far more sharply delineated in historical records than in the materials anthropologists and sociologists commonly use (Barraclough 50).

Social-scientific interpretations of New Testament documents are directly concerned with history, not social science. Yet as sociologist John A.
Coleman has pointed out, they have made some significant contributions
to the social sciences (Coleman 1999). At present, the use of the social
sciences in the historical enterprise of New Testament interpretation is
evident by the exegetes' use of explicit, testable, and systematic conceptualizations in place of the usual historical approaches typical of traditional
historical Jesus research rooted largely in the usually unwary adoption of
implicit, arbitrary, and unsystematic conceptualizations. Furthermore,
and most significantly, social-scientific approaches seek to set out the
underlying social structures that provided the meanings articulated in
the sources used in historical biblical interpretation.

Not surprisingly, the interpretation of documents from alien times
and cultures has always been multidisciplinary. Since the advent of the
sense of history in the eighteenth century, historically oriented biblical scholars have assumed mastery of a range of disciplines as fundamental to the toolkit of their craft. Consider the "disciplines" that are
generally brought to bear in the task of historical biblical interpretation: history (ancient, medieval, and modern), proficiency in ancient
languages (at least Hebrew, Greek, Aramaic, and Latin) and modern
languages (at least English and German – though most scholars trained
in European Catholic institutions handle Italian, Spanish, and French as
well), literary theory (ancient, medieval, and modern), theology (ancient,
medieval, and modern), and philosophy (ancient, medieval, and modern). The overall purpose of historically oriented biblical interpretation
is to discover what some ancient biblical document meant to its original
audience.

The social dimensions of human behavior became a focused center
of concern early in the twentieth century in departments of philosophy,
history, and ethics. Much confusion about social-scientific interpretation among New Testament interpreters derived from the labeling of
social philosophy or social history as sociology (see the definitions stated
previously). It seems that the source of this confusion stemmed from
the translation of a number of German works dealing with the social
philosophy and social history of early Jesus groups. The German words
soziologisch and *sozial* are often translated as "sociological." In fact both
words mean "social" and quite often have nothing to do with sociology.

(This is much like the German word *politik*, which means both policy and politics.) In any case, many works of social philosophy have been labeled "sociological" and a number of English-speaking scholars doing social history have called their work "sociological."

Be that as it may, it was around mid-twentieth century that disciplines such as sociology, cultural/social anthropology, and social psychology reached a level of institutionalization that required academic independence from other university departments. And, since the field of biblical interpretation was already drawing on such disciplines as philosophy, history, theology, and ethics, it was only a matter of time before it would draw on the "social sciences" as well. Awareness of the proliferation of field studies of foreign societies and the amassing of cross-cultural data in the social sciences made it all the more obvious that historical biblical interpretation was, indeed, a form of cross-cultural study. The distinctive systems of meaning of the various human societies referred to in the Bible derived from and maintained their distinctive social systems.

Recently, Ralph Hochschild sought to trace the course of what he calls "social historical exegesis," referring "to those scholarly investigations concerned with the history of the social world of early Christianity. Social historical exegesis analyzes the social dimensions of biblical texts from the viewpoint of their social and cultural context. It reconstructs this world and attempts to elucidate the influence of this social world on the belief and life of early Christianity, as it seeks to make this world understandable and conceivable for us today" (Hochschild 25–26).

To begin with, Hochschild divides social historical exegesis into four types, based on the different methods and intellectual interests of its practitioners: materialistic exegesis (sociology of literature, philosophical structuralism, and Marxist social theory), social descriptive exegesis (Palestinian archaeology, geography, and history of artifacts), social-scientific exegesis (sociology, cultural anthropology, and ethnology), and social kerygmatic exegesis (*Formgeschichte* [form criticism] and *Redaktionsgeschichte* [redaction criticism]).

Hochschild concludes with a summary explanation of how social questioning in New Testament exegesis emerged as a scientific enterprise, with these four perspectives marking the institutionalization of an academic discipline. The social-scientific and materialistic perspectives both utilize social-scientific models and are innovative in methodology. Social descriptive and social kerygmatic perspectives both renounce the explicit use of models and are conservative in methodology. The former interweaves social standpoints with exegesis, leaving theological data in the background. The latter adopts the developments of liberation theology, connecting with feminist exegesis. In materialist and social kerygmatic perspectives, theological interests dominate while New Testament passages are appropriated for the present. In social-scientific and social descriptive perspectives, theological interests retreat into the background, and New Testament passages are distanced from the present.

In his story of social-historical interpretation, Hochschild mentions American scholars only to the extent that they have influenced the German scene. However, as William F. Ogburn demonstrated in 1922, it is quite normal for two or more persons or groups to invent and discover new methods independently at approximately the same time, even in different parts of the world. In the U.S. version of this story, the framework is socio-rational empiricism (U.S. pragmatism), with stages marked by the pre–World War II rise of empirical (as opposed to philosophical) sociology, the emergence of cross-cultural anthropology in the 1950s, the Vietnam war period with awareness of U.S. cultural diversity, and growing interest in cross-cultural understanding. Further, a good number of U.S. scholars trained in the 1960s and presently devoted to social-scientific New Testament interpretation have lived and often taught in alien societies for extended periods. Moreover, in this period the setting and audience for New Testament research in the United States shifted away from seminaries to universities, where biblical scholars collaborated with professional colleagues in literature, ancient history, and the social sciences. The chart displayed in Fig. 5.1 has been adapted from the perspectives provided by Hochschild.

In sum, what the foregoing overview indicates is the history of the rise of social concerns in biblical interpretation. It obviously intimates the emergence of social concerns among exegetes working in these perspectives. The merit (or demerit) of social-scientific interpretation is the purposeful omission of explicit contemporary social concern, often called relevance. The whole goal of social-scientific research is the recovery of the ancient social system(s) in some comparative perspective, so as to discern what the writers said and meant to say to their audiences.

Explicit social-scientific interests
Explicit and examined models

Social-scientific exegesis based on comparative sociology, cultural anthropology, comparative social psychology, and any other cross-cultural, inductive methods. These methods make explicit the social system of the interpreter, e.g., U.S. sociology compared with other societies. Only persons in groups have a sociology – the study of human beings in groups. NT religion (and theology) is embedded in kinship and politics.	*Social-philosophical exegesis* (based on Weber and Marx) studying social groups comparatively, and with deductive methods rooted in explicit models. However, these methods usually keep the social system of the interpreter implicit; e.g., Weber's charismatic is a Teutonic type. Ideas have a "sociology," e.g., sociology of knowledge, of science, of music. Models articulated for social change in church or society. Explicit, deductive sociological models applied to the past simply reveal what past peoples would be like if they lived today, e.g., sect model, Marxist liberation theology models, economic class, and class struggle.

Distanced and   **Appropriated and**
strange for _____ **recontextualized**
today   **for today**

Social-historical exegesis (i.e., nonpolitical history, history of the past not focused on elites and wars). Thus narrative descriptions of peasants, their families, behavior, roles, etc., invariably drawn up on the basis of the historian's implicit models of how the ancients thought their societies worked. Interweaves social topics with exegesis, leaving theological data in the background. Often such history is ethnocentric and anachronistic, even if interesting.	*Social kerygmatic exegesis*: Twentieth century – geschichte, *Formgeschichte, Traditionsgeschichte*, and *Redaktionsgeschichte*, usually appropriated and recontextualized for ecclesiastic (church) purposes. Theological interests dominate, while NT interpretations are often ethnocentric and anachronistic, but quite relevant and appropriated to the present.

Explicit "social" concern
Implicit and unexamined models

5.1. Models for Varieties of Social Exegesis.

Presuppositions of Social-Scientific Approaches

The fundamental presuppositions of social-scientific approaches deal with belaboring the obvious yet often overlooked features of New Testament interpretation. The first fact is that New Testament study is rooted in the act of reading ancient documents written in ancient languages for ancient audiences. The first question, then, is how do languages work? Then, how do readers read? And, finally, to what sort of audiences were

the documents directed? These questions incidentally entail considerations of social systems and reflections on how understanding of the
ancient documents in question emerge.

HOW LANGUAGES WORK? The study of language in use is called sociolinguistics. The advent of sociolinguistics (another new tool in the
interpreter's toolkit) made it more than clear that language is a trilevel
affair. At its most concrete, language consisted of soundings and markings that consisted of somewhat abstract patterns called wordings (e.g.,
words, sentences, short pieces of language called paragraphs, syntactical
patterns, and the like). Thus, meaning is expressed in rather abstract
patterns of language (wordings) realized concretely in patterns of soundings (speech) and markings (writing). Sociolinguists insisted that the
meanings expressed in the patterns (wordings) and realized in the soundings and markings derive from the social system of the speaker. When
prospective hearers share the same social system as the speaker, they
can understand each other. If each shared a different social system, they
would either misunderstand or not understand each other.

In sum, language is a trilevel affair: concretely, language is squiggles
or sounds, put into patterned sequences called wordings. Wordings then
mediate meanings that come from the social system of the speakers/
hearers and writers/readers. The basic unit of language is a text, defined
as a meaningful configuration of language intended to communicate. In
New Testament studies, the texts in question are the whole "books" being
studied. In this particular study, the text is the anonymous work known
as the Gospel of Matthew. To realize his text, the writer of Matthew
used sentences to express thoughts, ideas, and concepts. When readers
share the same social system as the writer of Matthew, mutual understanding of his text is possible. Otherwise, the result is misunderstanding or nonunderstanding. This leads to a reflection on how reading
works.

HOW READING WORKS? Experimental psychologists have conducted a
battery of tests to investigate how individuals actually read. The outcome
in general is that what one brings to one's reading is far more significant
than what one presumably reads out of some document. Accordingly,
to be a considerate reader of ancient documents, one must bring to

one's reading a range of scenarios rooted in the social system of the writer/audience of the document to be read.

A fundamental presupposition of social-scientific approaches is that since the meaning of language derives from the social system of the speaker or writer, a mere knowledge of Hebrew, Aramaic, or Greek wording offers no direct access to the social systems that purvey the meanings mediated by those languages in the daily interactions of ancient speakers. Reading is a process through which a reader brings his or her understanding of how reality works to a document through which a writer attempts to reshape or manipulate the reader's understanding of a segment of the real world. Concretely, a reader comes with sets of scenarios based on his or her experience of reality to a reading interaction in which a writer reshapes the scenarios to provide new information, insight, or understanding. Such scenarios consist of scenes, schemes, and models of how and why people and things work the way they do.

This model of reading squiggles that encode wordings which realize meaning from a social system is not too different from the social psychology model of how human beings "read" situations. All human beings carry on an interpretive enterprise. As a rule, people carry in their heads one or more models of "society" and "human being" that greatly influence what they look for in their experiences, what they actually see, and what they eventually do with their observations by way of fitting them into a larger scheme of explanation. In this respect, every human being, tutored or not, is no different from any trained observer in our society (Garfinkel 262–83). For example, every scientist, like every other human being, holds some general conception of the realm in which he or she is working, that is, some mental picture of how it is put together, how it works, and how one ought to feel about it. Of course, the same is true for the biblical interpreter, professional and nonprofessional. Such general conceptions form the consensus reality of the society in which a given group of people are socialized.

The scenario model of reading begins with the fact that nearly every adult reader has an adequate and socially verifiable grasp of how the experienced world works. As readers, people bring this awareness to a text or text segment. In the linguistic interchange that is reading, a writer is allowed to present some distinctive sets of scenarios of the working world that in effect suggest and motivate the reader to rearrange the scenarios that he or she brings to the reading. Effective communication depends on the considerateness of the writer or speaker. Considerate writers attempt to understand their readers. As a result of such understanding, considerate writers will take up the scenarios shared by their readers and elaborate them. Beyond this, considerate writers will make an effort to develop scenarios by beginning with what the reader knows and coupling this to the new, unknown features they wish to impart to readers and hearers. This is the "given-new contract" that constrains a writer to consider what is "given" (what the reader knows or does not know) before presenting new information.

Judged by such standards the writer of Matthew and biblical writers in general "violate the contract" and are all inconsiderate from our perspective. They neither begin with what we moderns know about the world nor make any attempt to explain their ancient world in terms of scenarios that we might understand based on contemporary experience. The writer of Matthew presumes that his readers/hearers are first-century eastern Mediterraneans, sharing a social system poised on honor and shame, fully aware of what it means to live in a first-century city or village, totally immersed in a sick care system concerned with the well-being of unfortunates, believing in limited good assuaged by patrons and brokers, and the like. Given the fact that Matthew is a first-century work rooted in a specific time and place, it would be rather silly to expect the writer of that document to envision readers two thousand years removed. Hence it falls to *us* to close the gap by becoming *considerate readers*. The considerate reader of documents from the past will make the effort to bring to his or her reading a set of scenarios proper to the time, place, and culture of the biblical writer. The scholarly articulation of such scenarios has been the metier of social scientists.

In sum, a considerate reader is required to perform two tasks: (1) call to mind some appropriate scene, scheme, or model as suggested by the text and (2) then use the identified scene, scheme, or model as the larger frame within which to situate the meanings proposed in the text as far as this is possible. The reader uses the text and its segments to identify an appropriate domain or frame of reference and then rearranges that domain according to the arrangements suggested in the text being read. This larger appropriate domain or frame of reference is the social system or a segment of the social system. When readers and writers share the same social system, understanding is possible. However, when readers and writers live in different social systems, the act of reading (or speaking) most often results in misunderstanding or nonunderstanding.

HOW GENERAL SOCIAL CONTEXT WORKS? The perspectives produced by scenarios as described previously are rather crucial to any reading of the New Testament since these documents all derive from what Edward T. Hall has called high-context cultures (Hall 1976). *High-context societies* produce sketchy and impressionistic texts, leaving much to the reader's or hearer's imagination. In a high-context society, people believe few things have to be spelled out, and so few things are in fact spelled out. This is so because people have been socialized into shared ways of perceiving and acting. Hence, much can be assumed. People presume, for example, that helping out a person in dire need makes that person obligated for the rest of his or her life to the helper. There simply is no need to spell out all these obligations, as we would when we sign for a car loan. In high-context societies, little new information is necessary for meaning to be constant. Hall lists the Mediterranean, among other areas, as a region populated with high-context societies. Clearly the Bible along with other writings from ancient Mediterranean peoples fit this high-context profile.

Low-context societies produce detailed texts, spelling out as much as conceivably possible, leaving little to the imagination. The general norm is that most things must be clearly articulated; hence, information must be continually added if meaning is to be constant. Such societies are fine-print societies, societies "of law" where every dimension of life must be described by legislators to make things "lawful," even including, for example, detailed legal directions about how much fat is allowed in commercially sold sausage. The *Congressional Record* offers hours of low-context reading for whoever might wish to be entertained in this way. Hall considers the United States and northern European countries as typically low-context societies.

How different, then, it is for low-context, Western readers to read a high-context text such as Matthew's Gospel? Attuned to detail, they simply do not know what is assumed in a high-context society. Again, it is the purpose of social-scientific models to fill in the assumptions of the high-context writers, assumptions that the writer shared with high-context readers of his Mediterranean society.

It will help us understand Hall's observations about high- and low-context societies if we attend to their respective communication problems. The typical communication problem in low-context societies such as the U.S. is giving people information they do not need, hence "talking down" to them by spelling out absolutely everything. In contrast, the typical communication problem in high-context societies is not giving people enough information, hence "mystifying" them if they are outsiders. The parables of Jesus are a prime example.

HOW TO MAKE GENERALIZATIONS WHILE READING? The academic discipline of history attempts to span the temporal gap tracing our times to the past. The academic disciplines of social and cultural anthropology attempt the comparative study of contemporary social systems and, when outfitted with a historical lens, attempt the comparative study of a modern, contemporary social system and that of some ancient people. It is with lenses that might be called anthropological history that social-scientific researchers attempt to understand the very ancient and truly foreign documents in the New Testament and explain these documents to their modern contemporaries.

The procedure is circular, a process of reasoning called *abduction*. One begins by postulating some model (e.g., patron–client relations in the modern Mediterranean); then, one accumulates data from the New Testament to see whether the postulated model can cover most instances; finally, one formulates a hypothesis – in this instance, that the ancient Mediterraneans described in the New Testament documents practiced patron–client behaviors. The hypothesized model then serves as a lens for assessing further instances of the behavior in question. Gradually a number of such models are clustered together to form sets of scenarios to provide a picture of social systems relevant to the time and place of the New Testament. This collection of scenarios allows for the formation of polythetic models, in which features are catalogued under the same rubric.

Scholars using social-scientific methods have uncovered a number of models typical of first-century Mediterranean social systems. Some of the more prominent ones are kinship types, patronage, benefaction, hospitality, group development, embedded religion and/or economics, significance of money, perceptions of limited good, antilanguage, antisociety, alternate states of consciousness, person types, envy and the evil eye, gender division of society, challenge and riposte, and basic value orientations, for example, honor and shame. These scholars have also surfaced a number of terms in general use by historians who are, in fact, totally anachronistic: supernatural, miracle, religion, Jew, Christian, author, and the like.

In sum, the scenario model has empirical evidence to support it. It attends to meanings, not just wordings. And so, only the scenario model can avoid problems of ethnocentric or inconsiderate reading of texts. It alone takes into account the social dimensions of reading: the interpersonal dimension, whose strategy is explained by sociolinguistics. Given the way reading works, the goal of social-scientific methods is to provide the interpreter with sets of scenarios to enable a considerate reading of biblical documents. The development of such scenarios involves a sense of history with knowledge of history in order to eliminate anachronism. It likewise entails a knowledge of one's own social system as well as that of the ancient Mediterranean. Such knowledge is the metier of social/cultural anthropology, and the development of adequate scenarios for reading first-century documents is a type of historical anthropology.

GENERALIZATIONS FOR READING MATTHEW
IN SOCIAL-SCIENTIFIC PERSPECTIVE

We may now offer a number of simple historical observations of rather great significance for interpretation of the New Testament, including the Gospel of Matthew.

1. The social institutions known as religion and economics did not exist as discrete, self-standing, independent institutions in antiquity. In antiquity, there were only two focal, freestanding social institutions: kinship and politics. Economics and religion were embedded in kinship and politics, yielding domestic economy, domestic religion, political economy, and political religion. Religion, therefore, is always articulated in terms of the kinship and/or political institution. The "kingdom of Heaven," for instance, should be regarded as a political-religious theocracy. There was no notion that separated church and state (or, for that matter, that separated bank/market and state). This separation took place in the eighteenth century.

2. Mediterranean society was a society of subsistence economy, with focus on the present and a daily concern for obtaining daily needs. Anthropological history reveals that for human beings to develop a future orientation, they must have all their present needs more or less guaranteed. Food, clothing, and shelter must be easily available in the society; otherwise future or forward planning becomes impossible. Such ready availability of basic resources emerged with the economy of abundance in the late eighteenth century. In the ancient Mediterranean world, the future was not conceived in abstract terms, but in terms of actual experiences of what was forthcoming: pregnancy leads to childbirth; plowing and planting lead to harvest. Thus, people in subsistence economies are said to be present oriented, with the indefinite future (like the indefinite past) belonging to God alone. The modern concept of "eschatology" (a product of eighteenth-century thought) would make no sense to them. There could be no "delay of the parousia" (for example), since "on time" was, by definition, whenever the most important person arrives for some event.

3. There were no authors in the ancient world. The category of "author," as an individual who reveals his or her thoughts in self-expressive creative works, emerged only in the eighteenth century. In antiquity, written documents of whatever sort were produced by writers. If the documents filled readers/hearers with awe or enthusiasm or some other significant emotion, this was attributed to the Muses, to some deity, or to God, any of whom might be said to "inspire" the writing. Thus, it is historically anachronistic to speak of biblical writers as "authors." In antiquity, the word "author" referred to a person who stood as the source or beginning of some human experience (see "source of life" in Acts 3:15; Heb. 2:10, 12:2).

4. As noted at the outset, the person types of antiquity were collectivistic, with group goals and group expectations primary. There were individuals in antiquity, but these individuals were not individualistic, with self-determined goals or with expectations of standing on their own two feet. People were collectivistic, more concerned with group integrity than with individualistic self-realization. The very concept of self-interest had more to do with the concerns of one's in-group than with one's individual concerns. Equally, there was no individualistic introspection in antiquity. People were anti-introspective and not psychologically

minded. Concern for the subjective, the psychological, the introspective emerged with the rise of Romanticism in the nineteenth century.

5. People who might seem individualistic to modern readers were individuals at the top of the social hierarchy where there were narcissistically impelled individuals, as well as those at the bottom of the social hierarchy who where isolated, cut off from any group support. By modern standards such persons were pseudo-individualistic.

6. There was no sense of history in antiquity. A sense of history is an awareness that the past is qualitatively different from the present, not merely different in the sense that it occurred previously. The ancients believed that the past and present were simply of the same quality; persons were expected to live up to the past. Stories about the past could and must serve as norm and teacher for the present. This is decidedly different from the modern view that the present need not imitate the past.

7. The general view, furthermore, was not simply that the present was like the past, but that the present offers every indication of devolution. Things are getting worse day by day; crops are less year by year; children are smaller than their parents generation by generation.

8. The sky above, the land below, and the denizens of both form a single social environment. There was no distinction between nature and supernature, natural and supernatural. All entities acted according to their nature, from God down. Hence God's actions were as natural for God as human's actions were natural for humans. Categories such as miracle or supernatural would be misplaced in the first-century Mediterranean world.

9. The facts that Christendom arose in the fourth century with Constantine and that Jewishness emerged with the Talmud in the fifth century indicate that there were no Jews or Christians in the New Testament period. Meanings come from social systems, and social systems that articulate Christianity and Jewishness recognizable today emerged first in the fourth and fifth centuries. Thus, there were no Christians or Jews in the New Testament period in any sense that might be known from modern experience. Jesus was not what we today would call a Jew and neither was Paul, since there were no Jews in any modern, recognizable sense in the first century. The same is true of the label "Christian." The meanings that we ascribe to these terms come from social systems (Elliott).

10. Some general cues of perception include the following:

- All goods are limited. Every social interaction outside the group is a win/lose interaction.
- All persons are perceived in terms of in-group/out-group (for/against, either/or, true/false).
- Conscience is group perception; it lies outside the psyche of the individual.
- Individuals are defined stereotypically in terms of genealogy, geography, and gender (kin group, location of origin, gender).
- Every effect that counts is caused by a person, visible or nonvisible (not by some adequate cause). When some significant effect occurs, the question it evokes is "who did it?" (not "what did it?").

11. Israelite society had the political religion of the temple and its sacrificial and calendric Levitical norms that traced back to its ancestors. But in the home, the domestic religion was *ancestrism*. Since kinship was in fact the focal social institution, Israelite ancestrism was the focal domestic religious expression.

Let us develop this last point further. Ancestrism refers to reverence for those persons who have preceded us in our family and/or fictive family. Some call this *memorialism*. Such reverence is realized by activities that honor those to whom we effectively owe our existence and continued well-being. Israel's Passover is an instance of domestic religious ancestor reverence. The God of Israel is in fact an ancestral God: "the God of Abraham, Isaac and Jacob," and/or "the one who raised Jesus from the dead." A strong, positive ancestral cult is more likely to be found in a society where the father–son relationship is dominant (as in the ancient Mediterranean) than in one where the husband–wife dyad is dominant (as in modern Western societies). In Mediterranean antiquity, the virtue of religion (=*eusebeia*) dealt with willingness to show respect and to give honor to those who have given and/or maintained our existence in society: God, king, ancestors, parents. One was expected to reverence (worship) ancestral deities (God of Abraham, Isaac, and Jacob) and to observe ancestral tradition (Matt. 15:2, 3, 6; Mark 7:3–5, 8–9, 13; 1 Cor. 11:2; Gal. 1:14; Col. 2:8; 2 Thess. 2:1, 3:6).

In the Mediterranean world, ancestrism is an essential expression of the kinship system and of society in general. The father–son dyad so

prominent in that tradition exhibits social continuity, group inclusive-
ness, paternal authority, and asexuality. These values express an approach
to life characterized by maintenance of ties with the past, close links
between generations, high value accorded to age, the normality of intervention by elders in the affairs of younger members, duties and obligations between superiors and subordinates, and strong, positive ancestor
reverence. When it comes to spirit beliefs, the father–son dyad normally
attests to benevolent and rewarding ancestral spirits and deity. Societies in
which a husband–wife dyad is dominant are characterized by an absence
or inactivity of spirits and deity in daily life.

For evidence of ancestrism in the New Testament, note Matthew's
proverb: "No one knows a son except a father, and no one knows a father
except a son and any one to whom a son chooses to reveal him" (Matt.
11:27). The ancestral God of Israel is benevolent and just, rewarding,
and punishing. Ancestor Abraham (noted seventy-three times in New
Testament) receives the dead, rejoices with his offspring, is source of
merit for all his offspring, is the recipient of God's promises for his
offspring, and the like. In Matthew's story, Jesus is most concerned about
the House of Israel, his in-group (10:5, 15:24). A social in-group is a
collection of individuals who see themselves as members of the same
social category, sharing emotional involvement with others in the group
and having a common evaluation of their group and of their membership
in it.

Those not in the house of Israel were seen as out-groups. A social out-
group is a collection of individuals who are perceived to be members of a
different social category, to share some emotional involvement in some
common definition of themselves, and to have in common a number of
negatively evaluated traits typical of the group and of its membership.

Note here that subsequent Jesus groups held Jesus as the focal ancestor
of their fictive kin group: the Lord's Supper is an ancestral remembrance,
in "remembrance of me" (Luke 22:19; 1 Cor. 11:24; Justin, Apol. 1.66.3).
Jesus abides with his own: "For where two or three are gathered in my
name, there am I in the midst of them" (Matt. 18:20); "I am with you
all days" (Matt. 28:20); actions are done in his name (Acts 2:38, 3:6, 4:18,
5:40, 8:16, 9:27–29, 10:48, 16:18, 19:5, 26:9; 1 Cor. 1:13, 5:4, 6:11; Eph. 5:20;
Col. 3:17; 2 Thess. 3:6; James 5:10, 14; 1 John 3:23, 5:13). Those "in Christ"
formed an in-group and those not "in Christ" formed out-groups.

Cognitive in-group/out-group labels are intended to create a master status, a process often called "role engulfment." A person is expected to be caught up in the role indicated by the group label and to live out the demands of that role in face of any competing labels and roles. In the New Testament, this means to become and act like a consistent "in Christ" person. The roles, status, goals, and values of the kinship system were contextualized to fit the roles, statuses, goals, and values of brothers and sisters "in Christ." The father–son patterns of subjection prevailed, although group members were to subject themselves to each other "in Christ."

SOCIAL-SCIENTIFIC APPROACHES: INTERPRETATION OF MATTHEW 8:11–14

The specific dimensions of the social system of antiquity that Matthew 8:11–14 calls to mind are scenarios dealing with holy man, centurion and the military institution, and the healing system.

Jesus as a First-Century Holy Man

In Israel, a holy man is a person called by the God of Israel with a view to intimacy with the spirit world, endowed with the abilities to enter the spirit world without fear of possession, to take sky journeys, and to heal people. This is the general definition of a shaman, although the word is decried for its Siberian specificity. Yet holy man (hagios) in New Testament times was also culturally specific. The paradigmatic Israelite holy man was Elijah, replicated in John the Baptist (see Matt. 16:14). One of the first titles ascribed to Jesus of Nazareth in the Gospel tradition is "holy man." The demon in the synagogue at Capernaum shouted out: "I know who you are, the Holy Man of God" (Mark 1:24).

In all cultures, a holy person (man/woman) is characterized by two qualities. This person has ready and facile access to the realm of the deity, that is, to God and the spirit world; such a person has experiential familiarity with this realm. Second, this person brokers favors from that world to this one, favors that often include life-shaping information but most especially healing. In all cultures, the holy person is primarily a spirit-filled ecstatic healer.

Anthropologists identify six steps across all cultures in a person's call and initiation into being a holy person. Adapting these steps to the biblical world and to a contemporary believer's life is enlightening and challenging. The obvious first step is that the spirit world makes contact with the candidate. This can take the form of adoption or possession. In the life of Jesus, this contact took place at his baptism: "You are my Beloved Son; with you I am well pleased" (Mark 1:11). Related to this contact, of course, is that the spirit identifies self (second step). In the case of Jesus, since he is called son, the contact is from his father in the realm of God.

This, of course, is just the beginning. The holy person must now acquire the necessary ritual skills in dealing with the spirit world (third step). Jesus demonstrates this skill especially in the experience of his testing (Mark 1:12–13//Matt. 4:1–11//Luke 4:1–13). While traditionally called "the temptations of Jesus," they are strictly speaking not temptations. Moreover, since no other human being experiences such challenges (e.g., turn stone into bread), they are not intended to be imitated. Within the Gospel story, the point is that the compliment paid to Jesus at his baptism must be tested. Is he really beloved? Will he remain loyal to his father if he is tested? Thus, the next experience is that Jesus's loyalty is put to the test by a spirit. The test is cast in a form very familiar in daily Middle Eastern life: challenge and riposte. If a person is challenged, that person must respond like an expert in fencing (riposte), with a quick and winning thrust. Jesus demonstrates his mastery of this skill. It was likely not impromptu. He has been preparing for this moment, this kind of showdown, by honing his skills. The outcome is success. He defeats the spirit and is not defeated by the spirit.

How did Jesus acquire these skills? They were not innate. Like every human being on the planet, Jesus needed a teacher (fourth step). Like holy persons, Jesus would be tutored by both a spirit and a real-life teacher. Mark notes that after the test of Jesus's loyalty, "angels waited on him" (1:12). While scholars believe this means that angels fed him (see 1 Kings 19:1–8; Life of Adam and Eve 4:2), in the perspective we are taking here, the angels could well have been tutoring Jesus. Anthropologists would recognize them as "spirit guides" or spirit teachers. As for a real-life teacher, we need to look no further than John the Baptist, whose disciple Jesus was for a while (John 3:22–24). The holy man John the Baptist undoubtedly taught Jesus the requisite skills.

The fifth step is to develop a growing familiarity with the possessing/adopting spirit. In the life of Jesus, this is evident in the event called the Transfiguration (Mark 9:2–10/Matt. 17:1–9/Luke 9:28–36). This experience took place in an alternate state of consciousness (ASC). Human beings of all times and cultures routinely move in and out of different levels of consciousness (e.g., daydreaming, sleeping, and the like). In the biblical tradition, ASC trance visions and dreaming are God's favored medium for communicating with human beings (Jer. 1; Isa. 6; Ezek.; Matt. 1–2). At the Transfiguration, God assures Jesus in his ASC of the divine mission entrusted to him. God informs the disciples in their ASC of Jesus's importance: listen to him . . . more than Moses (the Law) and Elijah (the Prophets). The final step in becoming a holy person is to enjoy ongoing ASC experiences. This is certainly evident in the career of Jesus. The Father reveals things to Jesus (Matt. 11:25–27). Jesus is certain God hears him always (John 11:41–42). Jesus communicates with God often (John 12:27–30).

Mention of the spirit world, of demon possession, and of sky journeys may make the modern Bible reader think the world of first-century Palestine was a world quite different from our own: it must have been a magical world in order for so many people to believe in angels, demons, transmigrating spirits, dreams, the impact of living stars and planets, spirit-travel to upper or lower worlds, the evil eye, spirit-caused maladies, spirit possession, and the like. On the other hand, some Bible readers and their nonbelieving contemporaries may simply dismiss such a world out of hand as unworthy of credence for those who favor a "scientific" interpretation of the world. The Bible came from people whose alien beliefs and practices were simply deluded, wrong, confused, irrational, misinformed, or superstitious. But *another* approach is to take an anthropological comparative viewpoint and judge that the perceptions of the ancients were in some important sense real and objective. If we only understood the meaning of those concepts properly and learned how the ancients applied them to their experience, we too would experience events that can be interpreted using those categories – events rightly linked to ghosts, demons, witches, and spirits.

To say this is to acknowledge the existence of multiple cultural realities with divergent rationalities. The world is populated by groups of people who live in different realities. Recognizing this allows us to consider a few features of our world.

First, "how the world is" or "what reality is like" will always be, in part, subject dependent. Objectivity is culturally tutored subjectivity.

Second, in all cultural systems, a distinction is made between what is real and what is unreal, although the same distinction does not hold for every system. Therefore, in one system, spirits and demons or the evil eye would be real for cultural insiders but not for outsiders. So, do such phenomena objectively exist or not? The answer, of course, is "Yes."

Third, within each cultural system there is a consensus reality. A consensus reality is the culturally normal reality, namely that aspect or dimension of reality of which a person is most commonly aware most of the time. In consensus reality there exist many things, called intentional objects, that are real though not necessarily objective (e.g., racism and racial superiority).

Fourth, cultural systems do not all follow the same methods for obtaining reliable knowledge about the world. In some cultural systems, a variety of experiences, known as alternate states of consciousness (e.g., dreams and intuitions), provide what people take to be reliable knowledge about the world.

Finally, within each cultural system, beliefs and experiences mutually confirm and support each other. Within the framework of reliable meaning into which people are enculturated, they experience the entities that they believe in and they believe in the entities that they experience.

What these points indicate is that no cultural system exhausts the range of human experiences in the world. Further, apart from ethnocentrism, it is no longer possible to assume that everyone is talking about the same consensus reality. For Bible interpreters, this means that one must make the effort to avoid the "myth of realism" (Tonkin 1990:25), that is, the belief that any text we read always refers to realities in our world, ethnocentrically defined as "the" world.

Jesus as holy man healed people of their maladies. What will it look like if Jesus's healing activities were viewed as first-century Mediterranean cultural reality? All the passages describing healings will be taken as reports about a reality culturally conceived and containing entities culturally interpreted. The scenarios described by the Gospel writers imparted culturally reliable knowledge based on the prevailing consensus realities.

The holy man is an expert in entering ASC and can lead others to do the same as well. Examples of such ASC experiences in Matthew include, for Jesus, his baptism and testing by Satan, and for the disciples, Jesus walking on the sea, the transfiguration of Jesus, and experiences of the risen Jesus.

To understand this phenomenon, some clarification is necessary. First, the terminology. *Consciousness* is the "totality . . . of sensations, perceptions, ideas, attitudes, and feelings of which an individual or a group is aware at any given time or within a given time span." The apparent continuity of consciousness that exists in everyday normal awareness is in fact "a precarious illusion that is only made possible by the associative connections that exist between related bits of conversation, task orientation, etc." (Rossi 1986:111, quoting Milton Erikson).

ASCs are "conditions in which sensations, perceptions, cognition, and emotions are altered. They are characterized by changes in sensing, perceiving, thinking, and feeling. They modify the relation of the individual to the self, body, sense of identity, and the environment of time, space, or other people" (Bourguignon 1979:236). The presumption is that reality consists of two parts: culturally normal or "consensus" reality; and alternate or "nonconsensus" reality. Culturally normal or "consensus reality" is that aspect or dimension of reality of which a person is most commonly aware most of the time. Alternate or "nonconsensus" reality is that aspect of reality that is counted as not normal. For example, Krippner enumerated twenty states of consciousness: dreaming, sleeping, hypnagogic (drowsiness before sleep), hypnopompic (semiconsciousness preceding waking), hyperalert, lethargic, rapture, hysteric, fragmentation, regressive, meditative, trance, reverie, daydreaming, internal scanning, stupor, coma, stored memory, expanded consciousness, and "normal" (Krippner 1972).

In a number of cultures (90 percent of the 488 in the Human Relations Area Files studied by Bourguignon) alternate or nonconsensus reality likewise describes that dimension of reality in which the deity and spirits reside, which human beings from culturally "normal" reality can sometimes visit in an ecstatic trance (variously called "sky journey" or "soul loss" and the like), and to which people go when they die. Among these were Ancient Egyptian, Greek, Hebrew, and forty-one other circum-Mediterranean societies. Why do some recent societies appear to lack these latter ASC experiences? "Only the modern, secular West seems to have blocked an individual's access to these otherwise pan-human dimensions of the self" (Kleinman 1988:50). When science in the seventeenth century disrupted the bio-psycho-spiritual unity of human consciousness that had existed until then, Westerners developed an "acquired consciousness" whereby they could dissociate the self and look at the self "objectively." This metaself does not allow the total absorption in lived experience that is the very essence of highly focused ASCs. The basis for the pan-human potential lies in the human nervous system, as Clottes and Lewis-Williams (1996) argue.

The point is that people in the first-century Mediterranean were enculturated into a social system that included a consensus reality in which ASCs were normal, where holy man healed and had ready access to alternate reality and the world of spirits, where there was no "supernatural," since God and gods, spirits and demons, angels and stars all acted naturally, according to their nature.

Centurion and the Military Institution

The second person who figures prominently in Matthew 8:11–14 is the centurion. The high-context reference would have us understand that he was an officer in the Roman legion, in charge of a garrison in Capernaum. If ordinary people in the Eastern Mediterranean knew about Rome and Romans through the Roman commander in chiefdom (this is what empire means), it was through the presence of the Roman military.

So what is the military? How does it function? As a social institution, the military is a set of symbols. Military symbols, just as symbols in all institutions, adhere in persons, groups, things, time, space, and God.

As an institution, the military is a system of symbols that acts to establish powerful, pervasive, and long-lasting moods and motivations in people, formulating conceptions of power expended for effective collective action and clothing these conceptions with such an aura of factuality that the moods and motivations are perceived to be uniquely realistic.

As a *system of symbols* it is a set of interrelated parts arrayed in hierarchical structure. The symbols are attached to persons and objects invested with power. Power is a generalized symbolic medium of social interaction that has physical force as its sanction. As a generalized symbolic medium, power can be inflated (lots of troops working ineffectively) or deflated (few troops working effectively). For example, the United States in Iraq had inflated power; troops under Saddam Hussein had deflated power.

As a subset of the political institution, the purpose of this power is effective collective action as determined by those wielding political authority. The military deals with power clothed with an aura of factuality that exists so long as it is recognized by others. The appurtenances of the military – uniforms and arms – are meant to symbolize the sanction of power, that is, physical force.

As noted, the military is a subinstitution of the political institution. The political institution looks to effective collective action. Central personages in the institution are legitimate officeholders endowed with authority (acknowledged institutional ability to control the behavior of others). To guarantee and support the decisions and directives of legitimate authorities on behalf of effective collective action, political systems have the military to ensure that the decisions and directives of legitimate authorities are carried out.

Military might be, or force is, employed as negative sanction for noncompliance with commands of legitimate authority. This subinstitution serves as agent for authorized violence (offensive and defensive) on behalf of legitimate authorities. The military may be simple or complex in organization and function. A simple military deals with both internal and external affairs. A complex military has one or more set(s) to deal with internal affairs and another (or others) to deal with external affairs.

The goal of effective collective action varies, depending on the political system. In democracies (whether socialist or market), effective collective action is focused on behalf of all the citizenry. In aristocracy and plutocracy (e.g., the United States), effective collective action is focused on behalf of the elites and their goals. In dictatorships (whether imperial or local), effective collective action is focused on behalf of the dictator and members of his apparatus.

The ethnicity of the centurion of Capernaum is not specified. Most interpreters take him to be a Roman, and they then read Matthew 8:10–11 as words referring to a non-Israelite. The reason for this is that historians such as M. Goodman claim that "there is a striking lack of evidence for Jews joining the Roman army voluntarily," probably because they objected to the requirement to participate in the pagan religious ceremonies, especially sacrifice to the military standards, which were normal for Roman troops as demonstration of their loyalty to their commander-in-chief, the emperor. Josephus reports several Roman governors taking seriously a claim by the Hasmonean ruler Hyrcanus II in 43 B.C.E that Jews "cannot undertake military service because they may not bear arms or march on the days of the Sabbath; nor can they obtain the native foods to which they are accustomed" (Goodman 117, citing Josephus, *Antiquities* 14.226–27). Goodman fails to note, however, that the famous Israelite governor of Alexandria (and later Palestine) Tiberius Julius Alexander was the nephew of the equally well-known Israelite of Alexandria, Philo, and was a significant Roman political figure in his own right (see Josephus, *War* 2.487). Safrai and Stern also note the following: four thousand Judeans of military age were dispatched from Rome to Sardinia in C.E. 19 (p. 119); Judean military settlers were sent by the Ptolemies to Cyrene and Egypt, and by Antiochus III to Phrygia and Lydia (p. 134); in Judea, the main Roman auxiliary forces were from Sebaste and Caesarea – the Sebaste force served as Herod's army (p. 326); Herod settled Israelite Roman military veterans from Babylon in Galilee, who also served in the Herodian family army in the north (p. 329).[2]

First-Century Mediterranean Healing System

Relative to well-being and sickening, the basic Israelite belief was that God sent both (Exod. 15:26; Lev. 26). God was the one and only healer. With

[2] For more on Israelites in the Roman legions, see J. P. Roth, "Jewish Military Forces in the Roman Service" (paper delivered November 23, 2004, San Antonio, TX, at the annual meeting of the Society of Biblical Literature); M. Speidel, "Roman Army in Judaea under the Procurators," *Ancient Society* 13/14 (1982/83): 233–40; A. J. Schoenfeld, "Sons of Israel in Caesar's Service: Jewish Soldiers in the Roman Military," *Shofar* 24/3 (2006): 115–26; R. Scharf, "Regii Emeseni Iudaei: Bemerkungen zu einer spätantiken Truppe," *Latomus* 56/2 (1997): 343–59; D. Woods, "A Note Concerning the Regii Emeseni Iudaei," *Latomus* 51 (1992): 404–7.

the spread of Greek culture following Alexander the Great's conquests, Israelites had to wrestle with the idea that some human beings claimed to have an ability to heal. This struggle is evident in the reflections of Ben Sira (Sir. 38:1–15) on (Greek) healers (anachronistically called physicians in many translations). While this Sage repeats the traditional belief that God is still the one and only healer (Sir. 38:9), he advises consulting human healers to whom God has surely imparted relevant insight (Sir. 38:2a). Thus, in the Israelite tradition, a healer was a broker of God's healing, and Jesus as a healer ought to be understood as someone who brokers healing from God to sick people (John 9:3). When the passive voice occurs in New Testament healing reports, the subject of the activity is God. For example, when the text reports that Jesus said to a man with a skin problem, "Be made clean!" and the man "was made clean" (Mark 1:41–42), the meaning is "he was made clean *by God* (of course)." Likewise, in Matthew 8:13, the passive verbs "be it done" and "he was healed" point to God, the patron, as the agency of healing. Jesus is the intermediary, the broker. The sick person is the client and beneficiary of God's healing.

Ben Sira's reflections on healers is often interpreted as referring to "professional" healers. This word is also anachronistic since "profession" at the present time is ill-defined and often used solely to invoke prestige. The "profession" of medicine as known in the contemporary world came into existence only within the last one hundred and fifty years (Freidson 1970). In the ancient Greco-Roman world, the so-called "professional" healers were actually philosopher types.

Prior to van Leeuwonhoek's microscope (1674), it would have been impossible to know about germs and viruses, the major causes of sickness, so healers essentially reflected on presenting symptoms (Horstmanshoff 1990) (e.g., Mark 5:5, sick man howling and bruising himself with stones; Matt. 17:14, moon-struck young man falls into fire and into water). We cannot even be certain that blindness or paralysis (as in Matt. 8:11) in antiquity describes the same reality we know today.

Healing by holy men, by persons who were not "professionals," falls into the category recognized by social scientists as "folk healers," ordinary people in every culture who know the folk wisdom and utilize folk remedies to help sick people. Jesus the holy man healer is best understood as a folk healer in his culture. Some folk techniques that Jesus used were laying on hands (or touching the sick person; Mark 1:41), using spittle (Mark 8:23) or mud (John 9:6), pronouncing powerful words ("talitha cum" Mark 5:41; "ephphatha" Mark 7:34).

One final piece of information is necessary to understand Jesus as healer. What does healing mean? What does a healer do? Medical anthropologists provide us with answers to these questions and a very helpful set of definitions for understanding the healing activity of the Mediterranean holy man, Jesus. To begin with, *well-being* is that human experience in which everything goes well: the family is fine, the finances are in order, and so forth. Loss of well-being is a misfortune. For instance, a child becomes addicted to drugs or a partner proves unfaithful. Misfortunes in the area of human health are termed sickness. Sickness is a personal experience of ill-being, most often focused on some dimension of the human body. But in antiquity, the human body was not the entity depicted in modern physiology and anatomy. For the learned, it was composed of air (spirit, pneuma), earth, fire, and water – with air, fire, and water having the quality of liquids. Some of these features reached common knowledge. When people die, they give up the spirit, as in Matthew 27:50 ("And Jesus cried again with a loud voice and yielded up his spirit") and John 19:30 ("bowed his head and gave up his spirit").

Medical anthropologists have developed two concepts for understanding this reality: disease and illness. These are explanatory concepts that assist an analysis and discussion of the reality of sickening or loss of well-being. Disease and illness are not the reality, but ways of understanding it. *Disease* is a scientific, biomedical view of sickening. It is a way of understanding that involves identifying organisms with physical problems, discovering the cause of the problems, and proposing remedies for those problems. Such a remedy is called a cure. Curing a person consists of removing or arresting the cause of the physical condition in hopes of restoring the activities of the organism and thus returning a person to an approximation of well-being. As already noted, such a perspective was impossible before the invention of the microscope (1674). As a way of understanding ill-being, disease is a relatively recent concept, and it is a concept that changes often with advances in knowledge.

In contrast to this view, *illness* is a sociocultural perspective and interpretation of sickening that is concerned with loss of well-being and of meaningful life due to some impairment or loss of function. Healing thus means restoring well-being and meaningfulness to life, regardless of whether the negative condition improves or remains the same. The fever that afflicted Peter's mother-in-law impeded the fulfillment of her domestic role. When the fever left her, she rose and served the visitors (Matt. 8:14–15; Luke 4:38–39). Jesus the healer restored culturally significant well-being in the life of Peter's mother-in-law. The New Testament takes no interest in the cause of the problem, or in whether the problem ever recurred.

In sum, Jesus was an Israelite holy man, an influential intercessor with God, the one and only healer. Jesus's role was that of a folk healer who acted perfectly in accord with folk traditions of his Middle Eastern culture. The results of Jesus's healing activities in each case were that he indeed did heal people and restore meaning to people's life. We have no way of knowing, scientifically, the conditions which Jesus treated, nor do we have any "before and after" markers (tests, x-rays, and the like). Nor do we know whether any of the conditions recurred. In other words, biblical writers do not inform their readers about the disease because they did not know about it. They rather present instances of illness, reporting how the illness was managed by healer and client, and how it was healed by the God of Israel.

By the way, it is important to recognize that no English Bible translation reflects the concepts just presented. The words sickness, disease, illness, cure, and heal (among others) are used indiscriminately. The contemporary reader must determine in each case what the reality might have been and what the real outcomes were in terms of the consensus reality of the ancient Mediterranean (see Pilch 2000, 2004).

Analysis of the Text

The text segment opens with Jesus coming to Capernaum. Readers (hearers) of the Gospel text know that Jesus lived in Capernaum (Matt. 4:13, 9:1), although he was born in Bethlehem (Matt. 1:18–25) and spent his childhood in Nazareth (Matt. 2:22–23). Jesus was a Galilean. They also knew of Jesus's baptism by John to "fulfill all righteousness" and of the ASC experience he had at that time (Matt. 3:13–17; sky opening and voice of God). They knew of his testing in a wilderness by Satan as a son of God, that is, as a holy man and prophet. Unlike ancient Israel, God's son

Jesus (Matt. 2:15) passed the test, demonstrating both that he is new Israel
and a holy man approved by God (Matt. 4:1–11). Jesus then proceeded
to recruit some disciples (to assist him, Matt. 4:18–22). They ascended
an unnamed mountain where, like Moses, Jesus presented a discourse
on being a righteous Israelite (Matt. 5:1–7:27). After this first discourse
(of five – like Moses' Torah), Jesus acts as God's holy man and broker by
demonstrating the patronage of the God of Israel (who is Father), man-
ifested through Jesus, God's broker: the healing of a leper, a centurion,
and Peter's mother-in-law (8:1–17). The passage of interest here is the
central one, Jesus's interaction with a centurion. The translation used
here is from the RSV, with one repeated alteration as noted:

A 8:5   As he entered Capernaum, a **centurion came** forward to him,
beseeching him
B 8:6   and saying, "Lord, my boy ("servant" in RSV, NRSV) is lying paralyzed
at home, in terrible distress."
A` 8:7   And he said to him, "I will come and heal him."
B` 8:8   But the centurion answered him, "Lord, I am not worthy to have
you come under my roof; but only say the word, and my boy ('servant' in
RSV, NRSV) will be healed. 8:9 For I am a man under authority, with soldiers
under me; and I say to one, 'Go,' and he goes, and to another, 'Come,' and
he comes, and to my slave, 'Do this,' and he does it."
A`` 8:10   When Jesus heard him, he marveled, and said to those who followed
him, "Truly, I say to you, not even in Israel have I found such faith. 8:11 I tell
you, many will come from east and west and sit at table with Abraham, Isaac,
and Jacob in the kingdom of heaven, 8:12 while the sons of the kingdom
will be thrown into the outer darkness; there men will weep and gnash their
teeth."
A``` 8:13   And to the **centurion** Jesus said, "**Go**; be it done for you as you
have believed."
And the boy ("servant" in RSV and NRSV) was healed at that very moment.

Scholars using social-scientific approaches do, in fact, build on the accu-
mulated wisdom of the European exegetical tradition. They take his-
tory quite seriously, beginning their task with the literary emphases of
Formgeschichte (form criticism). In this case, a formal, literary analysis
indicates that the passage is a conversation, with an inclusio opening the
segment with Jesus *coming* to Capernaum and a *centurion* approaching,

and a matching inclusio closing the segment (8:13) with Jesus speaking to the *centurion*, telling him *to go*. The [come–go] words signal the inclusio.

Following the markings (A and B) in the aforementioned text, the conversational interaction proceeds with the centurion speaking to Jesus twice (B = 8:5b–6, 8–9) and Jesus answering twice (A = 8:7, 8:13). The literary unit is interrupted by 8:10–12, noting Jesus's amazement and an apostrophe directed to those following him.

By comparing the passage with the other Gospels in a synopsis, one can see that the passage shows traces of an original Q-tradition (Q 7–9) that is least developed by Matthew and somewhat more elaborated in Luke (7:1–10). A different version of the tradition is also recounted in John 4:46b–54.

Luke's developed version emphasizes the intervention of the centurion's clients who approach Jesus on the centurion's behalf. Nearly all commentators note that this was a healing at a distance. The other instance of such a healing is that of a non-Israelite (Canaanite woman's daughter, Matt. 15:21–28, also in Mark 7:24–30), with stress on the woman's faith, paralleling Jesus's stress on the centurion's faith here.

In keeping with his previous proclamation of the kingdom of God and his Sermon on the Mount, Jesus reveals his social role as an Israelite prophet. The present passage stands in a context of a series of passages in which Jesus performs the role of an Israelite holy man.

MATTHEW 8:5–6. Capernaum was located at a significant crossroad and taxes were collected from those who traveled through the city or who engaged in fishing or other business activities there (Matt. 17:24). As an honorable Israelite holy man and prophet, Jesus enters accompanied by an entourage (8:10), the presence of which indicates his honorable social standing. Jesus is an Israelite holy man known to the local centurion, presumably a Roman military official. Both of them were town mates, living in Capernaum (4:13; 9:1 for Jesus; 8:8 for the centurion). Since they lived in the same small town, they were members of an in-group relative to outsiders. Further, they surely knew of each other. As an officer representing Roman elite interests, a centurion would often broker imperial resources for the local population (a point noted by Luke 7:4–5). The fact that the centurion approaches Jesus himself might readily be interpreted as a challenge to Jesus's honor, as so frequently with the approaches of

scribes of the Pharisees in Matthew's story. However, the centurion's calling Jesus "lord" indicates that he acknowledged Jesus's social role as an
Israelite holy man and means to deal with him with respect and proper
self-abasement. It also points to the centurion's attachment to the sick
boy in his house (the RSV and NRSV both use "servant" for the Greek
pais ["child"] without further explanation; they may be influenced by
Luke 7:2, 3, 10 which has *doulos*, "slave"; John 4:46b has *huios*, "son").

Since the writer makes no mention of the centurion's ethnicity, it
would seem that the centurion here was a member of the house of Israel
(explained previously). As noted previously, he was like so many Israelites
who served in the auxiliary Roman legions (although Luke 7:5 states that
he is not one of "us"). The significant social fact is that the centurion, a
person of high social standing due to his political rank, turns to Jesus for
assistance.

MATTHEW 8:7. After being so honored, Jesus proposes to come to heal
the boy. Jesus's proposal is, of course, a high-context statement. The one
who will heal is the God of Israel, whose healing power is mediated by
the Israelite holy man. That Jesus so readily agrees to come is further
indication that the centurion was an Israelite since in similar circumstances (the case of the Canaanite woman's daughter in Matt. 15:21–28),
Jesus notes, "I was sent only to the lost sheep of the house of Israel."
As for the healing that the centurion requests, one must appreciate the
consensus reality that both the centurion and Jesus shared. Jesus, like the
centurion, was a first-century Middle Eastern person fully enculturated
in the beliefs and values of his culture, including their health-care delivery
system, delivered in this case by the folk healer, the Israelite holy man.

MATTHEW 8:8–9. The centurion responds with the courteous "lord,"
and continues by stating his unworthiness to have Jesus enter his house
(8:8). The centurion makes it clear that even though he is a Roman
officer, as far as he is concerned Jesus is in no way his social inferior. This
is underscored by his protestation of unworthiness (like John the Baptist
in Matt. 3:11): "I am not worthy to have you come under my roof." The
category "worthy" nearly always has to do with social status, not with any
moral quality. Furthermore, in such an in-group/out-group world, being
"worthy" indicates social worthiness, signifying location or permission to

be in the in-group. "O Lord I am not worthy" duly situates the centurion in the out-group in this encounter (Q = Matt. 8:8; Luke 7:1).

As previously noted, however, there is reason to believe that the centurion may have been an Israelite in the Roman auxiliary legion. As such he has no right to step into Jesus's space and Jesus need not humiliate himself by stepping into his space (interpreted as Roman presence in Capernaum). The same would apply to the designation of John the Baptist as not worthy (Mark 1:7 and parallels; similarly, the "worthy" in the hymns of Rev. 4:10, 5:9, 12). He is a person qualitatively different from Jesus, in a qualitatively lower status on a social ladder. Once more, then, the centurion proclaims Jesus's social superiority in relation to himself.

With "for" (Greek *gar*), 8:9 offers the reason for the centurion's confidence that the boy will be healed if Jesus simply says the word. He himself is under authority and in turn wields authority over the soldiers in his military unit as well as over his slaves. Authority means the recognized social ability to control the behavior of others. The centurion emphasizes that his authority is always met with compliance. Jesus, the Israelite holy man and healer, is likewise under the authority of the God of Israel, and as healing broker, has authority over the personal forces causing sickness. The next two verses serve as an aside in this passage. Jesus turns to address his entourage, ever present around the holy man to witness his actions and praise the God of Israel. Their presence also gives Jesus a grant of honor, that is, publicly acknowledged worth.

MATTHEW 8:10–12. As a rule, in the culture of the first-century Mediterranean, there is no internal state without some corresponding external expression. The writer can assert Jesus's amazement here because of Jesus's words. Jesus acknowledges that the centurion's display of loyalty to the God of Israel (faith) is the trigger of his amazement: "Truly, I tell you, among no one else have I found such faith in Israel" (my literal translation; the RSV translation "not even in Israel," as well as the NRSV with its rendering "in no one in Israel," is inaccurate, giving the impression that this centurion was not an Israelite).

The phrase "Truly I say to you" is a word of honor; Jesus gives his word of honor to underscore the truth and sincerity of his judgment. A word of honor expresses sincerity of intention, a willingness to commit one's honor to what one says. To demonstrate this sincerity of intention, a person can give a word of honor, which functions like making an oath or swearing with God as witness. But the word of honor engages only the individual himself or herself, not God or others. People in the first-century Mediterranean could expect sincerity and loyalty only from in-group members. There was no presumption that some out-group person would be telling the truth. From the out-group, insincerity, deception, and lying were quite normal (as with twenty-first century U.S. government officials). Even in the in-group, however, a word of honor may be appropriate when those who find what a person says or does to be ambiguous or incredible. Jesus's characteristic "truly, I say to you" or "I say to you" function as a word of honor (cf. Matt. 5:18, 26; 6:2, 5, 16; 8:10; 10:15, 23, 42; 11:11; 13:17; 16:28; 17:20; 18:3, 13, 18, 19; 19:23, 28; 21:21, 31; 23:36; 24:2, 34, 47; 25:12, 40, 45; 26:13, 21, 34; Mark 3:28; 8:12; 9:1, 41; 10:15, 29; 11:23; 12:43; 13:30; 14:9, 18, 25, 30; Luke 4:24; 12:37; 18:17, 29; 21:32; 23:43; John 1:51; 3:3, 5, 11; 5:19, 24, 25; 6:26, 32, 47, 53; 8:34, 51, 58; 10:1, 7; 12:24; 13:16, 20, 21, 38; 14:12; 16:20, 23; 21:18). It seems that what was incredible here was that a centurion, even if an Israelite, could profess such loyalty to the God of Israel. Given such loyalty to God the Patron, Jesus then brokers God's healing power as requested.

In high-context Matthew, the word "many" (Greek *polloi*, 8:11) invari-ably requires the reader to supply the words "in Israel" or "Israelites." Jesus's political religious movement was quite Israelite specific (see Matt. 10:5, 15:24). Matthew's recollection of this is to be found in all the "many" over against "all" statements in his Gospel. To put those statements in their proper social location in Matthew, for example, one must read "many in Israel." Thus:

- "Enter by the narrow gate; for the gate is wide and the way is easy, that leads to destruction, and those who enter by it are many [in Israel]" (Matt. 7:13).
- "On that day many [in Israel] will say to me, 'Lord, Lord, did we not prophesy in your name, and cast out demons in your name, and do many mighty works in your name?'" (Matt. 7:22).
- "Truly, I say to you, many [Israelite] prophets and righteous men longed to see what you see, and did not see it, and to hear what you hear, and did not hear it" (Matt. 13:17).

- "But many [in Israel] that are first will be last, and the last first" (Matt. 19:30).
- "The Son of man came not to be served but to serve, and to give his life as a ransom for many [in Israel]" (Matt. 20:28; Mark 10:45).
- "For many [in Israel] are called, but few are chosen" (Matt. 22:14).
- "For many [in Israel] will come in my name, saying, 'I am the Christ,' and they will lead many [in Israel] astray" (Matt. 24:5).
- "And then many [in Israel] will fall away, and betray one another, and hate one another. And many [Israelite] false prophets will arise and lead many [in Israel] astray" (Matt. 24:10–11).
- "For this is my blood of the covenant, which is poured out for many [in Israel] for the forgiveness of sins" (Matt. 26:28; see Mark 14:24, who lacks the explicit expiatory motif).
- "But they found none, though many [Israelite] false witnesses came forward" (Matt. 26:60).
- "The tombs also were opened, and many bodies of the [Israelite] saints who had fallen asleep were raised, the holy city and appeared to many [in Israel]" (Matt. 27:52–53).
- "There were also many [Israelite] women there, looking on from afar, who had followed Jesus from Galilee, ministering to him" (Matt. 27:55).

What of Matthew's explicit *ethnos* replacement in 21:43: "Therefore I tell you, the kingdom of God will be taken away from you and given to an *ethnos* producing the fruits of it." The passage is addressed to the chief priests and Pharisees, who perceived "that he (Jesus) was speaking about them" (Matt. 21:45). Hence *ethnos* should not be translated as "nation" (as in many English Bibles) but rather as "political religious group." Dictionaries of ancient Greek indicate that the word bears such a meaning (e.g., Liddell and Scott, Moulton and Milligan).

So, too, in this passage (8:11–12): "I tell you, many [in Israel] will come from east and west and sit at table with Abraham, Isaac, and Jacob in the kingdom of heaven." In the forthcoming theocracy, many Israelites will come from East and West for table fellowship with the foundational ancestors of their ethnic group. The contrast is with the "sons" (NRSV "heirs") of the theocracy, those located in the land of Israel. Table fellowship among Israelites from among non-Israelite regions as well as those in Israel will characterize the new community (see Matt. 7:22–23).

On the other hand, some of "the sons of the kingdom" are described as publicly shamed; this is what the "weeping and gnashing of teeth" refers to. The phrase describes the externals indicating the internal state of being shamed or dishonored (a favorite phrase of Matthew (13:42, 50; 22:13; 24:51; 25:30; also found in Luke 13:28; see also Ps. 112:10; Sir. 30:10).

MATTHEW 8:13. The passage concludes with Jesus in control, significantly commanding the centurion to go. And he notes that it was the centurion's trust in the God of Israel, expressed in his confidence in Jesus as a broker, that marked the healing of the boy. As is well known in New Testament study, the passive voice is used to specify that God is the doer, since to utter the name of God was forbidden. Here the passive-voice verb "be it done" indicates an activity of God; God does to you as you believed. The same is true of the passive verb "was healed": God is the healer.

WORKS CITED

Barraclough, G. 1978. *Main Trends in History*. New York: Holmes & Meier.

Bourguignon, E. 1979. *Psychological Anthropology: An Introduction to Human Nature and Cultural Differences*. New York: Holt, Rinehart and Winston.

Clottes, J. and D. Lewis-Williams. 1996. *The Shamans of Prehistory: Trance and Magic in the Painted Caves*. Text by J. Clottes translated from the French by S. Hawkes. New York: Harry N. Abrams, Inc.

Coleman, J. A. 1999. "The Bible and Sociology." *Sociology of Religion* **60**: 125–48.

Elliott, J. H. 2007. "Jesus the Israelite Was Neither a 'Jew' Nor a 'Christian': On Correcting Misleading Nomenclature." *Journal for the Study of the Historical Jesus* **5.2**: 119–54.

Freidson, E. 1970. *Profession of Medicine: A Study of the Sociology of Applied Knowledge*. New York: Harper & Row.

Garfinkel, H. 1967. *Studies in Ethnomethodology*. Englewood Cliffs, NJ: Prentice Hall.

Goodman, M. 2007. *Rome and Jerusalem: A Clash of Civilizations*. Baltimore: Penguin.

Hall, Edward T. 1976. *Beyond Culture*. Garden City, N.Y.: Doubleday.

Hochschild, R. 1999. *Sozialgeschichtliche Exegese: Entwicklung, Geschichte und Methodik einer neutestamentlichen Forschungsrichtung* (NTOA 42). Fribourg: Editions universitaires; Göttingen: Vandenhoeck & Ruprecht.

Horden, P., and N. Purcell. 2000. *The Corrupting Sea: A Study of Mediterranean History*. Oxford: Blackwell.

Horstmanshoff, H. F. J. 1990. "The Ancient Physician: Craftsman or Scientist?" *Journal of the History of Medicine and Allied Sciences* **45**: 176–97.

Kleinman, A. 1988. *Rethinking Psychiatry*. New York: Free Press.

Krippner, S. 1972. "Altered States of Consciousness." Pages 1–5 in *The Highest State of Consciousness*, ed. J. White. New York: Doubleday.

Murdock, G. P. 1980. *Theories of Illness: A World Survey*. Pittsburgh: University of Pittsburgh Press.

Ogburn, W. F. 1922. *Social Change with Respect to Culture and Original Nature*. New York: B. W. Huebsch.

Pilch, J. J. 2000. *Healing in the New Testament: Insights from Medical and Mediterranean Anthropology*. Minneapolis: Fortress.

Pilch, J. J. 2004. *Visions and Healing in the Acts of the Apostles. How the Early Believers Experienced God*. Collegeville, MN: Liturgical.

Rossi, E. L. 1986. "Altered States of Consciousness in Everyday Life: The Ultradian Rhythms." Pages 97–132 in *Handbook of States of Consciousness*, ed. B. B. Wolman and M. Ullman. New York: Van Nostrand Reinhold Co.

Safrai, S., and M. Stern, eds. 1974. *The Jewish People in the First Century: Historical Geography, Political History, Social, Cultural and Religious Life and Institutions*. Philadelphia: Fortress.

Tonkin, E. 1990. "History and the Myth of Realism." Pages 25–35 in *The Myths We Live By*, ed. R. Samuel and P. Thompson. London: Routledge.

6

$\downarrow$

Postcolonial Criticism and the Gospel of Matthew

FERNANDO F. SEGOVIA

*P*OSTCOLONIAL BIBLICAL CRITICISM ENTERS THE THEORETICAL and methodological repertoire of the discipline in the latter half of the 1990s. Among critical approaches, therefore, it is of late vintage, marking the turn of the century – emerging, as it does, at the very end of the twentieth century and establishing a solid foothold only with the beginning of the twenty-first century. At first, it does so largely among critics from the non-Western world living and working in diaspora in the West and thus fitting the category of non-Western racial–ethnic minorities within the West. Such critics come to biblical criticism after the fateful developments in the discipline of the 1970s, which involved not only fundamental changes in method and theory but also incipient trans-formations in visage and voice.[1] Soon, however, postcolonial criticism would become a major area of interest for non-Western critics outside the West, similar newcomers to the discipline, as well as for Western critics.

The present exposition of this still-developing critical approach proceeds in two steps. The first part offers an overview of the approach as a whole in terms of historical path, theoretical foundations, and

[1] I have described the field of biblical studies today as encompassing four paradigms or umbrella models of interpretation: historical, literary, sociocultural, and ideological. These classifications, which encompass a broad variety of methods and theories, I see not as mutually exclusive but as pointing to the principal focus of research. I have further described the field today as reflecting a profound demographic transformation. Such developments I trace back to the mid-1970s. For a brief introduction, see F. F. Segovia, "Methods for Studying the New Testament," *Reading the New Testament Today*, ed. M. A. Powell (Louisville: Westminster John Knox, 1999), 1–9. For more extensive treatment, see F. F. Segovia, *Decolonizing Biblical Studies: A View from the Margins* (Maryknoll, NY: Orbis, 2000).

methodological configuration. The second part examines its particular application to the Gospel of Matthew, beginning with an overview of postcolonial interpretations of the Gospel in general and concluding with postcolonial readings of Matthew 8:5–13 in particular, the episode traditionally known as "The Healing of a Centurion's Servant."

POSTCOLONIAL BIBLICAL CRITICISM: AN OVERVIEW

In this first part, then, I begin with an overview of the approach: first, an account of its historical path, tracing its origins and following its trajectory within the discipline; second, an exposition of its theoretical foundations, in both disciplinary and interdisciplinary terms; lastly, a description of its methodological configuration, addressing issues of demarcation as well as of procedure.

Historical Path: Tracing Origins and Trajectory

With the privilege of hindsight, looking back over ten years of critical development, I would draw a distinction between two periods of time. These divisions are not meant as hard and fast, nor should they be regarded as self-evident and indisputable. They are simply offered for analytical purposes. For the first such period, I would propose 1996–99, a phase of formation and definition – a time of disciplinary and professional "firsts." My criterion for such delimitation is as follows: the year 1996 marks the first attempt to bring together biblical studies and postcolonial studies; this discursive confluence gains formal professional footing in 1999. For the second period, I would propose 2000–2007, a phase of expansion and consolidation – a time of multiple experimentation and growing sophistication. My rationale for this demarcation runs as follows: the year 2000 ushers in a variety of efforts to apply the postcolonial optic across the various constitutive dimensions of the discipline; such work reaches an iconic climax with the publication of *A Postcolonial Commentary on the New Testament Writings* in 2007. In the account that follows I concentrate on the first period, with a word on a precursor to the movement and brief comments on the second period. I do so because I find that the essential concerns and interests of the postcolonial optic are already set in place within the initial phase of definition.

A CRITICAL HARBINGER. A work from the first half of the 1990s may now be seen, in retrospect, as an immediate antecedent for the yet-to-come outbreak of the postcolonial optic in biblical criticism. The volume in question, published in 1994, is a collection of essays under the title of *Postcolonial Literature and the Biblical Call for Justice*, edited by Susan VanZanten Gallagher.[2] Strictly speaking, this is not an exercise in, nor does it deal with, biblical criticism as such. Its editor is a professor of English, with an interest in the relationship between religion and literature, and its contributors all hail from departments of literature, mostly English, and are all based in the United States. Its primary object of attention, however, is postcolonial literatures, across a broad range of areas and authors – Latin America, the United States (Native American), Africa, and the Middle East. And, the volume does deal with the relationship between biblical texts and postcolonial writings.

The overall context addressed is described as the conflicted legacy left behind by Christianity in colonialism – more specifically, the biblical codes and their use for evil or for good. Against this background, the concrete focus lies on the use of this legacy in postcolonial literatures in the interest of freedom and justice, through analysis of the theme of justice as formulated in the biblical texts and appropriated by postcolonial authors. In bringing together the Bible and the postcolonial perspective, analyzing how postcolonial writers interpret biblical texts on justice and reflect on the demands and tensions of such a call for justice, the volume clearly points the way to – and demands more critical attention than it has received from – postcolonial biblical criticism. The move from analysis of the postcolonial take on the Bible to a postcolonial analysis of the Bible as such would not take long – a mere two years.

PERIOD OF FORMATION AND DEFINITION (1996–99). It is the journal *Semeia* that takes pride of place in leading the way, as it did in so many other instances since the key transition period of the mid-1970s. The point of origin is the volume entitled *Postcolonialism and Scriptural Reading*, published in 1996 and edited by Laura E. Donaldson.[3] Quite

---

[2] S. VanZanten Gallagher, ed., *Postcolonial Literature and the Biblical Call for Justice* (Jackson, MS: University of Mississippi, 1994).

[3] L. E. Donaldson, ed., *Postcolonialism and Scriptural Reading, Semeia* 75 (Atlanta: Scholars, 1975). See, especially, her introduction to the volume, "Postcolonialism and Biblical

interesting is the fact that this foray is spearheaded, as was the case with the forerunner collection of VanZanten Gallagher, not by a biblical critic but (this time) by a literary and cultural critic based in Literary Studies, Women's Studies, and American Indian/Native Studies. In seeking to bring postcolonial and biblical studies together, Donaldson, a scholar of Native American (Cherokee) roots, argues for the need to examine the varied and complex legacies of colonialism on the discipline of biblical studies and on biblical interpretation. Postcolonial criticism, described in terms of "reading like Canaanites," is conceived in oppositional terms: to rescue the voices in the text silenced by the dominant readings of the text. This opposition is further conceived as multidimensional in orientation, keenly attentive to the intricacies of the colonial situation in terms of culture, race, class, and gender.

This is what the volume sets out to do at various levels of inquiry: analyzing texts from both scriptural canons, the Hebrew Bible and the Christian Testament; turning to later texts and contexts of interpretation; examining various hermeneutical frameworks and projects. The range of topics is broad and unrelated. For this task, the volume draws on contributors and respondents from both inside and outside biblical criticism: for the main essays, in approximately equal numbers; for the critical evaluations, mostly from biblical studies, with the one exception of VanZanten Gallagher. The gamut of faces and voices represented is, in standard *Semeia* fashion, quite broad, nationally as well as globally.

What follows this first discursive conjunction is a steady flow of publications and ventures. These develop in varying ways the different levels of inquiry already pursued under the postcolonial optic in the collection – biblical texts and contexts; interpretations and contexts; frameworks of interpretation. In order to bring out the lively character of this formative stage and the early articulations of definition, I shall trace such a flow on a year-by-year basis.

(1997). The year 1997 proves significant: two important publications see the light of day, and a major publishing project is launched.[4] The

---

Reading: An Introduction" (pp. 1–14). Donaldson, based at the time in the University of Iowa, had already published an influential volume on the intersection of gender, race, and colonialism (*Decolonizing Feminisms: Race, Gender and Empire Building* [Chapel Hill, NC: The University of North Carolina Press, 1992]).

[4] Although not focused on the approach as such, the juxtaposition of interpretation and postcolonialism is pursued at the AAR–SBL Annual Meeting in a section of the Asian

volumes – neither of which is grounded in postcolonial theory, although both are acquainted with this discursive framework – reflect different critical perspectives. One represents a first attempt to relate the past of the text and the present of interpretation within the postcolonial optic, with ideological critique in mind, while the other signifies the first effort to foreground the reality and experience of empire in early Christian writings. The former is written in the tradition of Liberation Hermeneutics; the latter, indebted to Liberation as well, bears the traces of Empire Studies. The publishing project signals an ambitious undertaking.

Thus, Sheffield Academic Press – like *Semeia*, a leading venue in newer modes of interpretation – brings out *The Bible and Colonialism: A Moral Critique*, authored by Michael Prior.[5] In this work Prior sets out to examine the motif of land possession and conquest in the biblical texts as well as in the use of such texts in a variety of colonial enterprises (Latin America; South Africa; Palestine). His goal is to offer a moral critique of such traditions, and hence of the Bible, in the light of the claims advanced and their ramifications for indigenous populations. In addition, Trinity Press International publishes *Paul and Empire: Religion and Power in Roman Imperial Society*, the first of Richard Horsley's volumes, both authored and edited, on the interface between early Christianity and the Roman Empire.[6] Emphasizing the relegation of politics, especially imperial politics, in traditional criticism, Horsley argues for just such a foregrounding in both texts and interpretations, in the light of similar developments in other fields and with specific reference to various postcolonial studies

and Asian-American Biblical Studies Consultation. This session featured a position paper by A. C. C. Lee on the subject of "Returning to China: Biblical Interpretation in Postcolonial Hong Kong," four responses (P. Chia, K. Pui-lan, K. D. Sakenfeld, and F. F. Segovia), and a final rejoinder by Lee. The proceedings were published in *BibInt* 7 (1999): 156–201.

5 M. Prior, *The Bible and Colonialism: A Moral Critique*, The Biblical Seminar 48 (Sheffield: Sheffield Academic Press, 1997). At the time, Prior, a Roman Catholic priest and member of the Vincentian Order, was chair of the Department of Theology and Religious Studies at St. Mary's University College, the University of Surrey. Active in the theology and hermeneutics of liberation and very much interested in Palestinian Christianity, he had published a few years earlier *Jesus the Liberator: Nazareth Liberation Theology (Luke 4.16–30)* (Sheffield: Sheffield Academic Press, 1995).

6 R. A. Horsley, *Paul and Empire: Religion and Power in Roman Imperial Society* (Harrisburg, PA: Trinity Press International, 1997). Horsley, a professor of Classics and Religion at the University of Massachusetts, Boston, had previously penned a number of studies on the political context and character of early Christian texts.

from the early 1990s. To this end, he fashions an anthology of studies, from classics as well as biblical scholars, having to do with the dynamics of Roman imperial society and the role of Paul within such a framework.

At the same time, Sheffield Academic Press, with R. S. Sugirtharajah as a catalyzing agent, announces the beginning of a new series, "The Bible and Postcolonialism."[7] For this long-term project, Sugirtharajah is designated as general editor, a broad editorial board is assembled (Marcella Althaus-Reid; Ralph Broadbent; Kwok Pui-lan; Sharon Ringe; Fernando F. Segovia), and an initial slate of volumes is devised and commissioned. This series, the first example of institutionalization by way of publishing venues, would play a key role in the spread of postcolonial criticism for years to come.

(1998). The following year, 1998, turns out to be no less significant: two further publications and a colloquium within a professional context. The volumes, both from the pen of Sugirtharajah, pursue different angles of the postcolonial optic. While one volume represents the first attempt to circumscribe postcolonial biblical criticism as such, the second signals the first sustained effort to bring postcolonial theory to bear on biblical criticism. The colloquium marks the arrival of the postcolonial optic in professional circles.

Thus, the inaugural volume in "The Bible and Postcolonialism" series appears, *The Postcolonial Bible*, edited by Sugirtharajah.[8] Here, as a foundational manuscript for the series, Sugirtharajah sets the tone for the enterprise as a whole: the replacement of colonial reading by postcolonial reading.[9] The latter would seek to overturn not only the assumptions of the former (superiority of Western culture; the Western male as subject; the Other as in need of domination and subordination) but also its

---

[7] R. S. Sugirtharajah, a native of Sri Lanka and an ordained minister in the Methodist Church, was then based at Selly Oak Colleges in Birmingham, England. He had earlier published a widely used volume on non-Western biblical interpretation, *Voices from the Margin: Interpreting the Bible in the Third World* (Maryknoll, NY: Orbis, 1991) and had by this time published a series of articles on postcolonial biblical criticism.

[8] R. S. Sugirtharajah, ed., *The Postcolonial Bible*, The Bible and Postcolonialism 1 (Sheffield: Sheffield Academic Press, 1998).

[9] R. S. Sugirtharajah, "Biblical Studies after the Empire: From a Colonial to a Postcolonial Mode of Interpretation," in *The Postcolonial Bible*, 12–22. A succinct definition of postcolonial reading is provided: "What postcolonialism does is to enable us to question the totalizing tendencies of European reading practices and interpret the texts on our own terms and read them from our own specific locations" (16).

practices (replacement of indigenous strategies; negative representations of the Other; exegetical strategies for imperial control). A postcolonial reading would thus function as a challenge to and an alternative for standard biblical scholarship by foregrounding issues of empire, nation, ethnicity, migration, and language in both texts and interpretations, thereby exposing and correcting the implication of the discipline in colonialism. The volume – drawing on an expansive variety of faces and voices – focused on readings of texts, analyses of critical spaces, and refigurations of biblical stories. In addition, Sugirtharajah brings out a collection of essays, *Asian Biblical Hermeneutics and Postcolonialism*, in which he pursues the interpretive agenda set forth in his Introduction to *The Postcolonial Bible* by means of a focus on the turns and dynamics of biblical interpretation in Asia.[10] This agenda – carried out by attention to modes of interpretation, critical commentaries, and practices of translation – is phrased in terms of contestation and resistance: postcolonial criticism as writing back and working against colonialism – its assumptions, representations, and ideologies.

Lastly, at the AAR–SBL Annual Meeting, a featured session on *The Postcolonial Bible* is held, the first example of institutionalization by way of professional association. This session, a panel discussion, was scheduled within the framework of an ongoing program unit formed a few years earlier, The Bible in Africa, Asia, Latin America and the Caribbean Section.[11] The colloquium marked a formal shift from a contextual approach to the Bible in the non-Western world, with emphasis on location of readings and readers, to a postcolonial approach, with attention to the geopolitical situation of non-Western readings and readers, their experience and reality within imperial–colonial formations and relations. This colloquium proved a sign of things to come within the Society of Biblical Literature itself.

(1999). The trend intensifies in 1999: two publications – a special issue of a major journal and another colloquium within a professional context. The volumes again pursue different angles of the postcolonial optic.

[10] R. S. Sugirtharajah, *Asian Biblical Hermeneutics and Postcolonialism: Contesting the Interpretations* (Maryknoll, NY: Orbis, 1998). See especially the introductory remarks in "Rethinking an Interpretive Agenda" (pp. ix–xii).

[11] The proceedings for the session were subsequently published; for the four reviews, see *JSNT* 74 (1999): 113–21; for a response, see *JSNT* 75 (1999): 103–14.

One focuses on indigenous traditions and practices of interpretation, the first attempt to do so in sustained fashion; the other carries out a postcolonial reading of an entire biblical writing, the first example of such a full-fledged exercise. The special journal issue, the first of its kind as well, provides a general introduction to postcolonial criticism, in applied rather than theoretical fashion. The colloquium signals ongoing professional institutionalization.

One of the volumes constitutes the second contribution to "The Bible and Postcolonialism" series, entitled *Vernacular Hermeneutics* and edited by Sugirtharajah.[12] The interpretive agenda of resistance and contestation outlined in the first volume continues here as well, now formulated, however, in terms of a hermeneutical contrast within the Third World. Non-Western hermeneutics, argues Sugirtharajah, is either liberation- or culture-focused: the former, unlike the latter, is well known and popular in the West. The reason is simple: liberation hermeneutics shares the foundations and practices of standard interpretation, while vernacular hermeneutics relies on indigenous practices and traditions. As such, it proves more effective in disrupting and displacing existing interpretation; hence, the volume, a compilation of such strategies from around the globe, is intended as a strategic sortie in this regard.

The second volume, Tat-siong Benny Liew's *Politics of Parousia: Reading Mark Inter(con)textually,*[13] is a monograph with postcolonial criticism at its center. Such criticism is situated within the broader theoretical ambit of postmodernism, defined as a terrain of resistance, where knowledge is viewed as perspectival, truth as constructed, and discourse as political. Thus, Liew advances an oppositional and liberational view of biblical criticism, grounded in and driven by a commitment to social change and liberation for the oppressed. For such sociopolitical criticism Liew proposes, drawing on the postmodern reading strategy of intertextuality, an "inter(con)textual" reading: a view of texts as proactive agents in context; a view of critics as proactive agents in context; a view of criticism as interchange between such (con)texts with transformation in mind. Within this interchange, then, the postcolonial turn is highlighted, so that

[12] R. S. Sugirtharajah, ed., *Vernacular Hermeneutics*, The Bible and Postcolonialism 2 (Sheffield: Sheffield Academic Press, 1999).

[13] Tat-siong Benny Liew, *Politics of Parousia: Reading Mark Inter(con)textually*, Biblical Interpretation 42 (Leiden: E. J. Brill, 1999).

colonialism emerges as fundamental to postmodernism, and race/ethnicity become essential categories in postmodernism. In effect: Mark as a colonial subject within Roman colonization; Liew as a subject in diaspora within Western colonization; Liew's inter(con)textual reading of Mark as a dialogical relationship (with a focus on authority, agency, and women) in search of change – social and economic justice. As a result of such dialogue, Liew argues for a move beyond the colonial mimicry at work in Mark (anticolonial reproduction of colonial program) toward a recognition of hybridity in the contemporary pursual of resistance and change for all.

Sugirtharajah also functions as the editor of a special issue on "Postcolonial Perspectives on the New Testament and its Interpretation" in the *Journal for the Study of the New Testament*.[14] Here the interpretive agenda receives a somewhat different formulation: on the one hand, the element of resistance is preserved – postcolonial criticism is said to open up a space for the once-colonized to engage in reclamation, redemption, and reaffirmation; on the other hand, such opposition is now nuanced – postcolonial criticism is also said to acknowledge the complexity of the colonial contact.[15] Such criticism is described as multidimensional: reviewing the biblical texts, reimagining the reading strategies, and revisiting interpretations – all from the perspective and concerns of the colonial relationship. The volume, made up entirely of biblical critics, is designed as a strategic exercise in this respect, focusing on concrete texts and specific reading contexts.

Finally, a proposal for a new program unit, conceived and formulated by Stephen Moore and myself as cochairs, is submitted to the Society of Biblical Literature, a consultation on "New Testament Studies and Postcolonial Studies"; the unit is approved and scheduled for a three-year term (2000–2002). Its initial gathering is held at the 1999 AAR–SBL Annual Meeting as a featured session, again within the framework of The Bible in Africa, Asia, Latin America and the Caribbean Section, then coming to the end of its scheduled run. This session, bearing the title

[14] R. S. Sugirtharajah, ed., *Postcolonial Perspectives on the New Testament and Its Interpretation*, Special Issue, *JSNT* 73 (1999).

[15] See his own description of this dimension ("A Brief Memorandum on Postcolonialism and Biblical Studies," in *Postcolonial Perspectives*, 3: "What the current postcolonialism tries to do is to emphasize that this relationship between the ruler and the ruled is complex, full of cross-trading and mutual appropriation and confrontation."

of "Postcolonial Biblical Criticism: Delineation and Configurations," is designed as an introduction to the approach by way of comparison with other critical angles of inquiry in the discipline bearing similar cultural and ideological concerns.[16]

(1996–99). At the turn of the century, therefore, postcolonial biblical criticism finds itself well represented in both the discipline and the profession. Its basic concerns and interests have by this time been voiced as well. With the beginning of a new century, its position would become further entrenched, as publications and projects, papers and gatherings, multiplied. In the process, its conceptualization and application would also become more sophisticated.

PERIOD OF EXPANSION AND CONSOLIDATION (2000–2007). I do not proceed with a year-by-year account in this second phase, for that would require too much time and space. I confine myself instead to a general outline of particular paths of development.

The focus on the interface between the Roman Empire and the early Christian assemblies on the part of Horsley continued apace.[17] This focus was also amplified to cover, along the lines of Prior, parallels between Rome and modern imperial powers, especially the United States.[18] It was taken up in other directions as well, as in the case of *The Gospel of Matthew in Its Roman Imperial Context*, brought out by John Riches and David C. Sim in 2005.[19] This work begins with a historical section on Rome and imperial frameworks and then proceeds to examine various aspects of Matthew against that background.

Several more volumes were published as part of the "The Bible and Postcolonialism" series. First, *Interpreting beyond Borders*, for which I

---

[16] The presentation involved postcolonialism (Segovia); feminism (Donaldson); poststructuralism (S. D. Moore); liberation (Sugirtharajah); Marxism (D. Jobling). Donaldson and Sugirtharajah were members of the Steering Committee, which also included Kwok Pui-lan.

[17] R. A. Horsley, *Jesus and Empire: The Kingdom of God and the New World Disorder* (Minneapolis: Fortress, 2003); R. A. Horsley, ed., *Paul and Politics: Ekklesia, Israel, Imperium, Interpretation. Essays in Honor of Krister Stendahl* (Harrisburg, PA: Trinity Press International, 2000); *Paul and the Roman Imperial Order* (Harrisburg, PA: Trinity Press International, 2004).

[18] R. A. Horsley, *Religion and Empire: People, Power, and the Life of the Spirit* (Minneapolis: Fortress, 2003).

[19] J. Riches and D. C. Sim, eds., *The Gospel of Matthew in Its Roman Imperial Context*, JSNTSS 276 (London: T&T International, 2005).

served as editor, appeared in 2000.[20] Its focus was on another dimension of imperial–colonial formations and relations, the condition of
diaspora, the result of large-scale migration of the non-Western world
into the West, and its effects on interpretation. The readings, all from
first-generation diasporic critics, addressed both the diaspora itself and
the diasporic optic. Second, Roland Boer's *Last Stop before Antarctica*
came out in 2001.[21] The focus here is on Australia as a lightning rod
for the confluence between postcolonial discourse and biblical criticism.
Third, *John and Postcolonialism* appeared in 2002, edited by Musa W.
Dube and Jeffrey L. Staley.[22] This was a multifaceted postcolonial exercise in reading the Gospel of John, involving for the most part scholars
from racial–ethnic minority groups and from the non-Western world. It
brought together analyses of individual passages, essays of a theoretical
nature, and analyses of reading locations in relation to the Gospel. Two
more volumes have been published within the series, but these I prefer
to treat separately, given their import.

The monographic tradition continued apace as well. A second work
on the Gospel of John comes out in 2004, Jean Kyoung Kim's *Woman
and Nation*, which follows the intercontextual approach developed by
Liew and which also brings the optic of feminism to bear on postcolonial
criticism.[23] Two studies on Matthew also appear. First, in 2000, Dube
published *Postcolonial Feminist Interpretation of the Bible*, a work closely
associated with the contextual approach of the 1990s.[24] From her base
in sub-Saharan Africa, Dube seeks to formulate a postcolonial feminist
method and then apply it to Matthew. Second, in 2001, Warren Carter
published *Matthew and Empire: Initial Explorations*, a work very much in
the tradition of Empire Studies.[25] From a historical exposition of Roman

---

[20] F. F. Segovia, ed., *Interpreting beyond Borders*, The Bible and Postcolonialism (Sheffield: Sheffield Academic Press, 2000).

[21] R. Boer, *Last Stop before Antarctica: The Bible and Postcolonialism in Australia*, The Bible and Postcolonialism (Sheffield: Sheffield Academic Press, 2001).

[22] M. W. Dube and J. L. Staley, eds., *John and Postcolonialism: Travel, Space and Power*, The Bible and Postcolonialism (London: Sheffield Academic Press, 2002).

[23] Jean Kyoung Kim, *Woman and Nation: An Intercontextual Reading of the Gospel of John from a Postcolonial Feminist Perspective*, BIS 69 (Leiden: Brill, 2004).

[24] M. W. Dube, *Postcolonial Feminist Interpretation of the Bible* (St. Louis, MO: Chalice, 2000).

[25] W. Carter, *Matthew and Empire: Initial Explorations* (Harrisburg, PA: Trinity Press International, 2001).

imperial ideology, Carter moves to examine the figure of Jesus in the Gospel and then analyze a number of passages characterized as "counternarratives." My own volume on *Decolonizing Biblical Studies* came out in 2000, portraying critical developments within the discipline, as it moved from historical through literary and sociocultural to ideological paradigms of interpretation and as it begins to undergo a demographic transformation in its ranks, as a move toward decolonization.[26]

As the work by Dube and Kim on the intersection with feminist criticism readily shows, postcolonial criticism began to expand in interdisciplinary fashion as well, making connections with other ideological approaches. The next volume in "The Bible and Postcolonialism" series, *Postcolonial Biblical Criticism: Interdisciplinary Intersections*, was designed as a deliberate move in this regard; it was published in 2005 and edited by Stephen Moore and myself.[27] This volume, in itself an expanded version of the colloquium held at the 1999 AAR–SBL Annual Meeting, sought to clarify the postcolonial optic in two ways: by tracing the path of postcolonial discourse and by exploring its intersections with a variety of other discourses – poststructuralism, feminism, economics, and race–ethnicity. The other contributors were all active figures in the movement (Boer; Donaldson; David Jobling; Liew).

The multifocal work of Sugirtharajah continued. Three volumes of essays appeared in rapid sequence. First, in 2001, *The Bible and the Third World*.[28] This is a look at the trajectory of the Bible in the Third World in three phases: before, during, and after colonialism – reception, embrace, reclamations. Second, in 2002, *Postcolonial Criticism and Biblical Interpretation*.[29] The field of vision here is ample: from the intersection of postcolonial studies and biblical studies, through the issue of Bible translation, to the problematic of diasporic criticism. Third, in 2003, *Postcolonial Reconfigurations*.[30] This work offers a mixed bag of essays of

[26] Segovia, *Decolonizing Biblical Studies*.
[27] S. D. Moore and F. F. Segovia, eds, *Postcolonial Biblical Criticism: Interdisciplinary Intersections*, The Bible and Postcolonialism (London: T&T Clark, 2005).
[28] R. S. Sugirtharajah, *The Bible and the Third World: Precolonial, Colonial and Postcolonial Encounters* (Cambridge: Cambridge University Press, 2001).
[29] R. S. Sugirtharajah, *Postcolonial Criticism and Biblical Interpretation* (Oxford: Oxford University Press, 2002).
[30] R. S. Sugirtharajah, *Postcolonial Reconfigurations: An Alternative Way of Reading the Bible and Doing Theology* (London: SCM Press, 2003).

both postcolonial criticism and the use of the Bible in a postcolonial world.

The use of special issues of scholarly journals is found again in the journal of Union Theological Seminary of New York, *Union Seminary Quarterly Review*, which dedicated a whole issue in 2005 to the theme of "New Testament and Roman Empire." The volume contains the proceedings of a major conference and is organized around four topics: Rome and the New Testament, specific stances of early Christian texts, discussion of paradigms, and consideration of contemporary empire and resistance.

As a concluding symbolic marker to, if not climax to, such sustained critical activity, I would posit the publication in 2007 of *A Postcolonial Commentary on the New Testament Writings*, edited by Sugirtharajah and myself – yet another volume in "The Bible and Postcolonialism" series.[31] This massive undertaking brings together a large and varied number of critics with postcolonial readings of all texts of the Christian Testament. It also captures the present and looks to the future of postcolonial criticism. The Introduction sets the scene. It reveals a wide spectrum of positions on fundamental features of the approach: configuration of meaning and scope; mode of approach and argumentation; description of interaction between the Roman Empire and the early Christian churches; interpretive stance toward critical findings. Such diversity of opinion witnesses to the ever-growing complexity and sophistication of postcolonial criticism. The conclusion envisions new directions. On the one hand, it identifies new areas of research: the noncanonical writings of early Christianity, the Jewish-Aramaic context of early Christianity, the relationship between monotheistic and polytheistic religions, and the realm of cultic and liturgical practices. On the other hand, it issues a challenge to critics: the need to address ethical issues and practices of the day, such as suicide bombings and asylum seekers.

Theoretical Foundations: Disciplinary and Interdisciplinary Moorings

In the light of this historical path, with its manifold attempts at definition and its multiplying lines of research, I proceed to examine the theoretical

---

[31] F. F. Segovia and R. S. Sugirtharajah, eds, *A Postcolonial Commentary on the New Testament Writings*, The Bible and Postcolonialism (London: T&T Clark, 2007).

foundations of the postcolonial optic. I do so from two perspectives: first, the disciplinary formation of biblical studies; then, the interdisciplinary movement of postcolonial studies. My objective in this inquiry into discursive moorings is to see how postcolonial criticism fits, at the time of its appearance in the mid-1990s, within both biblical criticism and postcolonial discourse.

POSTCOLONIAL CRITICISM AND BIBLICAL STUDIES. In addressing the relation of postcolonial criticism to the discipline of biblical studies, I take as point of departure major concerns and interests as well as particular caveats and instructions expressed in early expositions of the approach. The following set of concerns comes readily to the fore:

- Retrieving silenced voices in texts and exposing dominant voices in interpretation.
- Exposing oppressive voices in texts and their ramifications in interpretation.
- Foregrounding the political in texts and interpretations.
- Challenging dominant scholarship by foregrounding empire and related issues in texts and interpretations.
- Contesting the presuppositions, convictions, and practices of colonialism in interpretation.
- Destabilizing established scholarship by opting for the vernacular.
- Opening up interpretive space for voices of the once-colonized.
- Framing texts, reading strategies, and interpretations within the ambit of colonial relations.
- Commitment to social change.

Needless to say, a tall order! In fact, given such an expansive list of concerns, a series of caveats is regularly advanced as part of these expositions as well. The following can be readily outlined:

- To mind the intricacies introduced by culture, race, class, and gender in the colonial situation.
- To acknowledge the complexities of colonial contacts.
- To move beyond binarism into hybridity.

Postcolonial criticism is thus viewed, in terms of interests, as revolving around texts and interpretations, issues of domination and resistance, and the politics of the imperial and the colonial. In terms of instructions, it is regarded as calling for attention to layering and intersections. This combination of interests and concerns as well as instructions and caveats place it within the ambit of ideological criticism.

A note of explanation is in order in this regard. It would be altogether inaccurate to say that it was only by way of postcolonial criticism that the problematic of the imperial–colonial was introduced into the discipline. Such a claim would be tantamount to arguing that prior to the advent of literary and sociocultural criticism, there had been no focus on the literary features or the social dimensions of texts among critics, or that prior to the emergence of feminist and liberation criticism, there had been no attention to matters of gender and economy in criticism. The question is not whether such features and dimensions had been addressed but how. What literary criticism and sociocultural criticism as well as feminist and liberation criticism brought into the discipline was a combination of sustained and systematic analysis of the specific focus in question and recourse to an established and ongoing body of work, both theoretical and applied, in such studies.

As such, postcolonial criticism forms part of the array of ideological approaches finding their way into the discipline since its fundamental shift in the mid-to-late 1970s. All such approaches foreground and theorize a relationship involving domination and subordination – unequal formations and relations of power. Their trajectory in the discipline can be outlined in three phases:

1. To begin with, as the discipline moves toward literary criticism and sociocultural analysis for anchor and guidance, certain pressures from without make themselves felt. With the influx of women scholars comes a focus on gender, male–female formations and relations – the beginnings of feminist criticism. With the advent of non-Western scholars comes a focus on political economy, the formations and relations of social class – the beginnings of liberation criticism.

2. Subsequently, in the 1980s, as the discipline moves beyond formalism in both the literary and the sociocultural domains and enters the realm of cultural studies, further pressures from without impinge on it. With the advent of minority scholars comes a focus on race and ethnicity, dominant–minority relations and formations. With the entry of gay and lesbian scholars comes a focus on sexuality, the formations and relations of sexual orientation – the beginning of queer criticism.

3. In the 1990s, then, as cultural studies expand and impact on all aspects of the discipline, a further focus on geopolitics, imperial–colonial formations and relations, comes to the fore – the beginnings of postcolonial criticism. This is initially propelled by non-Western migrant scholars in the West and is readily taken up by racial–ethnic minorities in the West.

Thus, in the late 1990s, postcolonial criticism enters the discipline as a further current in ideological criticism, through the problematizing of another differential relation of power, now at the geopolitical level of imperial–colonial frameworks.

Such problematization accounts not only for the concerns but also for the caveats raised from the beginning of the approach. The latter are especially important: due attention must be given to the intricacies and complexities at work in imperial–colonial interchanges. In foregrounding and theorizing geopolitical power, postcolonial criticism necessarily enters into dialogue with feminist and liberation as well as minority and queer criticisms, all of which focus on unequal relationships of power. Likewise, these other criticisms must not proceed without a sense of how geopolitical dynamics affect their areas of interest. Thus, while postcolonial criticism's principal focus on imperial–colonial frameworks and its intense analysis through a postcolonial optic apply, both have to be properly nuanced by way of gender, economics, race–ethnicity, and sexual orientation – plus any other dimension of human existence – in order to avoid a facile collapse of categories into the single binomial of imperialism and colonialism.

POSTCOLONIAL CRITICISM AND POSTCOLONIAL STUDIES. In attending to the relation of postcolonial criticism to the movement of postcolonial studies, I use as point of departure two distinguishing features of its early deployment. First, it is critics from the outside, such as Van-Zanten Gallagher and Donaldson, that introduce the problematic to the discipline. Such a development is not surprising, given the fact that postcolonial discourse had been active in Literary Studies and Cultural Studies for some time. Second, it is biblical critics from outside the center that first come on and latch onto the postcolonial problematic.[32] This

---

[32] Sugirtharajah, *Voices from the Margin*; F. F. Segovia and M. A. Tolbert, eds., *Reading from This Place. Vol. 1: Social Location and Biblical Interpretation in the United States*

turn of events should not prove surprising either, since such critics had been active for some time already in pursuing the question of social location in interpretation and since such research concentrated on the global context of the non-Western world and the local context of racial–ethnic minorities in the West, both domains in which postcolonial discourse had been active. For a proper understanding of postcolonial criticism, therefore, a sense of the problematic, its origins and trajectories, is also in order. This, however, is a task easier said than done, given the enormous volume of scholarly literature, the wide range of critical positions, and the high intensity of discussions present in such studies. What follows provides but a basic summary of this historical path.

Where do postcolonial studies begin? The answer is at once straightforward and problematic. On the one hand, it is the publication of Edward Said's *Orientalism* in 1978 that is generally marked as *the* point of origin.[33] On the other hand, such precise identification and dating tend to isolate such studies from various preceding concerns and developments.

Said's analysis of the juncture of power and discourse in the representation of the Orient in the West, with its view of the Orient as the Other – static, enigmatic, inferior – as grounding for political conquest and domination, leads to the formation of what is initially characterized as "colonial discourse theory." In this critical enterprise, primarily undertaken at first within Literary Studies and under the influence of various poststructuralist influences, the name and work of Said are joined eventually by those of Homi Bhabha and Gayatri Chakravorty Spivak.[34] These three figures constitute the core of what eventually becomes known as "postcolonial discourse," as this critical movement expands across the

---

(Minneapolis: Fortress, 1995), *Reading from This Place. Vol. 2: Social Location and Biblical Interpretation in Global Perspective* (Minneapolis: Fortress, 1995), and *Teaching the Bible: The Discourses and Politics of Biblical Pedagogy* (Maryknoll, NY: Orbis, 1998).

[33] E. Said, *Orientalism* (New York: Pantheon Books, 1978).

[34] Bhabha's literary production, in the nature of essays, begins in the early 1980s and is brought together in *The Location of Culture* (New York: Routledge, 1994). Spivak's literary production, also by way of essays, dates from the mid-1980s, and is brought together in various volumes: *In Other Worlds: Essays in Cultural Politics* (New York: Routledge, 1987), *The Post-Colonial Critic: Interviews, Strategies, Dialogues*, ed. S. Harasym (New York: Routledge, 1990), and *Outside the Teaching Machine* (New York: Routledge, 1993). A collection of her most important studies and introductions to her work may be found in D. Landry and G. MacLean, eds, *The Spivak Reader* (New York: Routledge, 1996).

disciplinary spectrum through the 1980s and 1990s. As such, they become the primary object of attention in treatments of the field, the requisite center of reference in scholarly developments, and the principal target of attack in critical discussions. In this process of taking account, expanding boundaries, and calling to task, the core figures and their publications are joined by an ever-growing list of names and works analyzing, extending, and revising the postcolonial angle of inquiry in ever-new directions.

With the unfolding of this disciplinary path and corpus, a number of exclusionary side effects become, in time, increasingly evident. First, this movement, given its close theoretical links with poststructuralist thinking, becomes curiously separated from the anticolonial struggles and writings of the 1940s through the 1970s. Thus, insufficient dialogue is established with such figures as Aimé Césaire and C. L. R. James, Amilcar Cabral and Kwame Nkrumah, Frantz Fanon and Albert Memmi – to mention but a few. Second, given its overriding concern for cultural production, the movement remains strangely removed from analysis of the material matrix. As a result, the long-standing analysis of imperialism and colonialism within the Marxist tradition is largely bypassed. Lastly, the movement, given its consuming attention to the world of the British Empire, remains eerily divorced from other such formations, most noticeably perhaps in terms of the anticolonial writings and struggles in the Americas from the beginning of the nineteenth century through the end of the twentieth century. One looks in vain, therefore, for any sort of critical contact with figures from the francophone, lusophone, and hispanophone world of Latin America.

In sum, not only does the emergence of postcolonial studies stand as both certain and muddled, but also its subsequent development emerges as intensely multifarious, convoluted, and conflicted. Consequently, in the late 1990s, postcolonial criticism enters the discipline by drawing on a problematic that had been introduced in the academy in the late 1970s, that had experienced widespread diffusion and gained considerable sophistication through the 1980s and into the 1990s, and that had spawned throughout countless debates, sharp controversies, and profound critiques. It was clearly only a matter of time before such a problematic would find its way into biblical criticism. That it should do so in full plenitude, with all its achievements and disputations, is, needless to say, imperative. This is highly important: due attention must be given at all times to this variegated and tensive historical path. As such, postcolonial biblical criticism should take nothing for granted; rather, all critical moves are to be explicitly grounded. It should not advance any particular procedure as *the* postcolonial way of interpretation; rather, it should keep other options in view and in dialogue. Only then will it avoid a monolithic understanding of both the problematic and the approach.

Methodological Configuration: Demarcation and Procedure

Having shed light on the theoretical foundations of the postcolonial optic, I turn to consider its methodological configuration. I have deliberately used the term "approach" throughout rather than "method" in order to make the point that a postcolonial optic does not present, and should not claim, a set way of going about the task of interpretation. Such openness is in accord with the diversity at work within the postcolonial problematic itself. For example, a look at the ways in which the various authors of the *Postcolonial Commentary* set about their task brings out such diversity. There is simply no point that is settled and no consensus to be had. In what follows I confine myself to two key areas of consideration: demarcation (the question of meaning and scope) and procedure (the question of dynamics and mechanics in argumentation); and I conclude with a personal vision for postcolonial criticism.

DEMARCATION: MEANING AND SCOPE.[35] The question of meaning involves the definition of postcolonial criticism. Five elements are relevant here: the force of the term, the relational configuration of imperialism and colonialism, the terrain of inquiry, the referential reach, and the mode of encounter. In each case I summarize the main options presented by the literature and express my own judgment regarding their application in biblical criticism.

1. Regarding the term "postcolonial" itself, the temporal denotation has been approached from both a historical–political perspective, marking the time after either the beginning or the end of colonization, and

---

[35] For an extensive analysis of the meaning and scope of postcolonial studies, see F. F. Segovia, "Mapping the Postcolonial Optic in Biblical Criticism," in *Postcolonial Biblical Criticism: Interdisciplinary Intersections*, ed. S. D. Moore and F. F. Segovia (London: T&T Clark, 2005), 23–78.

a psychological–social perspective, signaling awareness of colonization. My preference is for conscientization: the problematization of a geopolitical relationship of domination and subordination, regardless of existing historical and political conditions.

2. On delimiting "imperialism" and "colonialism," two main options present themselves: a sequential relation, in which colonialism precedes imperialism as a less defined civilizational or economic system; and a spatial relation, in which imperialism is taken to refer to the center and colonialism to the periphery. I prefer the spatial understanding: imperialism and colonialism apply to all that has to do with center and periphery, respectively.

3. Concerning the terrain of inquiry, one finds a spectrum of positions: emphasis on the material matrix underlying imperial–colonial frameworks, as pursued in Marxist criticism; concentration on the discursive production emerging from such frameworks, as favored by postcolonial discourse; or due consideration of both. My preference is for critical attention to both the social and the cultural perspectives as interrelated and interdependent.

4. On referential reach, a spectrum of positions is again evident: concentration on the relation between the imperial and the colonial; concentration on the colonial, untying its umbilical cord to the imperial; or due consideration of both. I prefer a broad understanding: analysis of the periphery not only in terms of the center but also in its own terms.

5. Regarding interaction between the imperial and the colonial, the mode of encounter reveals several options: uniform application across imperial–colonial frameworks, regardless of time and culture; unique application to a particular framework, with no comparative analysis across frameworks; and multifarious consideration of similarities and differences, not only between/among centers and peripheries in different frameworks but also between a center and its peripheries in any particular framework. My preference is for comparative analysis: rigorous stocktaking of differences and similarities throughout.

The question of scope has to do with the range of postcolonial criticism. Two elements are pertinent here: operative breadth and underlying rationale. In each case, again, options are summarized and a preference is set forth for application in biblical criticism.

1. With respect to operative breadth, the spectrum comes across as functional rather than theorized: limited (imperial–colonial frameworks within the modern West); expanding (frameworks in the premodern West as well); expansive (frameworks across historical epochs and/or cultural contexts, from antiquity through the present, both within and outside the West). My preference is for the expansive vision.

2. With respect to underlying rationale, the spectrum ranges from the restricted to the inclusive: from confinement to the political and economic frameworks of modernity and capitalism to embrace of other frameworks, alongside or preceding capitalism and modernity. I prefer the inclusive vision.

PROCEDURE: DYNAMICS AND MECHANICS. The question of dynamics has to do with overall mode of analysis in postcolonial perspective. Here one finds work in all umbrella paradigms of contemporary criticism: from the historical through the literary and the sociocultural to the ideological. A first approach is to draw the historical context of imperial power and then to show how a particular text or group fits within such a context. A second is to elicit how the texts themselves represent the imperial context and fashion a corresponding response. A third is to call on social models of imperial–colonial formations and relations and then to apply such models to specific texts or groups. A final approach is to invoke postcolonial discourse and to filter texts through the lens in question. Such modes are not mutually exclusive but admit of varying combinations. The question of mechanics has to do with concrete angles of analysis. Here one finds a substantial degree of variation in strategies and techniques within each overall mode.

POSTCOLONIAL BIBLICAL CRITICISM: A VISION. From this exposition of methodological configuration, I view the deployment of the postcolonial optic in biblical criticism as entirely justifiable and decidedly open ended.

To begin with, the range of positions regarding demarcation fully warrant such application. That is certainly the case in terms of scope. One finds in postcolonial studies ample room for a conceptualization of its envisioned domain as transhistorical and transcultural and of its proposed task as fundamentally comparative in nature. Not all would agree, to be sure, but the theoretical space is there, even if largely unexplored. From this perspective, postcolonial biblical criticism is justifiable, since no imperial–colonial formation would be ruled out of consideration on historical or cultural grounds and no underlying framework deemed out of bounds in political or economic terms. Such is also the case in terms of meaning. One also finds ample room in postcolonial studies for a properly informed articulation and execution of its proposed comparative task in transhistorical and transcultural fashion. Such deployment can be readily instituted along the major lines of reference indicated earlier:

- Foregrounding conscientization of the geopolitical problematic in texts and interpretations alike, irrespective of existing historical–political conditions.
- Adopting a spatial designation of the "imperial" and "colonial" nomenclature, and related set of terms, with reference to center and periphery, respectively.
- Taking up both the social and the cultural realms as object of analysis.
- Attending to the imperial and the colonial not only in terms of their mutual relations but also in terms of each formation by itself.
- Taking seriously into account similarities and differences in comparing imperial–colonial formations as well as in contrasting variations within a center–peripheries formation.

In addition, the range of possibilities regarding procedure, in terms of both dynamics and mechanics, allow for such application to be cast in any number of general modes and concrete angles of inquiry.

At this point, then, I would like to offer my own vision for postcolonial biblical criticism as a critical project. From the first, as the account of its irruption in the field has shown, this project has been conceived in terms of texts and interpretations. I would concur wholeheartedly.

Indeed, I would argue for a threefold application, with a view of the various levels at work as interrelated and interdependent: (1) analysis of the biblical texts, whether of ancient Israel or early Christianity, both within and vis-à-vis their respective imperial–colonial formations; (2) analysis of interpretations and interpreters of these texts and contexts in the Western tradition, again within and vis-à-vis the imperial–colonial formations at the heart of Western hegemony and expansionism; (3) analysis of interpretations and interpreters of the biblical texts and contexts on a global scale, once again within and vis-à-vis the imperial–colonial formations at the core of contemporary globalization. Thus, postcolonial biblical criticism would embrace analysis of the geopolitical relationship of power in the worlds of antiquity, modernity, and postmodernity.

At all three levels, moreover, such analysis should involve attention to both the material matrix and the discursive production of the imperial–colonial framework in question. Emphasis in this regard will depend, of course, on the nature and objective of the inquiry in question. Postcolonial biblical criticism would thus have as its domain the remains, representations, and artificers of biblical antiquity. At all three levels, lastly, such analysis may be pursued in any variety of modes and any number of angles of inquiry. Choice in this regard should always be advanced and grounded in explicit and theorized fashion.

POSTCOLONIAL BIBLICAL INTERPRETATION: THE GOSPEL OF MATTHEW

I turn now, in this second part, to the application of the postcolonial optic to the Gospel of Matthew. Keeping in mind the historical path laid out earlier, a postcolonial approach to Matthew begins in earnest during the second period of expansion and consolidation (2000–2007). While a couple of studies in this vein appeared earlier, it is at this point that a full-fledged approach to Matthew in terms of imperial–colonial context and stance begins to emerge. Pride of place in this regard belongs to Dube and her monograph *Postcolonial Feminist Interpretation of the Bible*, published in 2000. In fact, it is Dube who had penned the earlier studies on Matthew and the postcolonial.[36] I take the volume, however,

---

[36] A first such study addressed the question of authoritative travel, border-crossing, and nation-discipling in imperialist texts through the focus of Matthew 28:16–20: "'Go Therefore and Make Disciples of All Nations' (Matt 28:19a): A Postcolonial Perspective on Biblical Criticism and Pedagogy," in *Teaching the Bible: The Discourses and Politics of Biblical Pedagogy*, ed. F. F. Segovia and M. A. Tolbert (Maryknoll, NY: Orbis, 1998). A second study focused on issues of biblical translation in Africa by way of the Matthean use of "demons": "Consuming a Colonial Cultural Bomb: Translating *Badimo* into 'Demons' in the Setswana Bible (Matthew 8.28–34; 15:22; 10:8)," *JSNT* 73 (1999): 33–59. Preceding both, Dube had already published an essay in L. E. Donaldson's foundational *Semeia* volume of 1996 in which she pursued the question of method, through the eyes of John: "Reading for Decolonization (John 4:1–42)," in *Postcolonialism and Scriptural Reading*, 37–57.

as the point of origin in Matthean Studies for two reasons: its rigorous consideration of procedure and its combined attention to both the text itself and its tradition of interpretation.

A series of publications followed swiftly. In the following year, 2001, a second monograph appeared, Carter's *Matthew and Empire: Initial Explorations*. Then, in 2005, the aforementioned collection of essays entitled *The Gospel of Matthew in Its Roman Imperial Context*, edited by Riches and Sim, came out. This volume was broad in scope: a first group of contributions addressed the question of social models and the view of Rome in Jewish and Christian literature; a second group focused on the Gospel, both in general terms and in specialized fashion (Roman characters; Matt. 1:1 and imperial Christology). Two essays from this latter batch prove especially significant: a study of Rome's role in Matthean eschatology by Sim and a study of Matthean missionary strategy by Riches. Lastly, in 2007, the piece on Matthew for the *Postcolonial Commentary* was authored by Carter.

Taken together, these works bring out a pointed sense of the postcolonial problematic in the Gospel and provide keen insight into the diversity at work in mode and angle of inquiry within postcolonial criticism. On the problematic itself, the Matthean stance within the imperial context of Rome, the spectrum emerges, on the surface, as extreme: at one end, a decidedly imperializing text; at the other end, a resolutely anti-imperial text; in between, a text simultaneously anti-imperial and imperializing. In what follows I expand on each position by way of a particular exponent, bringing out their varying modes and angles of inquiry.

Matthew as Imperializing Text – Musa W. Dube

Dube's work is analytically innovative: its historiographical approach is unusual and path breaking, sophisticated in orientation and complex in execution. As is invariably the case with new critical orientations, it delves deeply into matters of theory and method. In fact, the volume devotes as much space to procedure, the grounding and elaboration of a postcolonial method, as it does to interpretation, the reading of Matthew from such a standpoint. The search for method involves a conjunction of postcolonialism and feminism, leading to the articulation of a "postcolonial feminist" approach. Its application to the Gospel deals with the Matthean point of view on the imperial–colonial framework of Rome as a whole, with sustained focus on Matthew 15:21–28, the story about the healing of a Canaanite woman's daughter by Jesus, as a key unit in this regard, given its insertion of gender at the heart of the geopolitical problematic.

Dube's work is explicitly perspectival, contextual, and theological. The volume represents, first of all, an exercise in ideological criticism, intersectional in character, with recourse to literary criticism (rhetorics, narratology, reader response) and sociocultural criticism (study of colonial/postcolonial societies). It inquires into geopolitical as well as gender relations of power in engaged rather than detached fashion. The volume is also rooted in Dube's reality and experience as a woman of the Third World (from the continent of Africa, the area of the sub-Sahara, and the country of Botswana) and a subject of the colonized world. For all such women, the "doubly colonized," geopolitics and gender prove, she contends, equally important, over against the single-minded patriarchal lens of Third World liberationism and the equally single-minded imperialist lens of First World feminism. The volume constitutes, lastly, a call for theological respect of and dialogue with the Other, seeking a space for the religious practices and beliefs of the colonized, Christian or otherwise.

Dube begins by setting both the biblical writings and the feminist movement within the context of a postcolonial historical–political world. In so doing, she introduces from the outset the challenges of imperialism and patriarchy for criticism as intertwined and calls for a hermeneutic that will take both dimensions of oppression jointly into account.

Dube takes up first the question of procedure. Her breadth of vision is expansive: appeal to anticolonial as well as postcolonial theory; attention to literary–rhetorical strategies in ancient as well as modern "imperializing" literature; and analysis of corresponding strategies in "decolonizing" literature. Its theoretical moorings are eclectic, drawing on both discursive and material studies; its literary parameters are broad, from Exodus and the Aeneid to English (Joseph Conrad) and Botswanan (Mositi Torontle) literature. The result is a proposal for a "decolonizing" method of reading the Bible, grounded in the "doubly colonized" women of the Third World – a method embodying resistance to imperial and patriarchal oppression and offering "liberating interdependence" for all. This method makes use of established discursive strategies, such as exposing imperial constructions or developing hybrid rereadings, but also goes beyond to include new spaces for self-representation and re-visioning of systemic structures and relations. Such a space Dube herself finds in the biblical reading of *Semoya* practiced by women of the African Independent Churches: a fresh hearing of God in the Bible, through the Spirit, with liberating existence in mind.

From such practices, a critical method emerges – "Rahab's reading prism," with reference to the combined gender and geopolitical status at play in the figure of Rahab. Its objective is to identify "imperializing" and "decolonizing" texts in the Bible. Its mode of analysis is to scrutinize the literary–rhetorical structures at work in texts in order to establish historical posture and ideological connections so that they can be properly marked as imperializing or decolonizing. For Dube, it should be noted, intertextuality is very much at work in both sets: structures and claims are liberally drawn on and creatively used anew within each set. Four questions function as filter in this process. The first one develops the historical angle: What is the stance of the text toward the political imperialism of its time? The other three pursue the ideological connection: Does the text encourage and justify travel to distant lands? Does the text construct difference by way of dialogical and liberating interdependence or by way of condemnation and alienation of the foreign? Does the text deploy gender and divine representations toward subordination and domination?

Dube then turns to a reading of Matthew following Rahab's reading prism. The result is a view of the Gospel as profoundly imperializing. Historically, as a work produced among the colonized Jewish margins of the Roman Empire, the Gospel presents Rome in positive fashion, while casting rival groups among the colonized in negative fashion. The implied reader so constructs characters, the issue of imperial taxation, and the trial of Jesus as to favor the Empire and its agents, while attacking the local religious leaders of Judaism, setting up thereby a relationship of domination and subordination between the Christian community and all outsiders within Judaism. Dube thus describes Matthew as the sort of postcolonial text that "certifies imperialism" and shifts the "root cause of oppression" toward "other victims" among the colonized. Ideologically, the Gospel subscribes to the foundational myth of Israel as the promised land and is thus geared toward fostering imperializing values. First, it sanctions travel to other lands and peoples, ascribing such a mandate to Jesus, in whom resides all authority in heaven and on earth. Second, it demands the submission of all peoples and lands, through obedience to the teachings of Jesus. The implied reader so uses historical figures of Israel's past – Abraham, David, and Rahab – as to set up a relationship of domination and subordination between the Christian community and all non-Jewish outsiders. Dube thus presents Matthew as imposing, through the mission, a "nonnegotiable cultural good" on "potential consumers". Taking both historical stance and ideological links together, Dube sees the Gospel as advancing a "partnership approach" with Rome, best captured by the pronouncement of Matthew 22:21 on God and Emperor.

In addition, the Gospel employs gender as part of its imperializing ideology, as the healing of the Canaanite woman's daughter shows. The unit is identified as a variation of the land possession type-scene in imperializing texts of the Hebrew Bible: a local woman functions as contact point with a traveling hero, a foreigner who has been divinely empowered; the local woman is represented as desiring or needing the traveling hero in some way; the traveling hero is depicted as responding in various ways. In Matthew 15:21–28, the Canaanite woman plays the role of the local woman – in need of assistance, while Jesus takes on the role of the foreign traveler – superior and divine. The implied author thereby constructs the mission to non-Jewish outsiders and the offer of salvation from the one God in terms of domination and subjugation, with a local woman as signifier for the conquest and colonization of a land and a people, indeed all lands and all peoples.

In conclusion, Dube unfolds a dialectical vision of texts as imperializing or decolonizing, not only in terms of the biblical texts but also with regard to the later readings and readers of such texts. Her postcolonial feminist approach is designed to serve as a decolonizing tool, yielding identification as well as critique, all in the interest of resistance and liberation. Its aim is thus twofold: exposing the intertwined geopolitical–gender agendas of texts and readings, and assessing accordingly with liberating dialogue and interdependence in mind. In the case of Matthew, Dube foregrounds the imperialistic and patriarchal oppression at work in the Gospel and classifies it as a thoroughly imperializing text: a text to be resisted, therefore. Analysis of its interpretive history in the West and the ramifications of such readings for society and culture prove equally wanting: a path to be similarly resisted. Matthew's Gospel is, therefore, not a work suitable for a vision of liberating dialogue and interdependence, whether for the doubly colonized or anybody else.

Matthew as Counter-Imperial Text – Warren Carter

Carter's early work, *Matthew and Empire*, is analytically straightforward: its historiographical approach is familiar and well established, yet intensely focalized and, within such focalization, broadly undertaken. The volume does not seek a new critical approach. It is not, therefore, much concerned with matters of theory and method. It is also not in dialogue with anticolonial or postcolonial discourse, aside from a ready appropriation of Said's territorial definition of imperialism. For Carter, rather, historical contextualization remains the primary task, but with a bent. The inquiry revolves around a twofold focus: the character of Rome as an imperial power, with analysis of its imperial–colonial formations and relations; and the reactions of early Christian groups to such power, with analysis of Matthew as one such instance. Thus, the volume is as concerned with a reconstruction of the Roman historical context as it is with a reading of Matthew against such a context. The reconstruction is widely based, attending to both social and cultural dimensions; the reading is widely cast as well, dealing with individual units as well as the Gospel as a whole.

Carter's work is neither openly perspectival nor contextual nor theological. There is, nonetheless, a definite, if underlying, agenda at work. First, the volume constitutes an exercise in historical criticism, with recourse to Classical Studies (Roman society and culture) and World-Systems Analysis as well as literary criticism (reader response: authorial audience) and comparative literature (other contemporary reactions, Christian and non-Christian). At the same time, its focalization pushes the geopolitical problematic to the center of interpretation. Its inquiry into geopolitical relations of power is thus detached but concentrated. Second, the volume conveys no concrete sense of its own social location or ideological agenda within the contemporary geopolitical world. Yet, Carter does characterize the present global situation as imperial, outlined as follows: implicit identification of the United States as the "one superpower"; explicit reference to the political economy of global capitalism; and pointed mention of cultural and religious expansionism. Consequently, he calls for critical attention to this imperial context in reading Matthew, a work deemed both "relevant" and "urgent."

Finally, the volume expresses no overt theological agenda in surfacing the religious beliefs and practices of the colonized. At the same time, in his call for critical consideration of the present-day imperialism when reading Matthew, Carter has Christian readers in mind, for whom, he explains, the Gospel is Scripture. As a result, he suggests various lines of approach: adopting its "suspicious" attitude toward all ruling institutions and practices, through consideration of who benefits and who does not; adapting its strategy of resistance to the ruling powers of today, through both theological engagement and social commitment; and weighing its vision of God's future as resistance to imperialism, through reflection on its (ironic) consequences. In the end, although in the background and general in tone, Carter's agenda remains undeniable.

Carter begins with a comprehensive account of the Roman imperial system in terms of social structures and cultural traditions. This he does in two steps: first, in empire-wide fashion; then, with respect to Antioch in particular, which he views as a "likely" location for the composition of Matthew, dated toward the end of the century, with the decade of the 1980s as "likely."

Materially, the system is classified as an "aristocratic empire." It is marked by the rule of an elite class (1–2 percent of the population) over vast areas of lands and peoples, with the figure of the Emperor at the top. Underneath this "aristocracy," a sharp gradation of social classes obtains: retainers (5 percent); peasants and artisans, with merchants as a small middle ground; the degraded and expendables (5–10 percent). Such rule was achieved and preserved by means of a "legionary economy," involving two interdependent components: the possession of enormous military force, strategically deployed and ready for action; and the amassing of great wealth, secured through control of the land and production and extracted through an extensive system of taxation and tribute. Such rule was administered by means of a limited bureaucracy and a far-flung network of provincial counterparts. Discursively, this system was unified and driven by a set of interrelated values: wielding power (connections, appointments, possessions, troops), acquiring wealth (land ownership and production), and displaying status (public recognition).

Taken together, Carter declares, the empire survived on domination and compliance, hierarchy and verticality, and exclusion and inequality. Further, what was true of the empire as a whole was true as well of Antioch, one of its largest and most important cities. Such was the underside behind the facade of the Pax Romana: a peace much vaunted – by those "from above"; a peace quite detrimental – for those "from below."

Further, at the intersection of all such structures and traditions, and playing a highly public role, lay the realm of religion. Indeed, its tenets, its practices, and its rituals were all filtered through the rule of Rome and the figure of the Emperor. Rome and the Emperor signified, therefore, the "sovereignty, presence, will, and blessings" of the divine realm in the human realm. There was thus, Carter argues, a clear "imperial theology." In such a narrative, it was the Gods who willed the rule of Rome, and it was the Emperor who embodied the presence of the Gods in general and, especially during and after the Flavian dynasty, of Jupiter in particular. In this narrative, moreover, the Emperor also served as the means for the distribution of divine gifts – specific and abstract, natural and supernatural. For such a narrative, therefore, the divine presence and largesse represented by Rome and Emperor demanded acquiescence as well as veneration, as institutionalized and disseminated through an intricate network of practices and rituals. Such, again, was the reality behind the surface of the Pax Romana: a peace of divine inspiration, mandate, and riches – from all those "from above"; a peace of human imposition, enforcement, and exploitation – on all those "from below."

Against this multidimensional portrayal of the Roman imperial system, its imperial peace, and theology, Carter undertakes a reading of Matthew. The result is a view of the Gospel as a text of radical resistance – a "counternarrative" to Rome. Materially, the author constructs a vision of Christian community that is egalitarian rather than hierarchical, merciful rather than exploitative, and inclusive rather than exclusionary. Discursively, the author constructs a set of Christian values unified and driven by commitment to the welfare and service of others – living as a "marginal slave, an outsider, on the edge, at the bottom" – rather than power, wealth, and status. Taken together, Matthew constructs a vision of peace grounded in justice. At the intersection of such envisioned structures and traditions, there is the realm of religion: a vision of an Empire of God that manifests itself – its sovereignty and will, its presence and benefits – in and to the world, in and through the figure of Jesus, his teachings and deeds. This Empire of God, for Matthew, is both present already, launched by Jesus and extended through his mission, and still to come, awaiting a final reconstitution through a return of Jesus. The author's vision of peace is thus grounded in justice as the will of God. From this Empire of God, the Empire of Rome (including local retainers, such as the religious leaders of Judaism) stands as its opposite, under the power of Satan – under judgment and destined for destruction.

In sum, Carter presents a dialectical vision of ancient social–cultural–religious narratives as imperial or anti-imperial. On the one hand, he draws out the dialectical vision of Rome as an imperial system: material and discursive, as well as religious – advantage for a small segment of the population, the elite and retainer social classes, who enjoy the narrative of imperial peace and theology; discursive and material, as well as religious – disadvantage for the great bulk of the population, the peasant–artisan and the degraded–expendable classes, who endure the underside of Roman peace and theology. Within any such system, Carter argues, resistance is likely, in some form or another. Rome is no exception; indeed, Carter reads Matthew as one such example and a rather stark one. On the other hand, therefore, he brings out the dialectical vision of the Gospel's own proposed imperial system: radical opposition between Rome and God; the Emperor with his agents and Jesus with his agents; the structures and values of the Pax Romana and those of the Pax Christiana – in effect, an anti-imperial text of the highest order. Yet, Carter brings out the irony inherent in such resistance. Matthew, he argues, remains captive to the "imperial mindset," framing the alternative community envisioned "in imperial terms," with recourse to images of domination and exclusion.

This point of imperial captivity Carter pursues but briefly and by way of conclusion. He asks his intended Christian "authorial audience" to ponder the consequences of God's future as constructed by Matthew and suggests a path through the dialectic that might preserve a middle stance between critique and vision. This path has four components: (1) looking for solidarity with others in the quest for justice, (2) bearing in mind that

God cannot be limited, (3) seeking alternative expressions for God's way, and (4) contrasting the mercy of God's present way and the violence of God's future way. For Carter, this last component provides the lead in reading Matthew: constructing a vision of God's future in terms of the vision of God's present.

Matthew as Conflicted Text – Warren Carter

Carter's later work, the piece on Matthew for the *Postcolonial Commentary*, is analytically more innovative: its historiographical approach, while preserving the central élan of contextualization, becomes broader, more complex, and sophisticated. Two developments account for this shift. The first is the foregrounding of the ironic character of Matthew's project of resistance, its opposition to the Roman Empire through an Empire of God. What had been pursued in *Matthew and Empire* by way of a concluding reflection is now introduced as a beginning orientation. The second is the deployment of a literary approach in the analysis of Matthew and its project of resistance, based on the character of the Gospel as a biographical narrative and highlighting the feature of plot. While the commentary does not set out to fashion a new critical approach as such, these developments, relatively modest in import, do mark a discursive shift: a new dialogue with postcolonial discourse and greater involvement with theory and method. To be sure, the task of contextualization, through reconstruction of both the Roman imperial system and the Matthean response, remains foremost. Consequently, such recourse to postcolonial and literary criticism stands as subordinate to and supportive of contextualization.

In the process, Carter's work becomes more openly perspectival. To put it differently, the underlying agenda at work from before now lies closer to the surface. To begin with, while the study still represents an exercise in historical criticism, its analysis of the geopolitical problematic in Matthew becomes more sharply ideological in tone – less detached, more engaged. First, a postcolonial reading of Matthew is justified on theoretical grounds. On the one hand, Roman rule qualifies as "imperial": as a "metropolitan center," Rome exercises "power over" other lands and peoples in various ways. Such "power over" – its means and dynamics, its impact and legacy – may thus be examined as a process of "imperialization." On the other hand, Matthew qualifies as a postcolonial text: as a textual–cultural expression within an imperial context, the Gospel is a "product of . . . interaction" between imperial and local cultures. Matthew is thus characterized as a "silenced provincial, a voice on the margins." Second, the depiction of Matthew's voice as one that both "contests and embraces" Roman power is given a postcolonial reading, along the lines of Homi Bhabha. Any process of interaction between the imperial and the local, including resistance, is said to involve a process of "complex negotiation," yielding a broad spectrum of options. As an example of such interaction, Matthew's project, grounded in an oppositional Empire of God, is portrayed as in "imitation" of Rome, its values and practices, and hence as signifying "ambivalence" and "ambiguity" in the face of Roman power. In addition, beyond Matthew itself, the reach of postcolonial analysis is significantly expanded to include the role of the Gospel in the imperial expansion of Europe, though not pursued.

Theologically, the essay becomes somewhat more explicit as well. The previous call for critical reflection on the part of Christian readers is now brought under the programmatic reach of postcolonial analysis. Such analysis extends not just to modern imperial systems but also to "contemporary readers in ecclesial contexts." Given their relation to the Gospel as Scripture, as a text for "guidance and formation," such readers must subject Matthew's particular mode of opposition to rigorous scrutiny so that, in their use of it, they avoid "imperial practices, mind set, and language." For this a reading of "suspicion," with specific strategic implications, is advanced. Contextually, however, the study actually turns less open: neither the contemporary imperial system nor the situation of ecclesial readers nor Carter's own location is pursued in any way.

Carter's reading of Matthew, while still firmly set against the Roman imperial system, is now pursued in formal literary terms, pointing out how both choice of genre and development of plot channel and advance the project of opposition to Rome. As ancient biography, the Gospel focuses on the life and teaching of a public figure; however, the figure in question, Jesus, is not someone who embodies and promotes imperial structures and values but rather a "provincial peasant," crucified by Rome, who overturns and replaces such values and structures. As narrative, the Gospel presents Jesus's life and teaching in terms of a crescendo unfolding of the Empire of God within the Empire of Rome, comprising six major stages in all: (1) identification of Jesus as God's agent – commissioned to make manifest God's saving presence within the Roman Empire, (2) execution of Jesus's commission to establish God's Empire – the nonviolent creation of an alternative community, (3) outline of popular reactions to Jesus's identity and commission – negative as well as positive, (4) focus on Jesus's collision with the local elite – the religious–political authorities of Judaism as retainers of Rome, (5) narrower focus on Jesus's final challenge to the elite and its consequences – rejection and, in league with Roman rule, death by crucifixion, and (6) laying bare the limitations of Roman power in the face of Jesus's resurrection, possession of all power in heaven and on earth – a worldwide mission. Throughout, Carter brings out the Gospel's twofold character of contestation and embrace.

In this later reading, therefore, the conflicted nature of the Gospel displaces, from the beginning and in a systematic fashion, the earlier foregrounding of Matthew as a counternarrative of radical resistance. Here, from the start and throughout, the emphasis is on the Gospel as a paradox, an "impure subject," in opposition to yet complicit with imperial power. From the first and in sustained manner, the dialectical opposition mounted by Matthew against Rome, while sharply reaffirmed, is also sharply exposed as "mimicry": the "power over" of the Roman imperial system is confronted and replaced by the "power over" of God's imperial system, evident in all categories comprising this vision of resistance. Such a consistent double-edged reading is directly responsible for the more explicit call to critical postcolonial reflection on the part of Christian readers today. In effect, while Matthew's critique of Roman rule should be praised, its vision of God's rule should be dissected, separating, as he puts it, what gives "life" from what maintains "death." Toward this end, then, Carter proposes, again, the earlier program for reading Matthew today and the set of strategies to be used in analyzing its vision of God's future and consequences.

Concluding Observation

As indicated earlier, the interpretive spectrum regarding the postcolonial problematic in Matthew is indeed dialectical. Yet, as also intimated earlier, such is the case at a surface rather than core level, for neither end of the spectrum ignores the presence of its opposite in the text. In both cases, Matthew is viewed as fully aware of Roman imperial power; in each case, however, Matthew's reaction emerges as radically different, yet nuanced. For Dube, Matthew responds by playing up to Rome, yet ultimately adopts imperializing values of its own toward all outsiders, drawing on Israel's foundational vision. For Carter, the Gospel responds with total opposition to Rome, yet ultimately mimics such imperial values with respect to all outsiders. Where the Gospel is placed within the imperial framework is thus, to my mind, a question of which narrative elements are emphasized and which are downplayed. In the middle, therefore, Carter's text-as-conflicted approach breaks through the dialectic by emphasizing both elements, accommodation and resistance, at once. Where Matthew is situated in the face of Rome depends, therefore, on mode and angle of inquiry, as activated by interpreters who are themselves situated and engaged within their own contexts in any number of ways.

READING MATTHEW 8:5–13 IN A POSTCOLONIAL KEY

At this point, I turn to an individual narrative unit of the Gospel as signifier for the postcolonial problematic in the Gospel. Theoretically, any unit, regardless of size, can serve in this regard. Practically, units in which official representatives of the Empire figure, directly or indirectly, provide a ready point of entry into the Matthean optic.[37] I shall use Matthew 8:5–13, Jesus's healing of the centurion's "servant"/"child," for this purpose on two counts; first, the centurion is the first such figure to appear in the narrative; second, the exchange between Jesus and the centurion provides a key insight into imperial–colonial relations from a Matthean perspective. I begin with various observations about the unit, its composition and placement; then, I place the unit within the interpretive spectrum earlier.

Matthew 8:5–13 as Narrative Unit

DELINEATION. The unit is brief and easily demarcated. The beginning (8:5) marks a shift away from the preceding unit, 8:1–4. Spatially, the

---

[37] Such units include: 8:5–13, a centurion's request for a healing; 22:15–22, the question of imperial taxation; 27:1–26, the trial of Jesus before Pilate; 27:27–31, 32–56, 57–61, the torture, the crucifixion, and the burial of Jesus; 27:62–28:16, the watch over the tomb.

action is now located in Capernaum, no longer in the area around the mountain where the long address of Matthew 5–7 had taken place. In terms of characters, a non-Jewish centurion replaces a Jewish leper as Jesus's main interlocutor. Whether there is a change in audience as well is uncertain: Is the group that now follows him (8:10) the same as the crowds that had followed him earlier (8:1)? The conclusion (8:13) anticipates another shift: a narratorial comment brings the action to a close, paving the way for a new unit to follow (8:15–16). Spatially, although presumably still in Capernaum, a specific locale is now identified, Peter's house. In terms of characters, Peter's mother-in-law takes center stage. Matthew 8:5–13 clearly constitutes a distinct unit.

GENRE AND PLOT. The unit can be readily classified as a miracle of healing. Such stories follow, in any number of variations, a pattern of development involving certain recurring components: a beginning description of context and illness; a request for a healing; the execution of the healing; a verification of the healing; and a reaction of the background audience. The present story, actually an example of healing at a distance, deploys all these components but one, the reaction of the bystanders, in three phases.

1. The first phase (8:5–6) combines introduction and request. A narratorial comment provides a general location ("When he had entered Jerusalem") and introduces the main characters: Jesus and a centurion ("a centurion came to him and begged him, saying," 8:5). The centurion's statement conveys the request for a healing (8:6). It is formulated in indirect fashion, by way of information: the subject in question is identified, introducing a third character, and the illness itself is described in vivid though general fashion: his "servant"/"child" (*pais*) lies severely ill at home – "a cripple, in terrible affliction" (8:6).

2. The second phase (8:7–12), more expansive, inserts an intermediate step between request and cure: an exchange between Jesus and the centurion that expands and qualifies the request. To begin with, Jesus offers, unconditionally, to come to the centurion's home and heal the individual in question (8:7). In response, the centurion seeks to alter such a plan by way of a comparative statement on power, its possession and exercise (8:8–9). The request is amended thereby to bypass a visit by Jesus to his house and to solicit instead a healing by a mere word on

Jesus's part from a distance. At this point, Jesus turns to a new character, "those who followed," and praises the centurion with a statement that also comments on the comparative eschatological fate of non-Jews and Jews in the Kingdom of the Heavens (8:10–12).

3. The third phase (8:13), quite brief, combines the execution and the verification of the healing. The cure is effected, following the centurion's express request, by a mere "word" from Jesus: "Jesus said to the centurion, 'Go, let it be done to you as you have believed'." It is confirmed by a narratorial comment: "The 'servant'/'child' was cured at that very hour."

In terms of formal arrangement and development, the author has constructed a marvelous deed on the part of Jesus. The first phase presents the illness as offstage. The second phase sets up the healing as offstage as well. The third phase offers not only a healing from a distance, as already channeled by the previous two phases, but also a healing that is immediate, taking place at the very utterance of a word from Jesus. The result is a demonstration of Jesus's extraordinary power and largesse.

CONTEXT. The unit is placed within the narrative section of Matthew 8–9, between the long address to disciples and crowds of Chapters 5–7 (Sermon on the Mount) and the shorter address to the core group of disciples of Chapter 10 (Mission Discourse). A narratorial statement in 5:23–25 summarizes the initial phase of Jesus's mission and points ahead to what is to follow. As Jesus moves about the Galilee, he teaches in synagogues, proclaims the Kingdom of God, and performs all sorts of healings. The consequences of such activity are immediate and far reaching: News of him spread throughout Syria. All sorts of ill people are brought before him and cured – including demoniacs, epileptics, and paralytics. Large crowds begin to follow from surrounding territories – the Galilee, the Decapolis, Jerusalem, Judea, beyond the Jordan. The narrative sections that follow expand on this statement: Chapters 5–7 provide a first, specific and detailed, look at Jesus's teaching, while Chapters 8–9 provide a first, concrete and extended, look at Jesus's deeds. A narratorial statement in 9:35–37 captures this phase of Jesus's mission and prepares for its extension through the disciples in Matthew 10. In so doing, this statement repeats the basic contents of 5:23–25. As Jesus goes about cities and villages, he teaches in synagogues, proclaims the Kingdom, and heals all kinds of diseases.

Jesus's activity in Chapters 8–9 does include teaching as well as conflict, but the emphasis is on miraculous deeds – not only exorcisms and healings, but also demonstrations of power over nature and death alike. Such activity has Capernaum as its focus: (1) beginning somewhere outside Capernaum (8:1–4); (2) in Capernaum (8:5–17), on and across the Sea of Galilee (8:18–9:1), back to Capernaum (9:2–34); (3) going on to cities and villages beyond (9:35–37). The unit is thus placed at the beginning of the first Capernaum cycle of events. Upon entering, Jesus heals the "servant"/"child" of a Roman centurion (8:5–13), Peter's mother-in-law (8:14–15), and a host of others, as conveyed by a narratorial statement that brings the cycle to an end (8:16–17). The centurion, therefore, is one of many who come to Jesus for assistance. He is, however, the first non-Jewish character to appear in the narrative and the first representative of the imperial system. He forms part of the military machine of Rome, in command of a company of soldiers (about 100 in strength). His appearance at the very start of Jesus's mission underlines his importance for the plot.

CHARACTERS. The unit highlights the encounter between the two characters on stage – Jesus and the centurion. This it does with minimal contribution from the narrator. Aside from setting and ending the scene, the narrator's role is limited to marking the change in speakers, with but a brief insight into each in the process. The characters, therefore, occupy center stage. Their encounter presents two phases.

The initial exchange is brief and pointed (8:5–6, 7). The centurion, whose concrete identity remains undisclosed, is portrayed as approaching Jesus directly with a request for healing. This request is not for himself but for a member of his household, a *pais*, whose concrete identity remains similarly undisclosed and, in fact, ultimately ambiguous, since the term could have a "servant" or a "child" of his in mind. The centurion does so without any sort of introduction, except for the use of the vocative *kyrie*, but, according to the narratorial description of his demeanor, with a sense of conviction and urgency (*parakalōn*). From the narrative thus far, it could be readily inferred that the centurion comes to Jesus as a result of Jesus's spreading fame and attraction, especially as a healer, which has somehow reached his ears. Such knowledge on his part would readily account for his use of *kyrie* in addressing Jesus, indicating respect and dependence. Aware of Jesus's power, therefore, the centurion lays before Jesus, in a veiled request for action, the particulars of the illness in question and its severity. Jesus's response is depicted as immediate and unconditional: "I will come and cure him."

At this point, a lower official in the military machine of Rome, a non-Jewish representative of the imperial system, has placed himself, for the sake of a healing, in the hands of a Jewish doer of wondrous deeds, Jesus. This official is received without questions and assured of a healing without conditions. What this official believes with regard to Jesus's identity and role as Messiah and Son of God is not disclosed.

The second exchange is more developed and complex (8:8–9; 10–12; 13). The centurion is now depicted as seeking to alter Jesus's plan of action. This he does by means of an extended statement regarding their comparative positions of authority and power. Jesus, in turn, is portrayed as amazed by such a declaration and as bowing to the proposed change. He does so by means of a twofold response: first, to the surrounding audience, in praise of the centurion; then, to the centurion himself, in answer to his request.

To begin with, the centurion responds to Jesus's resolve to come to his house with a proposed modification of such a plan (8:8b–e) and a justification for such an alternative course of action (8:9). The centurion seeks to bypass such a visit in favor of a healing by a mere "word" (*logos*) from Jesus – a healing from a distance. This proposal is conveyed, and hence justified, by a declaration of comparative status: he is not "worthy" (*hikanos*) of such a visit from Jesus, whom he again addresses as *kyrie*. The centurion then expands this initial justification through a declaration of comparative authority and power. This declaration is truncated: while his own authority is laid out, that of Jesus remains unverbalized. The centurion presents himself as a man situated within a chain of authority – both "under authority" and in authority, having "soldiers under him." As such, he points out, he has power: whatever he commands such soldiers, they do. Unexpectedly, the centurion further presents himself as a slave owner, with similar authority and power: his "slave" does as he commands. (Were the *pais* his "servant," he would have absolute authority over him as a slave.) The implication regarding Jesus is unmistakable: his authority and power are even greater than the centurion's! Indeed, Jesus not only has power over illness but can heal, as requested, from a distance. In fact, Jesus has power over the centurion as well – the power of granting his request.

Jesus responds first to the audience at hand, and he does so with "amazement" (*ethaumasen*). This reaction is twofold. First, Jesus offers a comparative evaluation of the centurion, as a non-Jew vis-à-vis Jews, regarding reaction to Jesus (8:10b). It is a striking statement. Such "faith" (*pistin*), he declares, he has found nowhere in Israel. This statement is descriptive, presumably covering the mission up to this point, and proves curious, given the positive reaction thus far. Then, Jesus offers a comparative assessment of non-Jews and Jews in general with respect to eschatological fate in the "Kingdom of the Heavens" (8:11–12). This is an even more striking statement. The banquet table in the Kingdom is portrayed in oppositional fashion: "many from east and west" – non-Jews – will be sitting alongside Abraham, Isaac, and Jacob, while the "sons of the Kingdom" – Jews – will be "cast out" into the "outer darkness." This statement is programmatic, presumably taking the mission of both Jesus and the disciples as a whole into account and positing a far greater welcome among non-Jews than among Jews. Jesus then turns to the centurion, providing the sought-after "word" of healing. It is brief and indirect. The centurion is instructed to return home, for what he has requested will be done for him "as he has believed." The healing, which had initially been promised unconditionally, is now tied to the centurion's "faith" in Jesus – that is, to his recognition of Jesus's status, authority, and power.

At the end, the centurion, as a military official of Rome and a non-Jew, has placed, directly or indirectly, Jesus's status, authority, and power above his own. In so doing, he sets the stage for an extraordinary display of power on the part of Jesus – healing at a distance. Jesus, in turn, places the centurion above everyone else in Israel thus far on account of his "faith," although what the centurion actually believes regarding Jesus's identity and role (beyond recognizing him to be a healer) remains unexpressed. Jesus further goes on to place non-Jews above Jews in the Kingdom of God. The centurion is dismissed without further ado, no instructions or demands.

Matthew 8:5–13 in a Postcolonial Key

What does this encounter between the centurion and Jesus signify with respect to the underlying encounter between the imperial system of Rome and the imperial system of God? How would the unit fare in the interpretive spectrum?

IMPERIALIZING READING. If one views Matthew as tending toward the accommodation pole, this text emerges as largely pro-Roman. That is precisely the reading of Dube. Two arguments lie at its core. The first focuses on Jesus's reception of the centurion and proceeds by way of comparative analysis with that of the Canaanite woman in Matthew 15:21–28, given key features they have in common: both are identified as outsiders (Gentiles), both request healing for dependents, and both receive praise for their faith. Whereas Jesus shows no hesitation regarding the centurion's appeal, the woman's pleading is first ignored, then rejected on the grounds of exclusionism, and finally granted only when the woman submits to self-humiliation. Such welcome of the centurion presents Jesus as positively disposed to the imperial powers. The second argument highlights the comparison between Jesus and the centurion, men of authority who make things happen by their "word," and the praise of the centurion over Israel. Such parallelism sanctifies the imperial powers; such commendation favors imperial officials.

For Dube, therefore, the unit not only disguises the exploitation and oppression of Rome but also pronounces imperialism righteous and acceptable. The unit, therefore, involves far more than the admission of outsiders, the Gentiles, into the Christian community. It is an exercise in courting the favor of the Empire, to the detriment of non-Christian Jews.

COUNTER-IMPERIAL READING. If one sees Matthew as tending toward the resistance pole, this text emerges as largely anti-Roman. It is in this direction that Carter moves.[38] To begin with, the centurion, although an agent and enforcer of imperial power, subordinates himself to Jesus.

---

[38] Carter focuses on Matthew 8:5–13 in *Matthew and the Margin: A Sociopolitical and Religious Reading* (Maryknoll, NY: Orbis, 1980).

First, in approaching Jesus, he, who holds authority over Jesus "as a Jew," places himself under Jesus's authority. Second, in the face of resistance on the part of Jesus, for Carter understands his initial response as a rhetorical question ("Will I come and cure him?"), the centurion, who belongs to a power that claims to rule the world, further submits to Jesus's authority: acknowledging the limits of his power, setting Jesus's power as far superior, and expressing absolute confidence in such power, as one "commissioned by God". In addition, by praising the centurion's "faith," Jesus places him within the circle of disciples: grasping Jesus's identity as God's agent and undertaking a life of "merciful and just actions." Lastly, while the healing does uphold slavery, for Carter takes the *pais* as a servant, Jesus anticipates, through the reference to the eschatological banquet feast, the Empire of God, which will reign over all and welcome all.

For Carter, therefore, the unit emphasizes the powerlessness of Rome before the power of Jesus, reveals the consequences of submission to and faith in Jesus, and provides a glimpse into the future Kingdom of God, where "all have access to adequate resources," through its restoration of an ill slave and its inclusion of outsiders. The unit thus has at its core a welcome not only of all "cultural nobodies" but also of the Gentiles alongside the Jews, who are warned thereby as well. It constitutes an exercise in cutting Rome down to size and pointing to the forthcoming triumph of God.

CONFLICTED READING. Should one situate Matthew within the middle of the accommodation–restoration spectrum, the unit emerges as highly controverted. Although Carter passes quickly over it in his postcolonial commentary, such a reading is not hard to imagine. On the one hand, the angle of resistance is evident. The Empire of the Heavens stands – in and through Jesus – over the Empire of Rome in authority and power, not only in the present but also in the future. Jesus reigns over all and welcomes all through "faith." On the other hand, the angle of accommodation is undeniable. The contrast between the Canaanite woman and the centurion is most telling: a military official of the Roman Empire is received, treated, and dispatched in more than exemplary fashion. The contrast between the Jews and the centurion proves equally telling: his "faith" is unsurpassed in Israel. The contrast between Gentiles and Jews is no less telling: "many" will be in the Kingdom over against the Jews as an unqualified group.

This conflicted reading is the one that I would espouse. It is a reading that brings together the different narrative strands of the unit outlined earlier without sacrifice. The unit most certainly offers opposition to Rome; there is no doubt about that. At the same time, however, the unit signals accommodation, a playing up to Rome (with submission in view) vis-à-vis a downplaying of Israel. In fact, this latter aspect is further intensified when one recalls the following two points: first, the unit never makes clear what exactly the centurion believes with regard to Jesus; second, the unit gives no indication of what demands are made of the centurion at the end, beyond the healing. The unit, therefore, is sharply conflicted, mixing opposition and accommodation in tensive and unreconcilable fashion, with lots of ambiguity to boot. That it should be placed so early in the plot is significant: there is a paradigm set forth for Rome and Gentiles here; this paradigm, however, is less than clear, if not Janus-like.

A CONCLUDING NOTE

A postcolonial optic has much to offer to biblical criticism, given its sustained, interdisciplinary as well as multidimensional, focus on the geopolitical problematic in general and on imperial–colonial formations and relations in particular. This is a line of inquiry that, while by no means unattended in the scholarly literature, has not been properly foregrounded, much less properly theorized or properly pursued. Postcolonial criticism does precisely that. It places geopolitics at the core of critical analysis. In so doing, it enters into critical engagement with fields of study that analyze such frameworks, like postcolonial studies or imperial studies. As such, it proves a decidedly interdisciplinary inquiry, involving a highly informed critical perspective. In so doing, moreover, it also takes into critical consideration the various imperial–colonial frameworks that underlie the different constitutive components of the discipline as conceived and practiced today: the texts and contexts of antiquity; the Western tradition of interpretation – the readings and readers of such texts and contexts – in modernity; the global tradition of interpretation – the readings and readers of such texts and contexts – in postmodernity. As such, it proves an intensely multidimensional inquiry, yielding a highly comprehensive critical perspective.

At the same time, in foregrounding the geopolitical problematic and pursuing it in highly informed and duly comprehensive fashion, the postcolonial optic should not proceed in isolation. It should remain, rather, in ongoing critical dialogue with other approaches in the discipline. Just as the geopolitical angle has an impact on other angles of inquiry, so do these other angles of inquiry – the historical, the literary and the sociocultural, the ideological – have an impact on the geopolitical. In foregrounding imperial–colonial frameworks, therefore, postcolonial criticism should keep in mind at all times how such formations and relations affect and are affected by historical situations and developments, social matrices and cultural production, and other differential relations of power, like gender and economy as well as race–ethnicity and sexuality. Such intersectional undertaking requires ever-greater sophistication in the biblical criticism of the future, already very much upon us. The role of postcolonial criticism, already highly creative and highly distinguished, in such a layered undertaking is absolutely essential and only just beginning.

Glossary

A list of how some key terms are used in Gospel studies:

abduction – in social-scientific study, a process of reasoning according to which one formulates a hypothesized model regarding social behavior on the basis of accumulated data and then uses that model as a lens for assessing more instances of the behavior in question.

alternative states of consciousness – conditions in which sensations, perceptions, cognition, and emotions are transformed.

ancestrism – reverence for predecessors in one's literal or fictive family.

androcentrism – a male-centered perspective.

anthropology – the study of human beings in groups, in foreign societies; cf. "sociology."

antipathy – in literary analysis, the phenomenon by which a reader feels unfavorably disposed toward a character in the narrative; cf. "sympathy."

authenticity criteria – in historical Jesus studies, the means by which traditions concerning Jesus are determined to be historically reliable or verifiable.

character groups – in literary analysis, characters who evince such consistency of traits and point of view that they are essentially treated as a single character throughout the narrative (e.g., "the disciples").

considerate reader – in social-scientific studies, a person who brings to his or her reading of a text a range of scenarios rooted in the social system of the document's writer and presumed audience.

cynicism – a system of Greek philosophy that encouraged *authenticity* through repudiation of shame and *independence* through renunciation of what cannot be obtained freely.

deconstruction – an interpretive strategy employed by postmodern critics that seeks to demonstrate the nonnormative character of proposed interpretations (e.g., by exposing dependence on contextually derived presuppositions).

discourse – in literary criticism, the rhetorical component of narrative related to *how* the story is told; cf. "story."

disease – in social-scientific studies, a scientific, medical understanding of "sickening" that would not have existed in the New Testament world; cf. "illness."

dissimilarity – in historical Jesus studies, a criterion of authenticity that holds that material that presents Jesus in a manner dissimilar to both his Jewish contemporaries and Christian followers is likely to be historically reliable.

dynamic characters – in literary analysis, characters whose traits or point of view change as the narrative progresses; cf. "static characters."

embarrassment – in historical Jesus studies, a criterion of authenticity that holds that material about Jesus likely to have proved awkward or embarrassing for the early church is likely to be historically reliable.

empathy – the phenomenon by which a reader identifies realistically or idealistically with a character and experiences the story from that character's point of view.

evangelists – traditional designation for the authors of the four New Testament Gospels.

expected reading – in narrative criticism, an interpretation or response to a text that appears to be invited by signals within the text itself; cf. "unexpected reading."

feminist criticism – the discipline of interpreting texts from the perspective of persons informed by feminism.

flat characters – in literary analysis, characters who exhibit consistent traits and a predictable point of view; such characters typically function as personifications of values; cf. "round characters."

form criticism – an academic disciple concerned with classifying material found in the Gospels according to literary form ("parable," "hymn," etc.) and with identifying the various purposes that diverse forms were intended to serve.

genre criticism – a discipline that seeks to identify the literary genre of the Gospels by comparing and contrasting them with other ancient works.

hermeneutical circle – a term used to describe paradoxically independent tendencies in interpretation; for example, the "whole" of a text must be understood in terms of its parts, but the parts must also be understood in light of the whole.

hermeneutics of creative actualization – in feminist criticism, a final step in biblical interpretation that utilizes imagination, art, liturgy, and so on, to enable texts to function for those opposed to patriarchal oppression.

hermeneutics of proclamation – in feminist criticism, a goal of interpretation that moves from uncovering androcentric and patriarchal tendencies of texts to a more positive assessment of how texts can be used theologically in contemporary communities of faith.

hermeneutics of remembrance – in feminist criticism, a goal of interpretation that seeks to reconstruct biblical history from a feminist perspective.

hermeneutics of suspicion – in feminist criticism, a stance that presupposes or assumes that biblical texts (and their traditional interpretations) are androcentric and will serve patriarchy; cf. "hermeneutics of proclamation."

high-context societies – societies that produce sketchy and impressionistic texts that spell few things out and leave much to the reader's imagination; cf. "low-context societies."

historical-critical method – an array of disciplines intended to enable scholars to arrive at the meaning of texts within their original context (typically, the meaning that was intended by the historical authors).

ideological criticism – an umbrella term for numerous disciplines that seek to interpret texts from the perspective of readers who occupy a specific social location and/or evince a particular ideology (e.g., womanist criticism, Marxist criticism, and Jungian criticism).

illness – in social-scientific studies, an understanding of "sickening" as loss of well-being and meaningful life due to some impairment; illness may be healed without disease being cured; cf. "disease."

imperializing texts – in postcolonial criticism, texts that lend themselves to the legitimation of subordination and domination.

implied author – in narrative criticism, the author of a text as reconstructed from the text itself.

implied reader – in narrative criticism, the reader presupposed by the text, who is to be envisioned as responding to the text with whatever knowledge, understanding, action, or emotion is called for.

in-group – in social-scientific analysis, a collection of individuals who see themselves as members of the same social category; cf. "out-group."

kernel events – in literary analysis, events that are integral to the narrative, such that they could not be removed without destroying the logic of the plot; cf. "satellite events."

kyriarchy – in feminist criticism, a term sometimes employed as an alternative for "patriarchy," to emphasize that oppressive social systems involve more complex subjugations than the power of men over women.

low-context societies – societies that produce detailed texts that spell out as much as possible and leave little to the reader's imagination; cf. "high-context societies."

monumental time – in literary analysis, broad or sweeping concepts of time that may provide temporal settings for a narrative (e.g., "in those days"; "that generation"); cf. "mortal time."

mortal time – in literary analysis, chronological or typological references to time as it is measured by characters within a narrative (e.g., "on the sabbath" and "at night").

multiple attestation – in historical Jesus studies, the claim that a saying or action attributed to Jesus can be confirmed through its appearance in two or more independent sources.

narrative criticism – a method of literary analysis used in Gospel studies that seeks to interpret texts from the perspective of their implied readers.

out-group – in social-scientific studies, a collection of individuals who are perceived to be members of a different social category than one's own.

patriarchy – a social construction based on androcentrism that is often institutionalized as a social-political system that favors the subjugation or oppression of women.

point of view – in literary analysis, the norms, values, and general worldview that govern the way a character looks at things and renders judgments on them.

postcolonial interpretation – a discipline that seeks to interpret texts from the perspective of those who have experienced the oppression of "colonialism" (being dominated by a foreign power).

postmodern interpretation – a discipline that seeks to demonstrate the instability and inaccessibility of meaning and to decry the establishment of any particular interpretation of any text as normative.

reader-response criticism – broadly, an umbrella term for all varieties of literary analysis that seek to interpret texts from the perspective of a reader (however that might be defined); more narrowly, the term is sometimes equated with ideological criticism and/or postmodern criticism.

reading strategy – in literary analysis, the manner in which a text is received, such as, whether it is heard, or read out loud, or read silently, or whether it is read as an independent document or as part of a larger work.

redaction criticism – a discipline concerned with the final stage of the formation of the Gospels, focusing on the evangelists' editorial work in arranging their material and editing their sources.

rhetorical criticism – a discipline concerned with understanding the Gospels from the perspective of the historical persons for whom they were first written, focusing on what the rhetoric of the Gospel would have communicated to those original readers.

round characters – in literary analysis, characters who exhibit inconsistent traits and a sometimes unpredictable point of view; such characters serve as potentially realistic options for reader empathy; cf. "flat characters."

satellite events – in literary analysis, events that fill out the story with aesthetic appeal but that are not absolutely necessary for the logic of the plot; cf. "kernel events."

Semitisms – sayings or deeds reported in the Gospel that reflect the Hebrew or Aramaic language.

Semoya – a method of Bible reading practiced by certain women of Botswana that brings to the fore a fresh hearing of God, through the Spirit, with liberating effect.

social institutions – fixed phases of social life, such as kinship, politics, economics, and religion.

social location – the description of any person (e.g., a reader of a narrative, an interpreter of a Gospel, an author of a Gospel, or a character in a narrative) in terms of features that would be shared with some, but not all, other people (race, gender, age, nationality, social class, etc.).

sociology – the study of human beings in groups, in one's own society; cf. "anthropology."

source criticism – the discipline devoted to identifying and, if possible, reconstructing the sources used by the evangelists in composition of the Gospels.

static characters – in literary analysis, characters whose traits and point of view remain constant throughout the narrative; cf. "dynamic characters."

story – in literary criticism, the "content" component of narrative (e.g., the events, characters, and setting that make up the plot); cf. "discourse."

sympathy – in literary analysis, the phenomenon by which a reader feels favorably disposed toward a character in the narrative; cf. "antipathy."

Synoptic Problem – the question of how the Synoptic Gospels (Matthew, Mark, and Luke) are related to each other, in light of the extensive similarities between them.

traits – in literary analysis, persistent personal qualities that describe a character in a narrative.

unexpected reading – in narrative criticism, an interpretation or response to a text that ignores or resists signals intrinsic to the text and so is incompatible with the perspective of the implied reader.

wirkungsgeschichte – a discipline concerned with tracing the "history of influence" for a text, noticing how it has been interpreted (and with what effect) throughout history.

womanist criticism – a variety of ideological criticism that seeks to interpret texts from the perspective of African-American women.

Annotated Bibliography

HISTORICAL-CRITICAL METHOD

Barton, John. *The Nature of Biblical Criticism.* Louisville: Westminster John Knox, 2007. Offers a balanced discussion of biblical criticism in light of both historical realities and current trends in interpretation.

Erickson, Richard J. *A Beginner's Guide to New Testament Exegesis: Taking the Fear out of Critical Method.* Downers Grove: InterVarsity Press, 2005. Perhaps the most accessible guide available to the practice of the historical-critical method, with remarkable clarity of explanation and in-depth discussion of things to emphasize and pitfalls to avoid.

Ferguson, Everett. *Backgrounds of Early Christianity,* 3rd ed. Grand Rapids: Eerdmans, 2003. A thorough guide to the historical context of the New Testament, covering every aspect of Roman, Greek, and Jewish thought, society, politics, and religion; also a good source of bibliographies.

Green, Joel B., Scot McKnight, and I. Howard Marshall, eds. *Dictionary of Jesus and the Gospels.* Downers Grove: InterVarsity Press, 1992. Excellent articles presenting history of scholarship, summaries of the ideas, and good bibliographies for form criticism, tradition criticism, genre, redaction criticism, and the Synoptic Problem. A number of articles also illumine aspects of the historical and cultural context out of which the Gospels arose.

Krentz, Edgar. *The Historical-Critical Method.* GBS. Philadelphia: Fortress, 1975. A classic introduction to the practice of the historical-critical method.

Sanders, E. P. and Margaret Davies. *Studying the Synoptic Gospels.* London: SCM, 1989. Contains in-depth discussions of source criticism, form criticism, redaction criticism, and the genre of the Gospels. Noting strengths and weaknesses in the work of various scholars, the authors guide the reader to a thoughtful application of these and other methods.

LITERARY APPROACHES

Adam, A. K. M. *What is Postmodern Biblical Criticism?* GBS. Minneapolis: Fortress, 1995. A basic introduction to postmodern reading strategies, including deconstruction and ideological criticism.

Kingsbury, Jack Dean. *Matthew as Story*, 2nd ed. Minneapolis: Fortress, 1988. The first and, to date, the most important narrative-critical study of Matthew's Gospel.

Powell, Mark Allan. *What Is Narrative Criticism?* GBS. Minneapolis: Fortress, 1990. The standard textbook for introducing students to the principles and procedures of narrative criticism. Cf. Resseguie, *Narrative Criticism.*

Powell, Mark Allan, *Chasing the Eastern Star: Adventures in Biblical Reader-Response Criticism.* Louisville: Westminster John Knox, 2001. An introduction to reader-response criticism that uses Matthew's Gospel as the primary "sample text" for illustrating the method and hermeneutic in practice.

Powell, Mark Allan, with the assistance of Cecile G. Gray and Melissa C. Curtis, *The Bible and Modern Literary Criticism: A Critical Assessment and Annotated Bibliography.* New York: Greenwood, 1992. A fairly comprehensive (though now dated) list of works that employ modern literary criticism in the study of biblical literature.

Resseguie, James L. *Narrative Criticism of the New Testament: An Introduction.* Grand Rapids: Baker Academic, 2005. An alternative textbook to Powell's *What Is Narrative Criticism?* for introducing students to the principles and procedures of narrative criticism. Resseguie employs more examples from secular literature than does Powell, and is a bit more insistent on employment of the method in line with a text-oriented hermeneutic.

FEMINIST APPROACHES

Anderson, Janice Capel. "Matthew: Gender and Reading." *Semeia* **28** (1983): 3–27. This article was the first explicit feminist reading of Matthew's Gospel, using "patriarchy" as its key analytic category.

Cheney, Emily. *She Can Read: Feminist Reading Strategies for Biblical Narrative.* Valley Forge: Trinity Press International, 1994. Cheney takes a literary-critical approach to selected Matthean texts, offering a reading supported by nuanced dialogue with literary critics.

Deutsch, Celia. "Jesus as Wisdom: A Feminist Reading of Matthew's Wisdom Christology." Pages 88–113 in *A Feminist Companion to Matthew*, ed. Amy-Jill Levine. Sheffield: Sheffield Academic Press, 2001. Celia Deutsch employs a specifically feminist lens to read Jesus as Wisdom in the Matthean construction of Jesus.

Dube, Musa W. *Postcolonial Feminist Interpretation of the Bible.* St. Louis: Chalice Press, 2000. Feminist approaches have been challenged within the last decade by women of color and M. Dube's book represents and outlines such challenges, highlighting the necessity of multidimensional hermeneutics.

Levine, Amy-Jill, ed. *A Feminist Companion to Matthew.* Sheffield: Sheffield Academic Press, 2001. Levine brings a Jewish feminist perspective to her own study of Matthew's Gospel, but in this volume she gathers articles representing a range of feminist approaches to the Matthean text, providing the Matthean feminist reader with a rich array of resources.

Wainwright, Elaine M. *Towards a Feminist Critical Reading of the Gospel According to Matthew.* BZNW 60. Berlin: de Gruyter, 1991. This was the first full-length study of the Matthean Gospel from a feminist perspective and it combines new literary and historical critical approaches to texts in which women function as characters in the narrative.

Wainwright, Elaine. M. *Shall We Look for Another? A Feminist Rereading of the Matthean Jesus.* Maryknoll: Orbis, 1998. In this volume, Wainwright turns her feminist reading lens to the character of Jesus in the Matthean Gospel narrative.

HISTORICAL JESUS STUDIES

Borg, Marcus J. *Jesus in Contemporary Scholarship.* Valley Forge, PA: Trinity Press International, 1994. An account of modern Jesus studies up through the early 1990s, presented in an apologetic style favorable to the work of the author's own work as part of the Jesus Seminar.

Charlesworth, James H. *The Historical Jesus: An Essential Guide.* Nashville: Abingdon, 2008. A brief overview organized as answers to popular questions about Jesus and about historical Jesus studies.

Evans, Craig A., ed. *Encyclopedia of the Historical Jesus.* New York: Routledge, 2008. A major reference work with contributions from numerous scholars.

Evans, C. A. *Fabricating Jesus: How Modern Scholars Distort the Gospels.* Downers Grove, IL: IVP, 2008. An exposé of popular misconceptions and faulty research that have plagued historical Jesus studies.

Gowler, David B. *What Are They Saying about the Historical Jesus?* Mahwah, NJ: Paulist, 2007. A brief and accessible introduction.

Powell, Mark Allan. *Jesus as a Figure in History: How Modern Historians View the Man from Galilee.* Louisville: Westminster John Knox, 1998. An introduction to the field of historical Jesus studies, with extended treatments on the work of the Jesus Seminar, John Dominic Crossan, Marcus Borg, E. P. Sanders, John Meier, and N. T. Wright.

Theissen, Gerd, and Annette Metz. *The Historical Jesus. A Comprehensive Guide,* trans. J. Bowden. Minneapolis: Fortress, 1998. A textbook for training students in the art of conducting Jesus research.

SOCIAL-SCIENTIFIC APPROACHES

Elliott, John H. *What Is Social-Scientific Criticism?* GBS. Minneapolis: Fortress, 1993. Scholarly overview of the field at the time, with full bibliography.

Malina, Bruce J. *The New Testament World: Insights from Cultural Anthropology,* 3rd rev. ed. Louisville: Westminster John Knox, 2001. General orientation and specific scenarios for reading the New Testament: honor and shame, person types, limited good, envy and the evil eye, purity rules, marriage, and Jesus group development; with exercises at the end.

Moerman, Daniel. *Meaning, Medicine and the "Placebo Effect."* Cambridge: Cambridge University Press, 2002. Valuable explanation of cross-cultural medical systems.

Neyrey, Jerome H., ed. *The Social World of Luke-Acts: Models for Interpretation*. Peabody: Hendrickson, 1991. Collection of essays by Context Group members dealing with specific features of New Testament Society applied to Luke-Acts.

Neyrey, Jerome H. *Render to God: New Testament Understandings of the Divine*. Minneapolis: Fortress, 2004. One of the few books dealing with theology (understanding of God) in the New Testament, facilitated by the application of social-scientific models.

Pilch, John J. *Healing in the New Testament: Insights from Medical and Mediterranean Anthropology*. Minneapolis: Fortress, 2000. Insights from the study of cross-cultural medicine applied to New Testament passages.

Pilch, John J. *Visions and Healing in the Acts of the Apostles: How the Early Believers Experienced God*. Collegeville: Liturgical Press, 2004. Modern scholarly understanding of alternate states of consciousness in cross-cultural settings applied to the many instances of the phenomenon in the New Testament.

Rohrbaugh, Richard L., ed. *The Social Sciences and New Testament Interpretation*. Peabody: Hendrickson, 1996. A collection of essays by Context Group members dealing with honor and shame, person types, kinship, purity rules, city, economy, patronage, food rules, and millennialism.

POSTCOLONIAL CRITICISM

Carter, Warren. *Matthew and Empire: Initial Explorations*. Harrisburg: Trinity Press International, 2001. Emphasizes the role of Matthew's Gospel as a "Counter-Imperializing Text," one that encourages a suspicious attitude toward all ruling institutions.

Dube, Musa W. *Postcolonial Feminist Interpretation of the Bible*. St. Louis: Chalice, 2000. A major monograph linking postcolonial studies and feminist studies, significant for Matthean studies due to its rigorous claim that the Gospel of Matthew is an "Imperializing Text" that needs to be resisted by those committed to liberation.

Moore, Stephen D., and Fernando F. Segovia, eds. *Postcolonial Biblical Criticism: Interdisciplinary Intersections*. The Bible and Postcolonialism. London: T&T Clark, 2005. Traces intersections of the postcolonial movement with a variety of other discourses, including poststructuralism, feminism, economics, and race–ethnicity.

Riches, John, and David C. Sim, eds. *The Gospel of Matthew in Its Roman Imperial Context*. JSNTSS 276. London: T&T International, 2005. Broad in scope, this volume contains articles by each of the two editors dealing with the role of imperialism in Matthew's eschatology and missionary strategy.

Segovia, Fernando F. *Decolonizing Biblical Studies*. Maryknoll: Orbis Books, 2000. An introduction to postcolonial biblical studies that traces the development of the field against the backdrop of profound demographic transformations in the scholarly guild.

Segovia, Fernando F., and R. S. Sugirtharajah, eds. *A Postcolonial Commentary on the New Testament Writings*. The Bible and Postcolonialism. London: T&T Clark, 2007. An ambitious project offering commentary on the entire Bible, this volume contains a study of Matthew by Warren Carter that regards that Gospel as more conflicted in its appraisal of empire than was evident in Carter's 2001 publication, *Matthew and Empire.*

Sugirtharajah, R. S. *The Bible and the Third World: Precolonial, Colonial and Post-colonial Encounters.* Cambridge: Cambridge University Press, 2001. A look at the third world biblical interpretation in three phases: reception (before colonialism), embrace (during colonialism), and reclamation (after colonialism).

Subject Index

abduction, 158, 169
alternate states of consciousness, 177–8, 180, 186
anachronism (social concept), 158, 164, 173
Anderson, Janice Capel, 84–5, 87, 90
androcentrism, 84–91, 93–5, 102, 104, 111, 115
angel(s), 37–41, 73–5, 115–16, 125, 127, 148, 157, 160, 176–7, 180
anthropology, 9, 17, 154, 156, 169, 171, 176–7, 184
  cultural, 30, 100, 109, 156–7, 162–4, 169–70
  historical, 157, 170
  medical, 184
  social, 156–7, 162, 169–70
anticolonialism, 221
anti-Judaism, 68, 101, 112, 128
Antioch, 1, 101, 125, 222–3
antipathy, 50
anti-Semitism. *See* anti-Judaism
Apocalypse of Peter, 124–5
appropriateness (social concept), 159–60
archaeology, 57, 119, 131, 136–7, 139, 145, 149, 152, 162
authenticity, criteria of, 138–42
author: as literary concept, 4, 14, 16, 45, 52–3
  as social concept, 171
authorial intent, 6–7, 14–15, 53, 63–4, 69, 81
author-oriented criticism, 54–5, 63–4

benefaction, 169
binarism, 207
biography, 23, 226

bios, 23
Buddha, 131

Caesarea, 124, 132, 182
Capernaum, 143–5, 149–50, 152–3, 175, 180, 182, 185–7, 189, 229, 231
Carter, Warren, 217, 221–8, 234
causal connections, 48
centurion: at the cross, 36n60, 103–4, 105n77, 106, 108–9, 111
  in Capernaum, 140, 143–50, 152–3, 175, 180–82, 186–90, 192, 228–236
challenge and riposte, 170, 176
characterization, 50, 68, 97, 101, 104, 111
characters (literary), 46–51, 67–9, 219
  dynamic, 49
  flat, 49, 68
  groups, 49–50, 67
  round, 49, 67
  static, 49
Christology, 41, 217
class (social concept), 51, 53, 88, 93, 98, 164, 197, 202, 207, 222, 224
Clement of Alexandria, 128–9
collectivism, 155–7, 171
colonialism, 88, 197, 200, 202, 207, 209, 211, 213
communicative event, 13–15
conflict: in literature, 46–7, 50, 69–70, 78
  in society, 155–6
context, 58, 88, 93
  historical, 13
  literary, 101, 229
  original, 15
  social, 216, 236–7
Cross Gospel, 127

251

Scripture Index